I0831416

James Joyce and the Exilic Imagination

The Florida James Joyce Series

UNIVERSITY PRESS OF FLORIDA

Florida A&M University, Tallahassee
Florida Atlantic University, Boca Raton
Florida Gulf Coast University, Ft. Myers
Florida International University, Miami
Florida State University, Tallahassee
New College of Florida, Sarasota
University of Central Florida, Orlando
University of Florida, Gainesville
University of North Florida, Jacksonville
University of South Florida, Tampa
University of West Florida, Pensacola

James Joyce and the Exilic Imagination

MICHAEL PATRICK GILLESPIE

Foreword by Sebastian D. G. Knowles, Series Editor

University Press of Florida
Gainesville · Tallahassee · Tampa · Boca Raton
Pensacola · Orlando · Miami · Jacksonville · Ft. Myers · Sarasota

Copyright 2015 by Michael Patrick Gillespie
All rights reserved
Printed in the United States of America on acid-free paper

This book may be available in an electronic edition.

20 19 18 17 16 15 6 5 4 3 2 1

Library of Congress Cataloging-in-Publication Data
Gillespie, Michael Patrick, author.
James Joyce and the exilic imagination / Michael Patrick Gillespie.
pages cm — (The Florida James Joyce series)
Includes bibliographical references and index.
ISBN 978-0-8130-6065-1
1. Joyce, James, 1882-1941—Criticism and interpretation. 2. Authors, Exiled.
3. Exiles' writings. I. Title. II. Series: Florida James Joyce series.
PR6019.O9Z533575 2015
823'.912—dc23
2014043922

The University Press of Florida is the scholarly publishing agency for the State University System of Florida, comprising Florida A&M University, Florida Atlantic University, Florida Gulf Coast University, Florida International University, Florida State University, New College of Florida, University of Central Florida, University of Florida, University of North Florida, University of South Florida, and University of West Florida.

University Press of Florida
15 Northwest 15th Street
Gainesville, FL 32611-2079
http://www.upf.com

For Asher Z. Milbauer
whose insight inspired and guided this work
and whose friendship made it possible

Think where man's glory most begins and ends,
And say my glory was I had such friends.

W. B. Yeats, "The Municipal Gallery Revisited"

Contents

Foreword

"Each exilic experience is as unique as the experience of any human life." Perhaps this is obvious, but sometimes it takes a critic with the special gifts of Michael Gillespie to hit what Lynch would call the "Bull's eye!" I have some personal interest in the subject, having left England at thirteen for the brave new world across the Atlantic, and so does Gillespie, who glances beautifully at his own family's part in the Irish diaspora ("when my grandfather left Achill Island"). So does Bloom, of course, and so does Joyce, and so do all of us. As the introduction shows, in a far-ranging study of the exile theme from Émile Zola to John Ford, from Joseph Conrad to Thomas Mann, exile is a "word known to all men." What Michael Gillespie brings to the long-worn subject of modernist exile is a double vision of sharpness and sensitivity, which is at once unafraid to take on the foolishness of received critical opinion and deeply attuned to the folly of the human heart. Time and again Gillespie gives us a less cynical, less hierarchical reading of the text, whether it is in a new validation of the intensity of Mr. Duffy's mourning, a new appreciation of the solicitude of the sisters of Reverend Flynn, or a new and warmer light shone on the machinations of Mrs. Mooney and Mrs. Kearney. This is a deeply sympathetic reading, but it is also coldly unafraid to tackle the prescriptive tenets of Joycean criticism, from the literary bases for Ellmann's biographical pronouncements to the standard readings of Stephen's encounter with Cyril Sargent in "Nestor." With this book, Michael Gillespie returns empathy to the center of Joyce's world, as any reader of *Ulysses* comes to understand is its rightful place.

The idea of the book, that Joyce's personal experience of exile was shot through with ambivalence about his native Ireland, an ambivalence that expresses itself in both his life and his work as hostility and sentimentality in equal measure, is everywhere compelling. The oscillating perspectives

(Gillespie borrows the term from Riquelme) of rancor and nostalgia perfectly map onto the exilic authors and characters that Gillespie discusses, and provide the reader with a clear path right to Joyce's doubled heart. This book is written clearly and sensibly, unblinkered by theoretical commitments, and achieves exactly what it intends in providing a timely and useful intervention in Joyce studies. This is an open work in the best sense: welcoming, evenhanded, and open-minded. What results is nothing less than a vital regeneration of Joyce's prose work.

Sebastian D. G. Knowles
Series Editor

Acknowledgments

In addition to the debt of gratitude I have toward Asher Milbauer, to whom this book is dedicated, I feel most grateful to my wife Paula and to our daughters Karen, Leigh, and Ann. Their support has sustained and made meaningful all that I have done as an academic.

I am grateful to a number of people at Florida International University. Deans Kenneth Furton, Meredith Newman, Gisela Casines, and Michael Heithaus have been constant in their encouragement. I have benefited greatly from the insights of colleagues in the English Department including Debra Dean, Ginny Gathercote, Paula Gillespie, Kenneth Johnson, Phillip Marcus, James Sutton, and Feryal Yavas.

I have also benefited from the support of colleagues elsewhere including Nancy Curtin (Fordham University), James Doan (Nova Southeastern University), James Fairhall (DePaul University), A. Nicholas Fargnoli (Molloy College), Anne Fogarty (University College Dublin), Andrew Gibson (University of London), Thomas Hachey (Boston College), Sean Latham (University of Tulsa), Vicki Mahaffey (University of Illinois), Timothy McMahon (Marquette University), James Rogers (St. Thomas University), and David Rose (Paris).

Finally, I am deeply indebted to my readers, Patrick McCarthy and John Paul Riquelme, for their rigorous, insightful, and generous assessment of my manuscript. I am also most grateful to Sebastian Knowles, series editor, who is simply the best book manuscript editor with whom I have ever worked, to Shannon McCarthy, assistant editor at the University Press of Florida, who is both insightful and patient. Finally, project editor Nevil Parker and copy editor Ann Marlowe provided crucial insights during the concluding stages of the project.

The chapter on *Dubliners* appeared in an earlier form in *New Hibernia Review*. The one on *Exiles* has previously appeared in *James Joyce Quarterly*. I am grateful to the editors of both journals for permission to reprint them here.

The Context of Exile

A Critical Introduction

We live in an aesthetic world where comprehension of any form of art cannot avoid inflection by attitudes that emphasize subjectivity, immediacy, and materialism—in short, in a world conceived as operating without elements that would clearly define a center or its periphery. From that perspective, any term seeking to encompass a concept that goes beyond describing an individual's feelings during a self-contained moment might seem to overreach. Conventional political, cultural, and social designations may seem at best arbitrary. The boundaries they asserted that made it possible in earlier eras to distinguish the exile from the society from which he or she had been cut off no longer enjoy the same legitimacy that gave them credence in a premodernist society.[1]

At the same time, ample evidence exists that fundamental issues of the exilic experience continue to resonate strongly within the postmodern world. One need only look to scenes in Samuel Beckett's drama *Waiting for Godot*, the literary paradigm of twentieth-century alienation, for an illustration of the continuing power of the exilic condition over individuals in our society. As Beckett's protagonists show throughout the play, alienation is inescapable for even the most solitary individuals surrounded by a void. From the bleak opening—"Nothing to be done"—through their repeated references to the pain of being alone, Vladimir and Estragon reiterate how the absence of a larger community, beyond that formed by their mutual dependence, scars the individual.[2]

The postmodern way of thinking does not banish exile but rather extends its definition to cover us all. Like the numerous epistemologies that have preceded it, postmodern thinking sees attitudes of isolation and alienation as inherent features in the natures of contemporary individuals. More to the point, it sees those feelings coming directly out of a need for connection with a large social entity.

However one describes that condition, the trauma that comes from separation from community, concern for the consequences of such marginalization repeats itself in public commentaries from generation to generation, with little variation over changing social contexts. This makes the impact of liminality on creativity a force to consider as formidable in any artistic period and no matter what our own interpretive perspective, for no matter when it occurs—from *Oedipus Rex* to *Lord Jim*—exilic images in literature retain a consistent and powerful influence upon how the reader sees and understands the world surrounding him or her.

Admittedly, some argument is necessary to make the case for reading Joyce's works as the product of an exilic experience. He was not a victim of political persecution, expelled from his native country and barred from return by threats of death or imprisonment. Nor was he, like many rural Irish who a half century earlier endured the Great Famine, an economic exile whose alternative to departure was starvation. Instead, Joyce quite simply was a displaced artist who left the land of his birth of his own volition because he felt that he could neither live nor create as he wished in Ireland. For many readers, this decision may seem indistinguishable from those made by any number of emigrants who departed from their homelands at the beginning of the twentieth century and who are not commonly labeled as exiles, but in terms of a critical understanding of the canon, that seems to me very much beside the point.

Charting creative influences always proves to be a problematic endeavor, for it rests upon subjective views that do not always carry conviction across a range of readers. One can shore up such an argument if one keeps the artist's state of mind in the forefront of all considerations. Evidence as to the artist's self-image stands as a far more significant determinant of the applicability of a particular condition than does any other measure of it.

That becomes a key feature to understanding Joyce's relation to his Irish heritage and the motivations that shaped its depictions in his writings. Biographical details and direct statements made by the author in letters and conversations make a strong case for labeling him an exile. In the end the most convincing reason for seeing Joyce as an exile writer comes not because he fits any received view of the term but because events in his life made it possible for him plausibly to see himself as one.

In the next chapter I will take up in greater detail Joyce's connection to the exilic experience. Before exploring the implications of that perspective, however, it is useful to step back and go over the features delineating the concept of exile as I apply it throughout this study. Establishing the specificity of my language stands as an important step in justifying the logic of my approach. I understand that not every departure from one's native country is a movement into exile, nor do all exiles view their native countries in the same way. However, exiles do share certain broad tendencies, and keeping these in mind while reading Joyce's works can greatly enhance our comprehension.

First, let me clarify what distinguishes exile from other forms of separation from one's country. The clearest illustration of the features of exile emerges in contrasting it with emigration, a related but distinctly different condition. Overt agency, though a crucial determinant in a narrow understanding of these terms, does not strike me as a definitive feature of the concept that I am applying in this study to Joyce and to his writings. Indeed, identifying the articulator of the judgment that a person must leave the country—whether it come as a governmental decision, an economic exigency, or an individual's judgment—has less interpretive significance here than does the individual's perception of that determination. For that reason, the psychological, emotional, and even instinctive responses one makes to the severance of ties with one's native land stand for me as the essential components that distinguish the exilic experience. An external entity may impose the condition that a person's life in his or her native country has become insupportable, or the individual may come to that sense of intolerability from within. In either case, it is the conditions and one's perception of them, and not their source, that form one's sense of being an exile.

This brings me back to the function of subjectivity in delineating the process, for it stands as the initial determinant that informs all of the conclusions that follow. Throughout this study, I read Joyce's works from the presumption that individual perception defines to a large degree the broader context in which the person exists. This point of view implicitly colors all of the attitudes that Joyce took throughout his writings, and it becomes an explicit feature informing the narrative, as Joyce's own discourse makes clear in the initial musings of Stephen Dedalus as he walks on Sandymount Strand at the opening of the Proteus chapter of *Ulysses*: "Ineluctable modality of the visible: at least that if no more, thought through my eyes. Signatures of all things I am here to read" (*U* 3.1–2). The passage offers a compact illustration not simply of Stephen's efforts to understand the relationship of imagination and perception but, more broadly, of how disposition can reshape context in Joyce's process of creativity. As Stephen aptly demonstrates, interpretation rather than initiation is the key factor in bringing art into existence. More than whoever initiates a physical change, it is the perceiver of that change—the one who gives it meaning—who imposes meaning on the environment.

This means that for any understanding of the way exile works in Joyce's writing, the most important consideration is that Joyce left Ireland because he felt he was compelled to do so. He became an exile because he saw himself as such. He defined himself in just the way that Stephen Dedalus attempted to piece together the world he ran up against. The "seaspawn and seawrack, the nearing tide, that rusty boot" (*U* 3.2–3) are the artifacts jumbled together that inhabit the world that Stephen encounters. As he comes to understand on his walk, it is his imagination that has the power to identify, classify, and unify them.[3] This makes the need to understand the orientation of imaginative power, not just in Stephen but in his creator as well, a primary function in any interpretive process. Understanding the influence of the exilic experience in turn provides important insights for discerning that orientation. In keeping with my view that the essence of the exilic experience is essentially psychological rather than physical, I believe that in any analysis the traumatic elements of this condition need to be emphasized to distinguish it from other circumstances in which individuals leave their countries of origin.

Emigration, though often materially similar to exile, has transcendent components that clearly distinguish it from exile. The emigrant, voluntarily and often eagerly, leaves his or her native home seeking an alternative situation. A young clerk in Manchester in 1845, for example, might have chosen to leave Britain to go to America seeking a better life, but the clerk would have made the decision knowing full well that it would be possible to remain in England in expectation of a reasonably comfortable situation, and that it would be possible to return home should prospects abroad prove disappointing.

In direct contrast, exile replaces inclination with compulsion, an animating force that violently initiates the condition and remains an influence on all subsequent actions. In this manner a young farmworker living on Achill Island in rural Ireland in the same year as the Manchester clerk, seeing widespread starvation after the country's potato crops had been devastated by blight, would have been faced with the choice of leaving to find sustenance in another country or remaining to face dying of hunger. Either course of action would have been irreversible. Comparing the two cases makes the distinction between emigration and exile exceedingly clear despite any similarities in the actual displacement.

Whatever the circumstances surrounding a specific decision to leave, the reality at the heart of the matter is that exile is thrust upon individuals who can no longer sustain themselves in the lands that they have considered their homes. Exile may be actively forced on a person, like Ovid's expulsion from Rome, or it may be the result of an individual's self-imposition when no alternatives seem to exist, like Lord Byron's departure from England. In every case a perceived threat to one's existence, defined in a variety of ways, propels one from one's country, and the consequences of displacement—a traumatic separation from the political, cultural, and social environment—radically reconfigure the way that the individual conceives his or her public identity.

It is this metaphysical impact of exile on the individual's consciousness, considered both in its immediacy and in its long term, that is the most important feature distinguishing the experience. Exile stands as a traumatic event whose duration and repercussions can hardly be overstated. Not just the act of being exiled but the enduring experience that unfolds as a consequence of being forced to leave one's home leads to visceral, emotional responses at the most fundamental level of understanding and comprehension, evoking sensations of expulsion, sundering, and alienation. An aura of violation—physical, emotional, and spiritual—surrounds the exile and inflects impressions of the exilic experience as profoundly as does the sorrow of separation. Exile quite simply is an event that fundamentally alters one's psyche, and its repercussions remain within the individual's consciousness for life.

At its heart, exile challenges identity. It does so by altering the individual's relationship to the cultural context against which the self has been measured. Exile redefines one's sense of the world from which one came. In the process it makes the individual far more deeply aware of dependence upon that world, and it creates sometimes sentimental and sometimes bitter feelings toward that now lost world.

This feeling is particularly evident in a number of writers whose postcolonial views are strongly influenced by postmodern thinking. It is a point well worth emphasizing, for it underscores how fundamental human feelings repeatedly trump ideological commitments. Even Edward Said, whose writings would seem to place him fiercely at odds with sentimentality, presents a softer version of the experience than one might expect:

> In a secular and contingent world, homes are always provisional. Borders and barriers, which enclose us within the safety of familiar territory, can also become prisons, and are often defended beyond reason or necessity. Exiles cross borders, break barriers of thought and experience.[4]

Said's prose does not succumb to the sentimentality that shades many exilic recollections, and his emphasis in the first two sentences focuses squarely on the claustrophobic qualities of nationhood. However, when he turns to the experience of exile, his language becomes more lyrical and a touch of romanticism tinges the exposition that follows. In this stylistic shift, the description of exile emphasizes it as more emotionally rewarding and more complex than one might expect in a mere materialist recapitulation of the events and the consequences of displacement. There is an understated but nonetheless powerful heroic element in Said's account that presents exile as a transformative and even enhancing condition.

In an essay published in the same year as the article quoted above, Said reiterates a commitment to this point of view. He comes back to the topic of displacement as a way of underscoring the deep-rooted, multifaceted influence of the exilic experience on every aspect of our lives. Said's description presents exile as anything but a crippling condition. Quite the contrary, he foregrounds it as an experience that reconfigures individuals and that leads to broad transformations of their environment. Said goes on to state unambiguously and perhaps, seeing himself also as a displaced person, with a sense of self-reflected pride: "Modern Western culture is in large part the work of exiles, émigrés, refugees."[5]

None of these observations can diminish the corrosive impact that exile exerts, nor are they intended to do such a thing. It is important to keep in mind that the experience of exile almost always has a profoundly traumatic or at the very least an insistently funereal quality to it. As Said himself knew, suffering starkly delineates the separation between theory and practice:

> Exile is strangely compelling to think about but terrible to experience. It is the unhealable rift forced between a human being and a native place, between the self and its true home: its essential sadness can never be surmounted.[6]

For Said, unique pain that one must endure, more than anything else, sets apart the exilic experience.

That, however, is not a sufficient summary of the exilic condition. Despite the directness and the confidence of statements by Said and others who have commented on the impact—psychological, spiritual, and creative—of the exilic experience, a great deal remains to be engaged when one takes up the issue of exile and art. Particularly in discussions of the impact of exile on creative expression, the point on how to understand expressions of exile embedded in authors' works remains open to debate. This is due in no small part to the fact that the conditions that precipitate writers' exiles and their consequent responses to their displacements cover a wide spectrum of possibilities. Even the broadest of categorizations regarding the displacement and its aftermath almost immediately suggest exceptions and provoke qualifications. The challenge to interpretive engagement comes from the diversity of experiences across the lives of different authors.

These transformative consequences of exile make it inevitable that the creations of artists who are compelled, for whatever reason, to leave their native countries will be informed by this condition. At the same time, the impact of the exilic experience is never simply apprehended by the individual who undergoes it or predictably discerned by others who observe it. Ann C. Colley, writing about Robert Louis Stevenson's separation from Scotland when his health forced him abroad, describes that author's complex and conflicted attitudes toward the country he left and by implication hints at its impact on the works he would produce.

> Stevenson's longing for Scotland is especially circumscribed by inversions and oppositions. Pride and mockery, admiration and deprecation permeated his commentary so that he alternately abhorred and respected, for instance the Victorian gentility of Edinburgh, and simultaneously esteemed and ridiculed the Scots dialect.[7]

Considering the life and writings of authors like Stevenson shows that the emotional, psychological, and spiritual duality that comes out of the experience of traumatic separation from one's homeland is by no means unique to a particular author or to particular works, and my study of Joyce will examine both the recurring attitudes that beset any exiled author and the features and attitudes unique to Joyce's experience that have shaped his work.

The artist's creative response to exile can take any of a variety of forms, but whatever the manifestation, it tends to adopt a point of view that replicates Stevenson's feelings of esteem and ridicule for the country that has been left behind. In consequence, despite the trauma inherent in the experience, it is a mistake to assume that the exile's feelings can be summed up sufficiently from a single, simple, negative perspective. Certainly, not every writer chooses to underscore the brutality inherent in exile, and critics show an equally broad sense of the condition. Indeed, some contemporary thinkers have configured descriptions of exile that demonstrate a more romantic sense of the broad experience than one might expect from critics of the cultural status quo.

Broadly speaking, whether they make exile a direct subject of their writing or bring it indirectly, even unconsciously, into their works, authors who have been compelled to leave the lands of their birth demonstrate both lasting and evolving connections with its transformative impact on their lives. Displaced authors go through the process of creating fiction refined through the influence, conscious or not, of the severed connections to the world that gave them identity. The subsequent accounts do not so much recapitulate the experiences of the exile as extend or anatomize them. This means engagements with exilic moments and attitudes that acknowledge a range of creative options and that stand as a crucial first step for anyone seeking to understand their works.

Even when a clearly discernible external force, like political oppression, brings about exile, almost any example one can produce will impose unique interpretive demands upon readers. Dante's *Divine Comedy* evokes a greater pathos when one understands that the spiritual journey of its protagonist parallels the profound suffering of its exiled author, articulated as early as the opening lines of the *Inferno*: "In the middle of the journey of our life, I came to myself, in a dark wood, where the direct way was lost." Madame de Staël's *Considerations on the Principal Events of the French Revolution* and *Ten Years of Exile* draw force from growing out of the confrontations with Napoleon that led to her peregrinations across Europe. Victor Hugo's nineteen years abroad—briefly in Belgium, then in Jersey, and finally in Guernsey—coincided with some of his strongest writing about life in his native country. To read *Les Misérables* without this biographical awareness is to deprive oneself of an important hermeneutic. And Lio Yiwu's *The Corpse Walker*, twenty-five interviews of people who exist on the margins—a professional mourner, a human trafficker, a public toilet manager, a leper, a grave robber, and a Falun Gong practitioner, among others—reflects the broader alienation across Chinese society and gains even greater power when one realizes the author's background of imprisonment and exile.

While these writers each suffered state-orchestrated oppression that profoundly affected their creative output, politics is not the only force propelling authors out of their native countries and informing their writings. Economic conditions have exerted equal pressure upon any number of artists, and displacement under those circumstances also uniquely inflects the works of that exilic category. Ireland is particularly rich in examples of writers compelled to leave for more amenable economic conditions. Though their departures were generally less violent and their responses less direct than is the case with political exiles, nonetheless our sense of their background gives us much stronger insights into their writings.

In the eighteenth century Oliver Goldsmith, after an undistinguished time studying at Trinity College Dublin and desultory wanderings around the Continent, went to London to write because there was no question of doing it in Ireland with anything like the same chance of success. Through the nineteenth century with Tom Moore and Oscar Wilde, and into the twentieth century with storytellers like Patrick MacGill and poets like Thomas Kinsella, a number of artists left because Ireland could not support them.[8] Goldsmith and Wilde all but effaced overt references to Irish sensibilities from their works, though a number of critics have seen Irish themes and attitudes particularly in Wilde's writings.[9] The others continued to use Ireland as a source of inspiration, even if it was no longer a basis for their income.

Two gestures stand as keys to understanding the art of these exiles: recognizing the parameters of the material world out of which these authors wrote and seeing the hardships of the world that they felt forced to leave in order to continue to write. (It is important to note before going further that such traumas—political, economic, or spiritual—do not inevitably produce harsh or negative responses. Shortly I will explore in greater detail the impact of nostalgia upon the exilic experience, discussing how recollections of homeland often become idealized, even fictionalized, accounts of the world left behind.)

In the post-Enlightenment era, the exilic impulse continued to evolve, and overtly self-imposed exile became increasingly common. The forces impelling one to leave expanded as the sense of national homogeneity eroded. Changing intellectual, emotional, and artistic environments placed authors in the conflicted position of being imaginatively rooted in the cultural context of their countries and yet, because of frustration with constraining cultural institutions, unable to bring their work to fruition in their homeland: Shelley, Byron, Keats, and D. H. Lawrence represent only a few of the best known. To a greater or lesser degree, all of these artists write out of their native experiences, yet no full understanding of their work can come without the sense that they also write from an exilic point of view.

As Said suggests in the passage quoted above, the experience of exile, though often melancholic, is not inevitably diminishing. Even with the exile pushed psychologically, emotionally, and spiritually to an existence at the margins of his or her native land, that position affords a unique point of view. It enables the exile both to enjoy an intimate sense of the country of origin and to experience a reflective detachment pulling any number of issues into perspective.

Often this can simply intensify creative ties to the homeland. One sees this, for example, in setting Émile Zola's year in England during the Dreyfus scandal against the output of subsequent years. The *Quatre Évangiles* project, truncated, by his death, at three of the four planned novels, reflects a renewed vigor in his naturalist renderings of French life and a sharpened critique of contemporary social institutions.

Each exilic experience is as unique as the experience of any human life. Nonetheless, despite a range of divergent forces bringing about the condition, a common creative feature characterizes the output of all exiled writers, setting their works apart from those of authors who are emigrants. Writers displaced from life in their native lands do not seek the integration of their artistic vision into the new environment, but rather continue to write out of the world from which they emerged. One sees this in the work of Henry James who, to the end of his days and despite living and gaining citizenship in England, remained as American a writer as his contemporary Mark Twain. In contrast, T. S. Eliot, through sheer force of will and a determined unwillingness to see anything ludicrous in his undertaking, had by the end of his life amalgamated himself into English society and had effaced from his works all of the social, cultural, and emotional features that made the writings of his fellow poet/businessman and literary contemporary Wallace Stevens quintessentially American.

All this is a long way around saying that the inherent referentiality of exile unifies the range of often dichotomous sensations, images, and attitudes to which a reader must be attentive. Despite the subjectivity of all artistic expression, creations shaped by the exilic experience come out of the same fundamental sense of separation, grounded in feelings of nostalgia and/or rancor. The exilic condition inclines the individual, particularly if that person is a writer, simultaneously toward backward and forward visions. The traumatic parting from the homeland severs the physical ties to a place even as the terms of that separation reaffirm an emotional bond to what is now lost. This oscillating perspective that stamps the work of the exilic writer also allows readers to see clearly the distinctions between authors who are emigrants and those who become exiles.

Joseph Conrad stands out as a paradigmatic emigrant writer, particularly along the lines laid down earlier in this chapter. At eighteen Conrad left home by choice to become a sailor, though living in Russian-controlled Poland may have influenced him. He remained in the merchant marine for nineteen years until poor health led him to settle in Great Britain. Although he may have considered himself Polish for his entire life, in practice he became English. Conrad integrated himself into the social ethos of his adopted country, took up its language, and made England and English life the topic of his art.[10]

Nowhere is Conrad's cultural commitment more evident than in fiction like his novel *Lord Jim*. There, although he makes his central character an exile, the descriptions of Jim and the longing he feels draw on Conrad's experiences as an expatriate rather than an exile. Conrad cuts his central character off from England while emphasizing its integral place in Jim's nature. The poignancy of Jim's loss testifies to Conrad's acquired sense of the deeply emotive features of ordinary English life. Paradoxically, in *Lord Jim* he writes movingly of exile and of the exilic experience, but only in reference to his adopted country.

In contrast, Thomas Mann stands as the paradigmatic exile artist. Like any exilic writer, his condition immediately evoked general characteristics of all exiles and presented the unique responses to what he endured. From his example, we see that dealing with exilic writers requires both a general awareness of the condition of exile and a specific attentiveness to manifestations of its effects in the literature produced by those forced from the homeland. It is important that interpretations remain balanced, rather than letting one condition overshadow the other.

Mann's life follows the pattern of the classic political exile. He was on holiday in Switzerland when Hitler came to power in 1933, and he felt that he and his wife could not return to Germany. At first Mann remained in Switzerland. He moved to America in 1938 and stayed until 1952. Mann then returned to Switzerland, where he remained until his death in 1955.[11]

During that time, Mann wrote as one cut off from his native country but with unbreakable emotional and imaginative ties to it. Whether offering his own account of the biblical story of Joseph and his brothers or presenting a scathing critique of contemporary political upheaval in nonfictional prose, his cultural, emotional, and spiritual commitment to the country where he was born remained clear and unambiguous. Mann wrote in his native language, and German life and culture stood at the heart of his artistic consciousness.

Conrad, the aspiring emigrant, worked to translate his past into representations of his current life. Mann, the consummate exile, strove to sustain his past through his works in the present. In both cases their artistic output became embodiments of the identities they acquired by leaving their native lands. Reading each demands not only a sense of their displacement but an awareness of the different responses they made to the experience.[12]

Certainly, all exiles are not writers, nor does writing inevitably lead one into exile. Nonetheless, the lives of exiled writers often mirror the experiences of the larger exile community through the reflection of their artistic consciousnesses. In consequence, understanding the fundamental features of the exile experience as it relates to an author's feelings and perceptions gives literary critics a clearer grasp of the achievement of a writer separated from his or her native land.

Before continuing, then, I want to elaborate on the common features that I have already associated with the condition of exile as well as noting the insistent and often strikingly diverse attitudes that they produce among all those who have involuntarily left their native country. Though they are common to almost anyone experiencing the trauma of exile, I will concentrate my attention, because of the emphasis of this study, on these manifestations in writers.

The most apparent and unrelenting consequences of this forced displacement are feelings of nostalgia and hostility toward one's country of origin. Manifestations remain stubbornly subjective, relating specifically to individual experiences and backgrounds, yet they trace broadly familiar patterns. Some exiles will privilege one over the other, and some will oscillate between the two. In either instance, while the origins remain the same, the natures of individuals will give a particularity to every expression. Each attitude comes out of a personal reaction to separation. Each incident exerts its own strong hold on the consciousness of the exile. And each proves to be a determining feature in the individual's perspective on his or her native land. At the same time, all these expressions come back to two fundamental feelings.

Nostalgia is an overt representation of the romantic ideas about separation that Said and other critics have articulated. It goes beyond simply a fond recollection of a place of origin. It reconfigures memory, supplanting the past with an idealized creation of a world that may or may not have existed physically but that has come to occupy a very real position in an individual's conceptions.

The subjective/objective dynamic of the experience is quite evident in the way it is labeled. All groups seem to recognize this attitude, and each captures it in a fashion that gives it a unique flavor according to a particular cultural context and to the romanticizing that recollection imposes on it. The Welsh, for example, sum up this feeling with the term *hiraeth*, roughly meaning a longing for a home that never existed, at least as it is being recalled. The word encompasses the feeling of sorrow and loss with an idealization for the place from which one is separated. In its specificity, it delineates a cultural attitude that nonetheless has a broad application from society to society, summing up the feelings of many exiles from different backgrounds who seek a means for articulating their pain.

The impact of idealization on the exile's recollections of home—and by extension on exilic writers' representations in their works—cannot be stressed too strongly. The nostalgia to which I refer will often produce a highly individualized portrait of the writer's native land. Its specificity makes it distinctly different from simply a general longing to return home. In the first chapter of *A Portrait of the Artist as a Young Man*, for example, Stephen Dedalus languishing at Clongowes Wood College does more than long to be back home in Dublin. He creates a vivid picture of the world there as he would like it to be.

The need to underscore the unique features of nostalgia as it characterizes an exile's reminiscences is especially crucial in light of the tendency of a number of commentators to conflate nostalgia and homesickness. Svetlana Boym, for example, sees nostalgia as restorative, a desire to return to a lost home, and reflective, that which feels a sense of loss.[13] For Boym those distinctions are both significant and sufficient. She makes an important point, emphasizing separation as the dominant feeling. From my point of view, however, that perspective does not give sufficient consideration to the way idealization functions in nostalgia and leads to distorted conceptions of the place from which one is separated and for which one longs. I find a more useful approach in the work of Jean Starobinski. Writing thirty-five years before Boym's study appeared, he showed that the notion of nostalgia was relatively new, with the term itself coined by Johannes Hofer in 1688 while studying the young Swiss mercenaries. Though he sees the two conditions as quite similar, Starobinski articulates the importance of distinguishing between the realistic evocations of homesickness and the idealized views of nostalgia.[14]

This awareness of their different connotations is particularly important in a study like this, for nostalgic views of Ireland abound both in readers and in writers, and any interpretation of Irish exilic literature needs to have a very fine sense of what those attitudes entail.[15] One of the best extended dissections of the deleterious effects of its excesses appears in John Ford's 1952 film *The Quiet Man,* where nostalgia is skillfully anatomized and mercilessly critiqued. Ford's motion picture offers a sophisticated elaboration of a short story by Maurice Walsh that appeared in the 11 February 1933 issue of the *Saturday Evening Post*. Unlike Walsh's short story, Ford's film presents a close examination of the protagonist's emotions, assumptions, and misconceptions relating to Ireland. Sean Thornton is the Yank returning to his ancestral home after his family has been forced from Ireland by economic exigencies. Time and again, to the amusement, puzzlement, and occasional frustration of the locals, he recollects his mother's eulogies on Irish life.

The naïve sentimentality of Thornton becomes all the more evident as incidents in the film illuminate the harshness lying just under the surface in rural Ireland. Xenophobia, spousal abuse, alcoholism, misogyny punctuate the rhythm of life in Innisfree, the town to which Thornton returns. Time and again, Thornton is told the Ireland of his imagination has no connection with the reality that surrounds him, most effectively done early in the film when the Widow Tillane sarcastically asks if he seeks to have White o' Morn, the cottage where he was born, turned into a museum celebrating his Thornton ancestors. However, the most devastating appraisal of his sentimentality is illustrated, not articulated. It comes at the end of the film when Ford shows that Thornton—after physically abusing his wife, fighting with his brother-in-law, and coming home drunk and unrepentant—has cheerfully embraced most of these vices and in the process has integrated himself into the community. Ford's assessment of Irish life and his characterization of those who have left and remember it ideally could hardly be more shattering.[16]

The antithetical attitude, the rancor of the displaced, often manifests itself with less fanfare but with no less intensity. I saw a powerful illustration of this feeling in Chicago in 1975 when my grandfather, Michael Masterson, was ill and on the verge of death. He had come to America as a young man in 1910 from County Mayo and had spent most of his adult life in Chicago. During one of my visits to his hospital room, I asked him why he never spoke of returning to Ireland, for it was something his wife, my grandmother, alluded to often though never carried out. The bluntness and the bitterness of his answer surprised me, for he was not a man given to open expressions of his feelings. "Michael," he said, "they couldn't feed me when I was there, and I am God damned if I'll go back and feed them now."

This is by no means an isolated example of bitter resentment toward the country from which one was forced to depart. Contemporary Irish literature abounds in examples of the deep scars inflicted by the forces that compel exile. In his poem "The Mule Duignan," Bernard O'Donoghue captures the poignancy and the bitterness of an Irish exile in Bristol recollecting a family crisis and the hostility it produced. Here is the portion of the poem that encapsulates harsh recollections from the speaker's childhood:

> I think back to a December night
> when my small sister crept into bed with me,
> shivering. We listened to our father's voice,
> emphatic and quiet: "If the cow does die tonight,
> we'll have to sell up and go." We prayed ourselves
> to sleep. In the morning the wind woke us
> and we all went out together to the stall.

The cow was standing up, eating hay.
And then for the first and only time I saw
my parents embracing. I hate that country:
its poverties and embarrassments
too humbling to retell. I'll never ever
go back to offer it forgiveness.[17]

The Irish experience of exile of course did not begin in 1910 when my grandfather left Achill Island for America, nor did it end with Bernard O'Donoghue's eloquent articulation of rage carried across an ocean and across a lifetime.[18] Rather it has a long, complex, and ongoing tradition reaching back well before England's eight-hundred-year occupation, and it mimics the pattern—political, economic, and intellectual displacement—that serves to characterize exile in general. Much of the exilic experience has been captured by Irish writers over that period, and that tradition of writing out of the trauma of separation stands as a strong feature in the literary heritage that shaped Joyce's work.

Exile has been an all too common experience in Ireland for at least fifteen hundred years, and writing about it has been a near constant occupation for Irish authors. One of the earliest recorded examples can be found in *Vita Columbae*, a hagiography of St. Columba or Columcille written by Adomnán (also known as Eunan) who served as the ninth abbot of Iona, the world-renowned abbey founded by St. Columba, until his death in AD 704. Adomnán recounts how, after the Battle of Cúl Dreimhne in AD 561, a clash between Celtic forces from the North and those from the South resulted in thousands of men being killed. St. Columba, who had supported the northern fighters, went into exile in Scotland as a sign of repentance for the loss of life caused by the fight.[19]

Exile took an increasingly cynical and ruthless role in political oppression from Elizabethan times to the early twentieth century as it became a popular tool used by English colonizers to rid themselves of nationalist agitators without creating martyrs. At various times over the next three hundred years, any native Irish considered by their English oppressors to be undesirables were transported wholesale to the West Indies, the American colonies, Canada, and Australia.[20] Banishment through colonial oppression continued to be a topic of Irish bardic poetry well through the nineteenth century with the Fenian John Locke's "The Exile's Return."

Politics, however, stood as only one of several prominent elements contributing to the writings of the Irish diaspora.

The tradition of economic exile, while often less immediately violent than political expulsion, proved to be just as painful and perhaps even more insidious. The occasion of forced economic departure from Ireland most familiar to general readers comes as the consequence of the potato blight that began in 1845 and lasted well into the next decade. It destroyed the staple element in the diet of most of rural Ireland and led to the catastrophic suffering and economic ruin across the country commonly called simply the Famine or the Great Hunger. Though precise numbers are difficult to determine, experts estimate that the loss of the potato crops caused approximately a million deaths. Landlord evictions and sheer desperation drove a million more from the country.[21] Unfortunately, though the most striking example of economic exile, it was not an isolated instance.

Until fairly recently, agriculture held pride of place as the dominant Irish industry, and even after the Industrial Revolution swept across England, it suited the colonial government to maintain this condition. In Ireland, farming remained a labor-intensive endeavor until well into the twentieth century, and the need for workers tended to be met most often through large families. However, to prevent endless subdivision, only one child was allowed to inherit the land, and there were few superfluous resources to support additional family members. In consequence, the other siblings had no choice in the matter. They had to leave once the property changed hands.[22]

The separation from family and community, whether in rural or urban settings, was every bit as painful as separation instigated by more dramatic social conditions or violent political change. It was seen as a traumatic sundering.[23] As recently as one hundred years ago, with the cost and conditions of travel as they were, such departures were akin to death. They stood as ruptures with no hope for reuniting. Indeed, when young people were compelled to go to the United States or Canada, the party traditionally held the night before they left was called an American Wake.[24]

As Ireland moved into the twentieth century and Irish society became increasingly diverse and complex, a new impetus, as effective as all the others at forcing individuals from their homeland, arose. It was tied to cultural rather than political or economic conditions, but the impact on the individuals involved in the upheaval was no less profound. The movement, aimed at renewing awareness and interest in traditional Irish arts, put a great deal of energy into fostering very particular kinds of creative endeavors. With the sponsorship of dynamic individuals like W. B. Yeats and Lady Augusta Gregory, it became extremely successful in a relatively short time. The inherent irony of the condition lay in the fact that, despite its avowed interest in strengthening awareness of a native artistic tradition, its conception of what that tradition might be was far narrower than many imaginative Irish artists could accept.

With the kinds of contradictions common to many new intellectual movements, the Irish Literary Revival had the dichotomous effects of energizing interest in Irish art while at the same time presenting a narrow, prescriptive sense of what that concept entailed. This was particularly true of the renewed attention given to Irish-themed literature.[25]

Though interest in native Irish writing had been growing over the final decades of the nineteenth century, W. B. Yeats's *The Celtic Twilight* and Douglas Hyde's *The Love Songs of Connacht*, both published in 1893, galvanized awareness of selected themes, events, and characters. Other writers sought to emulate their work, and those affiliated with this movement adopted very clear paradigms that highlighted lyrical celebrations of Irish mythology and idealizations of the lives of the peasantry. Simultaneously, they displayed an aggressive disinterest in the contemporary, Catholic, urban, middle-class Irish world. The founding in 1899 of the Irish Literary Theatre (the forerunner of the Abbey Theatre) by Yeats, Lady Augusta Gregory, and Edward Martyn and the subsequent dramatic efforts of Yeats, Lady Gregory, John Millington Synge, and a number of lesser playwrights solidified Revival attitudes, and they clearly delineated what was and what was not legitimate Irish writing.

The consequent prescriptive views of what constituted Irish art and the control that Revivalists exerted on the scope of writing that found approval created a need to find freedom for artistic expression outside the country. Joyce deftly satirizes the parochial, claustrophobic, and most significantly self-satisfied Revivalist mentality when he has Buck Mulligan parody the colophon that appeared in the Dun Emer Press edition of Yeats' *In the Seven Woods*: "That's folk, he said very earnestly, for your book, Haines. Five lines of text and ten pages of notes about the folk and the fishgods of Dundrum. Printed by the weird sisters in the year of the big wind" (*U* 1.365–76).[26] As Joyce's life attests, writers who did not share the Revival's idealized views of Irish life and antiquity or did not at the very least outwardly conform to them gave up any real hope of literary success in Ireland.[27]

George Bernard Shaw, Sean O'Casey, and Samuel Beckett stand out as only the most famous among scores of writers contemporary to Joyce who felt that they must leave Ireland because of its claustrophobic imaginative atmosphere. The degree to which they felt the need for separation and the anger at and/or longing for Ireland varied from author to author, but evocations of Irish life and customs, attitudes and biases, and hopes and disappointments run through their works and attest to the profundity of the choices and the tenacity of those effects. (W. B. Yeats, always the canny cultivator of his public image, managed to have things both ways. While he remained a figure dominant on the Irish literary scene—writing about forgotten myths, political chauvinism, rabid civil strife, and struggles for national identity—he spent easily as much time living outside his native country as he did residing in his famous tower in the west of Ireland.)

The individuals resisting what they saw as the artistic tyranny of the Celtic Revival did not endure the same level of physical duress as ancestors expelled by Cromwell or crushed by the potato blight. Nonetheless, the claustrophobic aesthetic atmosphere imposed by a literary movement with little tolerance for alternative modes of expression created a toxic environment as powerful as the one that forced the departure of those whose political views and economic conditions had made their lives insupportable in Ireland.

Each instance shaped the country's exilic tradition. The impetus for exile could and did change according to cultural and historical contexts, but the broad relief sought by the individual compelled to leave remained constant. Just as punishment for mid-nineteenth-century political violence put men and women on ships bound for Australia and the threat of starvation forced many from the middle of the nineteenth until well into the twentieth century into economic exile in America, Canada, England, and elsewhere, creative stagnation stood as a danger every bit as threatening to the imaginative lives of Joyce and his artistic contemporaries.

1

Joyce's Exilic Self-Conception

From 8 October 1904 to 13 January 1941—that is to say, for most of his years as an adult—James Joyce made his home outside Ireland. Ostensively his departure from his native country, as chronicled by Richard Ellmann and others, was of his own volition. Nonetheless, as the evidence that one finds in his letters and biographies and the memoirs of family members and friends makes abundantly clear, Joyce felt, with absolutely no hesitation, that irremediable social, cultural, and creative conditions compelled him to leave.[1]

The brief visits that he made back to Ireland in 1909 and again in 1912 only solidified these views, and he never again set foot on Irish soil. In 1922 he declined to accompany Nora and their two children on a visit there, and in fact actively discouraged their trip. In 1932 he felt it would be out of the question to return for his father's funeral.

The decision not to return did not come from any lack of opportunity. In his early years abroad he always managed to find ways to travel if it suited him, and in the two final decades of his life he traveled widely across Europe. Despite all this, he had no interest in returning to Ireland. Even after the outbreak of World War II, when the German occupation made it intolerable to live in France, Joyce chose in December 1940, just a month before his death, to go back to Switzerland rather than make his way to neutral Ireland.

At the same time, as his letters and the recollections of those close to him make very clear, he never lost touch with his family in Ireland, he welcomed visits from relatives and friends who came to the Continent, and he never lost his intense interest in the most ordinary rhythms of Irish life.[2] Over the course of his time abroad, Joyce amply demonstrated the ambivalence—oscillating between rancor and nostalgia—felt by many exiles, balancing criticisms with outbursts of sentimental longing and national pride.[3]

Though Joyce's decision to become an exile may seem straightforward and simple, his motivations were diverse and complex. Joyce made no secret of his broad resentment for the restrictive authority by which religious ardor, nationalist fervor, and colonial oppression shaped Irish life. Leaving Ireland was the only way he could see to escape the influence of the multiple cultural, social, and political institutions that had been curtailing a great deal of what he tried to do to establish an identity and that would circumscribe all that he hoped to achieve as an artist.

Time and again the customs, values, and practices of Irish life had thwarted his desires for making his way in the world. He resented the minute control of the most mundane of circumstances exercised by Catholic beliefs and traditions. He did not wish to submit to a marriage ceremony, religious or civil, yet at the same time he knew he could never have lived openly with Nora Barnacle in Ireland. (In fact, when they did marry in 1931, it was only to protect the inheritance rights of their children.) He chafed at the circumscription of Irish public life by the English colonial administration. And he could not help but wish to escape the implicit burden of the dysfunctional family that his father had allowed to sink into poverty and malnutrition. In these respects and in a dozen others in which his views challenged prevailing social attitudes in Ireland, he would have been fighting his whole life long against the parochial discipline then imposed on Irish society by the Catholic Church, the legal system, and dominant community values and customs.[4]

To understand this disposition toward self-imposed exile, let me elaborate on allusions made in the previous chapter to the attitudes dominating the Irish artistic environment as Joyce grew to adulthood. At the turn of the last century, for Joyce or any other young writer living in Ireland, a prerequisite for success would have been a willingness to adhere to the agenda of the Irish Literary Revival. Yeats and Lady Augusta Gregory, George Russell (AE), Edward Martyn, Katharine Tynan, William Kirkpatrick Magee (John Eglinton), and others with unshakable commitments to the tenets of the Revival had a strong influence on what was published and performed in Ireland.[5] John Millington Synge, Padraic Colum, James Stephens and numerous others followed their prescriptions with varying degrees of success.[6]

Joyce resisted the autocracy of the Revivalists and went so far, in the Scylla and Charybdis episode of *Ulysses*, as to satirize the system of flattery and habits of deference that he saw stifling Irish writing as many ambitious young Irish writers bowed to the system. Buck Mulligan, in a tone that mixes pragmatism and cynicism and does much to reveal his own willingness to accommodate, chides Stephen Dedalus, who has written a harsh review of a Lady Gregory book, for ignoring the opportunity to ingratiate himself and instead showing disdain for those who do.

> Longworth is awfully sick, he [Mulligan] said, after what you wrote about that old hake Gregory. O you inquisitional drunkenjewjesuit! She gets you a job on the paper and then you go and slate her drivel to Jaysus. Couldn't you do the Yeats touch? (*U* 9.1158–61)

As his brother Stanislaus attests in two memoirs of life at that time, Joyce's actual experiences with the Dublin literati were not far removed from this fictional representation, and they gave him ample reason for a rancorous recollection of his native land.[7]

At the same time, Joyce's views of Ireland and Irish life were not universally hostile but manifested themselves in a complex and diverse tone that characterized his view of his native land throughout his life.[8] The same evidence that shows his resentment over the specific circumstances that compelled him to leave also reveals Joyce's at times nostalgic fascination with the world of lower-middle-class Catholic Dublin that informed his consciousness from infancy through his maturation to young adulthood. Like the fictional Kevin Egan, the Irish nationalist forced by English displeasure over his political activities to flee his homeland, who appears briefly in Stephen Dedalus's recollections of Paris in the Proteus chapter of *Ulysses* (*U* 3.209–64), Joyce never forgot his native country, but the scene does more than show that Ireland was prominent in his mind while he live abroad. A tone of melancholic fondness for a range of features of Irish life permeates Joyce's representation of Egan's life in Paris, and it suggests, at the very least, the author's keen familiarity with such sentiments.[9]

Recognizing these feelings helps demonstrate why, despite his living abroad for more than thirty-six years, the ethos of Dublin at the turn of the last century remained keenly impressed upon his consciousness, and evoking it became a feature central to his artistic process. His brother Stanislaus sums up this attitude very nicely, saying, "The dearest of all things in Ireland is the memory of the past." Stanislaus goes on to talk about Joyce's particular fascination with Dublin:

> [My brother] always held that he was lucky to have been born in a city that is old and historic enough to be considered a representative European capital, and small enough to be viewed as a whole; and he believed that circumstances of birth, talent, and character had made him its interpreter.[10]

Stanislaus's close relationship with his brother produced unique insights into crucial features of Joyce's creative methods, but the full significance of this observation becomes clearer when one considers that Joyce's writing emerged from feelings shaped by the complex attitudes of the exilic experience. Joyce did not simply write about Dublin. Rather his fiction described a Dublin frozen in his imagination at the moment he left in October 1904. In his correspondence with friends and family members, Joyce would often ask for artifacts and recollections, collecting numerous mementoes and recording countless anecdotes that captured unique aspects of the period when he grew from a child to a young man and brought that time in Dublin back to the center of his recollections.[11]

Over the course of his artistic career, Joyce always showed a keen determination to maintain a connection with that time he spent as a boy and young man in Ireland. This became particularly apparent when he encountered any of his countrymen who were visiting Paris. The Irish actor Jack MacGowran, speaking of meeting Joyce there sometime in the 1930s, recalled the kind of interrogation that must have been quite common. "Although Joyce never came back to Dublin, anyone who came from Dublin Joyce was eager to know. Was such and such a shop still there? Was So and so still alive? Did Mrs. So and so still walk her dog at such an hour of night?"[12] Unlike émigré authors who chose to employ their craft to demonstrate and facilitate their own cultural assimilation, Joyce's art did not embrace the ethos of the world he entered, nor did he write his fiction in the language of the countries he inhabited. Like Dante, another displaced artist whose vernacular accounts were shaped by recollections of his past life in Florence, although he did not choose to evoke it directly, Joyce sustained an otherness in exile by writing accounts of his homeland in its vernacular.

As the MacGowran quotation illustrates, Joyce endeavored not simply to evoke but to sustain and then to reproduce the world that he left behind. One sees this impulse recurring in countless letters that he wrote to his aunt Josephine, to his brother Stanislaus, and to other relatives and friends who were still living in Ireland. In every instance he pressed them into service to illuminate, confirm, or correct, as precisely as possible, a variety of mundane details about daily life, events in the lives of friends and neighbors, and topographical features in Dublin at the turn of the last century.[13] The consequent encyclopedic quality of allusions embedded in his narratives—from the *Dubliners* stories onward—attests to the effectiveness of this research and at the same time calls out for a key that would provide an understanding of this aspect of his writing. One cannot fail to note the strong and varied emotions that color these descriptions, suggesting that Joyce's own sense of place and of people exerts a profound influence on his process of composition and on our acts of interpretation. Once one has made that connection, understanding the impact of the exilic experience becomes an essential concept for grasping Joyce's creative process.

Managing interpretive responses to this referentiality becomes easier when the reader recognizes the fundamental tendency on Joyce's part to ground his work in the emotional duality that comes directly out of his sense of displacement. One sees the transformations thrust upon his sensibilities as a writer by the exilic condition correlating with the writing he produced. Joyce's role as chronicler of contemporary Irish-Catholic bourgeois existence was uniquely defined by the life he came to live. He had assumed both the role of an intimate and that of an outcast, which created multiple perspectives and fostered complex emotional attachments to the past. Thus a reader's engagement with that life is a crucial first step toward understanding the works.

Such an approach demands we see Joyce not only as separate and free from the Irish society he had left but also as always engaging and engaged by it. From that perspective the contradictions defined by Joyce's relationships with Ireland serve to clarify rather than obscure his creative impulses. The everyday world he inhabited reminded him of his marginality. He continued to experience Ireland, if at all, from a distance and secondhand. At the same time, the ethos of Pola, Trieste, Rome, Zurich, and Paris brought to bear insistent pressures on his ways of seeing the world that he occupied.

As an exile, past and present challenged Joyce in ways different from what he would have experienced had he never left home, and his efforts, conscious or not, to reconcile them require in readers a particular attentiveness to the fluctuation of cultural contexts. No matter what changes he experienced in his life, Joyce could never erase his past or its impressions on him. He could leave Ireland, he could renounce the Catholic Church, he could abjure family ties, but he could never stop having been a Dublin Irish-Catholic son and brother. Like Yeats's horseman, Joyce can cast a cold eye on his country, but unlike the figure from the poem, he cannot pass by. He can never lose a sense of appreciation for the world he recollects, and to understand his writing we must understand this blend of nostalgia and rancor.

The concept of exile appears early on in published work relating to Joyce, and it has remained a consistent feature in subsequent inquiries from then until the present. Exile serves as a unifying narrative feature of the first biography, Herbert Gorman's *James Joyce: His First Forty Years*, published only two years after *Ulysses*. There Gorman situates Joyce's writing within the context of his coming to maturity in Ireland and living from young adulthood to middle age on the Continent. In the process, Joyce's residing in foreign cities emerges as having as important an influence on his imaginative perspective as his growing up in Dublin.

This emphasis on social milieu as a creative determinant was echoed in subsequent examinations of Joyce's published works, and in short order exile became an important theme in early critical studies. For example, Richard Kain's *Fabulous Voyager* explored the classical context of wandering that runs through *Ulysses*. In a contrasting perspective that nonetheless continued to focus attention on the condition of displacement and yearning produced by exile, Hugh Kenner's *Dublin's Joyce* showed that, even though Joyce lived outside his native country for most of his adult life, the displacement made him all the more attuned to the Irish world from which he emerged and which remained the formative influence on his creativity.

Following the lead of earlier commentators, in his 1959 biography and in its revised edition of 1983, Richard Ellmann repeatedly wove the theme of exile into his accounts of the different stages of Joyce's life. At various points in the biography, Ellmann also touched on the theme of exile as a feature characterizing the imaginative forces that propelled Joyce's writing. In keeping with his broad-stroke approach to Joyce and his works, Ellmann did not attempt a detailed exploration of the social, artistic, or emotional implications that adhere to such a highly charged term, but instead he left it to his readers and the literary critics who drew on the biography to complete the significance of the concept.

As Joyce studies became increasingly specialized, the theme of exile grew to be a critical commonplace and served as the starting point for a range of diverse approaches to the author's canon. However, like Ellmann, critics did not feel the need to parse its significance.[14] Rather, exile stood as a presumptive condition from which examinations of contingent issues emerged. With that same confidence in the stability in the term, and the consequent presumption of a universally shared sense of its implications, any number of recent interpretations of Joyce's canon have continued to rely upon the conception of exile as a generalized notion that could be similarly applied and understood by any number of different critics and readers. In this fashion, the exilic condition served as an anchoring metaphor for a wide range of studies broadly examining diverse influences of place on Joyce and on his writings.[15]

Even with this presupposition of a shared central assumption, however, a range of different critical views on the significance of the conjunction of Joyce and exile emerged. Previous studies have followed parallel approaches to how cultural, social, and spiritual contexts and traditions shaped Joyce's process of composition, but they often came to markedly different conclusions. James Fairhall and Robert Spoo, for example, have taken broad views of major social forces, examining the historical conditions bracketing and informing Joyce's life and works.[16] Enda Duffy, Vincent Cheng, David Lloyd, Emer Nolan, and Leonard Orr, to name only a few of the most prominent critics who have applied postcolonial approaches to Joyce's life and works, have all explored one aspect of his exile, that shaped by the influence of eight hundred years of British occupation of Ireland, with varying conclusions as to its impact on his work, although each succeeded in drawing important attention to unique aspects of the relationship between Joyce's life and his creative efforts.[17]

In significant ways, my study benefits from all of their endeavors. These approaches privilege the same broad epistemological assumptions about the impact on Joyce of the Irish context and social and cultural institutions. In my own understanding of both the author's creative efforts and the reader's interpretative endeavors, I have striven to keep in mind what these critics say about how location, experience, and emotion have exercised formative influences on the construction and consumption of Joyce's art.

Nonetheless, while these earlier studies have accomplished a great deal, giving any number of readers an important sense of how context shapes creativity, they have generally followed very specific and often highly ideologically oriented views of Joyce's relations with Ireland. I think it useful to make a distinction between those efforts and my own examinations of exilic features in Joyce's writings. In a general way, these critics all have explored Joyce's role as a public figure who represented, through his art, broadly held social feelings and whose own life mirrored widespread reactions to political conditions in Ireland. My approach narrows the scope of inquiry and seeks to emphasize the personal response, reflected in his writings, that Joyce made to his separation from his native country.

As I have indicated through references to other works, the perception of Joyce as a figure on the margins of a national consciousness is not new with this study, and in fact there is a long tradition among Joyce critics of seeing him in that extraterritorial imaginative state that allows one to examine as key both his position as an exiled writer and his disposition to make exile a central theme throughout his major works. Time and again critical approaches to his canon acknowledge this point of view in references to exile and to the exilic experience that appear in letters, in memoirs of friends and family members, and in biographies of Joyce, his wife, and his family.[18] Nonetheless, perhaps because of the frequency and duration of these allusions, it becomes too easy simply to take exile as a given, a familiar feature in his artistic makeup, and not explore the implications of that condition. This study aims to develop the implications of the relation of an exilic experience to Joyce's writing and by extension to readers' interpretations.

Scholarly attentiveness to images of or allusions to displacement on a national scale, the postcolonial view, has already led to important contributions to early comprehension of the thematic structure of Joyce's writings. Bringing a sociological perspective to thematic issues in Joyce's canon has illuminated the potential for a broad contextual understanding of the political and ideological impetus behind the composition of particular works. Now there is a need for adopting a view that acknowledges similarities in Joyce's experience of marginalization and those of countless other artists while at the same time moving the focus to the more personal consequences of such experiences, a methodology that combines biography and literary explication to illuminate general feelings that beset exiles—in this case rancor and nostalgia—while at the same time giving readers a more precise sense of how Joyce's individual responses to exile shaped the emotional forces evident in specific narratives.

It is a fairly straightforward proposition to assume that the exilic condition that was a daily factor in Joyce's life on the Continent informed his retrospective vision of Ireland as he recalled the Dublin of his childhood and young manhood, and indeed one finds in his own words clear explanations of how he sought to bring this hypostatic recollection to bear on all of his works: "For myself, I always write about Dublin, because if I can get to the heart of Dublin I can get to the heart of all the cities of the world. In the particular is contained the universal."[19] Though that passage is often quoted, it has to this point not provoked much interest beyond its citation as a default explanation for Joyce's selection of topics. I wish to expand engagement with that concept by focusing on the connections between creativity and the exilic experience in a way that develops a clearer sense of the often conflicting forces at work when one chooses to look back at one's homeland.

Joyce first left Dublin for the Continent in early December 1902, not as an exile but as a literary tourist. His ostensive aim was to take up medical studies in Paris. In fact he treated the time as an extended postgraduate course in the humanities, reading widely in the Bibliothèque nationale de France and familiarizing himself with the city. He gave language lessons, borrowed from his students, and wrote begging letters to his parents for money to make ends meet.

During the four and half months from December 1902 until his return in April 1903, Joyce gave no indication that he saw this move abroad as a permanent displacement, and indeed he broke up his time in Paris with three weeks back in Dublin, 24 December 1902 to 17 January 1903, for the Christmas and New Year's holidays. His correspondence with his family outlines life away from home for the first time, with predictable intimations of homesickness and fairly regular pleas for money (*Letters* II.18–41). The frequency of his writing and the affectionate tone that runs through his letters shows a young man who retains strong ties to his family and to the land he has left. Of course, the letters also reveal that Joyce, like so many students before and after him, was perpetually short of money and greatly dependent on regular financial supplements from home.

Joyce's tone a year and a half later as he prepared to elope with Nora Barnacle showed a markedly different perspective. In the weeks before his 8 October 1904 departure for the Continent, his letters to Nora are full of resentment for the Irish milieu and articulate an agitated desire to be free of that world. A long letter on 29 August lays out a number of grievances, real or imagined, that Joyce saw as engendered by life in Ireland. He ends with a categorical rejection of the authority and legitimacy of the institutions that he saw as defining the Irish life that surrounded him:

> My mind rejects the whole present social order and Christianity—home, the recognized virtues, classes of life, and religious doctrines. How could I like the idea of a home? My home was simply a middle-class affair ruined by spendthrift habits which I have inherited. My mother was slowly killed, I think, by my father's ill-treatment, by years of trouble, and by my cynical frankness of conduct. (*Letters* II.48)

He goes on to excoriate the Catholic Church in particular and Irish life in general, but that was only the beginning of his diatribes. In a 16 September letter he tells Nora of his views in somewhat broader terms and puts himself in the heroic role of one resisting crushing, enervating social forces:

> When I was waiting for you last night I was even more restless. It seemed to me I was fighting a battle with every religious and social force in Ireland for you and that I had nothing to rely on but myself. There is no life here—no naturalness or honesty. People live together in the same houses all their lives and at the end they are as far apart as ever. (*Letters* II.53)

Joyce declares himself in open revolt against his conception of the Irish way of life, outlining the impossibility of existing, much less thriving, under such conditions, and forming his determination to leave. Once he has arrived on the Continent, he will refer to himself as an exile, but it is clear from these expressions of rancor that he has already taken up that role and determined that circumstances are forcing him to leave his native land.

If anything, this animosity increases once Joyce has left Dublin and gone into exile. Expressions of rancor run through his letters with a reckless intemperance and an anger that he takes no trouble to conceal or modify. When criticized by a potential publisher for the coarse language and harsh descriptions running through the *Dubliners* stories, Joyce in a 23 June 1906 letter defends his tone, saying:

> It is not my fault that the odour of ashpits and old weeds and offal hangs round my stories. I seriously believe that you will retard the course of civilization in Ireland by preventing the Irish people from having one good look at themselves in my nicely polished looking-glass. (*Letters* I.63–64)

Three years later, while visiting Ireland, he writes to Nora on 22 August 1909 of his disgust for his native city: "How sick, sick, sick I am of Dublin. It is the city of failure, of rancor and of unhappiness. I long to be out of it" (*Letters* II.239). Two months later, on 27 October, he is even harsher as he sums up his animosity toward his countrymen and his sense of alienation from them:

> I loathe Ireland and the Irish. They themselves stare at me in the street though I was born among them. Perhaps they read my hatred of them in my eyes. I see nothing on every side of me but the image of the adulterous priest and his servants and of sly deceitful women. It is not good for me to come here or to be here. Perhaps if you were with me I would not suffer so much. (*Letters* II.255)

Of course, one must not forget that this trip was filled with frustration over his unsuccessful efforts to persuade an Irish publisher to bring out *Dubliners* and with soul-scorching doubt over his relationship with Nora because of the slanderous insinuations of a so-called friend, Vincent Cosgrave.

At the same time, Joyce showed himself equally capable of a range of far more positive views of his native land and of his countrymen—from genuine concern for the health of the national psyche to fond recollections of Ireland and the Irish nature. This became particularly evident in views expressed after he had passed the initial exhilaration of his departure from Ireland and settled into a routine that acknowledged the permanence of the separation. Writing on 20 May 1906 to Grant Richards, the recipient of the 23 June 1906 letter quoted above and the eventual publisher of *Dubliners*, Joyce, seeking to avoid cuts that Richards was demanding, characterized his work in a slightly less rancorous tone as an effort at improving the Irish consciousness:

> I fight to retain them [the passages under dispute] because I believe that in composing my Chapter of moral history in exactly the way I have composed it I have taken the first step towards the spiritual liberation of my country. (*Letters* I.62–63)

He wrote an even more upbeat assessment of his countrymen in a letter to his brother Stanislaus on 7 December 1906. "I think the Irish are the most civilised people in Europe, be Jesus Christ, I do" (*Letters* II.202). A month after he wrote to Nora the second harsh assessment of Ireland quoted above, he described on 19 November 1909 in almost lyrical terms his impressions on visiting Finn's Hotel in Dublin, where Nora had worked as a chambermaid:

> The place is very Irish. I have lived so long abroad and in so many countries that I can feel at once the voice of Ireland in anything. The disorder of the table was Irish, the wonder on the faces also, the curious-looking eyes of the woman herself and her waitress. A strange land this is to me though I was born in it and bear one of its old names. (*Letters* II.266)

All of these sentiments stop far short of the gushing views one would normally associate with nostalgia. Still, they are strikingly less acerbic than the attitudes found in the letters quoted immediately before. The point is fairly simple, but significant nonetheless. While Joyce may have been far too cynical to lapse into the sentimental exaggerations typical of others who had left their native land, he certainly was capable of poignant tenderness in some of his recollections of Ireland.[20]

Both attitudes exerted pronounced influences on his writings, and my study seeks to continue to explore that rich topic while quite frankly laying out a different area of interest. In the process, I wish to move from the political to the personal and to focus on what he wrote, not why he wrote it. Elements in Joyce's letters highlight his life abroad and the forces that sent him there from a deeply personal point of view even as they reflect the broad feelings that one can assign to almost any exile. I see these feelings as exerting a formative impact on his creations that has until now received too little attention. That has moved me to the creative and interpretive issues that I wish to explore here.[21]

At a fundamental level, my study takes up issues implicit but underexamined in Joyce criticism for decades. Even before he left Ireland, exile acted as an integral narrative feature in Joyce's work. The spiritual exile of Father James Flynn in "The Sisters," Joyce's first published story, stands as a haunting precursor to subsequent examinations, charged by experiences of living abroad, of social, cultural, and emotional displacement. Images of the condition become increasingly overt in later *Dubliners* stories, in *A Portrait of the Artist as a Young Man*, and in *Ulysses*. By the time he was writing *Finnegans Wake*, Joyce had moved to direct engagement with the consequences of physical displacement. Early in the book he describes Shem the Penman, a central character loosely analogous to the author, as one who "became a farsoonerite, saying he would far sooner muddle through the hash of lentils in Europe than meddle with Irrland's split little pea" (*FW* 171.4–6). As a result of such allusive gestures, for decades critics sensitive to these references have incorporated, in various forms, aspects of the concept into a wide range of epistemologies.[22]

My study explores that approach of dual, conflicting impulses shading Joyce's accounts of Ireland and Irish life. By taking into consideration how being an exile shaped Joyce's process of composition and how that affects a reader's sense of Joyce's writings in specific fashion, readers come away with a clearer sense of the range of attitudes embedded in the narratives. This in turn suggests nuances in familiar passages, and it offers a new orientation to Joyce's overall approach to writing. In the end, my aim is to augment current readings and to enhance our sense of the imaginative world from which Joyce's works emerged.

These oscillating perspectives have great significance for the way I advocate understanding Joyce's sense of who he was after he left Dublin and how that shaped his artistic outlook. They demonstrate how Joyce embraced the emotional point of view of an exile. In leaving Ireland he gave up traditional, conventional ties to the people, ideas, and institutions that had informed his life from infancy to maturity. He did not stop being someone from a middle-class Irish-Catholic Dublin family, but he did place himself on the margin of that world with a both/and view of its features and foibles.

This emotional, cultural, and social repositioning had an enduring and very specific impact on Joyce's process of composition. A reader's coming to grips with the imaginative perspective that such a state of mind produced in Joyce is the first step toward achieving a full sense of his writings. Thus, though my topic is the exile of James Joyce, a writer who spent his adult life outside Ireland, the central concern of this study is not physical displacement but rather its consequences as demonstrated time and again in the construction of his fiction.

Before turning to close analyses of Joyce's writing, it might be useful to lay out broadly the parameters of this study. I have settled on assessing the work that he composed once he had made the decision to exile himself from Ireland. This quite obviously includes *Dubliners*, *A Portrait of the Artist as a Young Man*, *Ulysses*, and *Finnegans Wake*. Joyce's only extant play, *Exiles*, both in subject matter and time of writing also falls within the bounds of exilic works. I reference some of the pieces in *The Collected Writings* but do not take up his other works in more than an oblique way, and it may aid a reader's orientation to explain why.

Joyce's first commercially published writing, the poetry collection *Chamber Music*, falls in a different category from the works under consideration here. Although it appeared in 1907, the verses were composed between 1901 and 1904, and their subject matter—love sought, gained, and ultimately lost—reflects a youthful romanticism and gives one insight into the topics and issues of interest to Joyce as an artist. While the poems can stand on their own merit, the time of their composition and the theme that unifies them ensure that they do not encompass the more mature issues that would occupy Joyce's creative attention once he went abroad.

I have also not taken up several other works that might seem to legitimately meet the standards for analysis laid down here, among them *Stephen Hero*, the novel that Joyce began to write on his twenty-second birthday, 2 February 1904, shortly after John Eglinton of the Irish journal *Dana* had rejected his essay "A Portrait of the Artist" as unsuitable for the magazine. By April 1904 Joyce had completed the first eleven chapters, and when he ceased work on *Stephen Hero* in June or early July 1905, he had written 914 manuscript pages, "about half the book" by his own estimate (*Letters* II.132). Whether one considers *Stephen Hero* an ur-version of *A Portrait of the Artist as a Young Man* or a tribute to Victorian fiction that Joyce needed to get out of his system before turning to the other novel, it does seem fairly certain that it was begun well before Joyce left Ireland, and its tone shows a marked variance from the sort of writing he undertook once he had become an exile.

Giacomo Joyce, written sometime around 1914, certainly falls within the period when Joyce was under the influence of the exilic condition.[23] Its relevance as a creative work remains an open debate. One can see it as a private journal, and there are legitimate questions as to whether good taste and a respect for privacy should have triumphed over the impulse to publish anything that Joyce wrote. In any case, it does not seem appropriate to this study.

Joyce's second collection of poetry, *Pomes Penyeach*, and various individual pieces like "Ecce Puer" were written well after Joyce established himself as an exile. There may well be exilic references in them that a critic skilled in the explication of poetry could bring to the foreground. However, I have found no evidence that they would offer literary satisfaction sufficient to merit such heavy lifting.

What this study does is comment on a range of Joyce's creative work from diverse periods in his life. It presents an overview, not a prescription. It does not seek to be an exhaustive assessment of exilic representations in all of his writings. For me the best criticism has not been attempts to present definitive understandings of literary selections but rather new approaches for individual engagement with the material. With that in mind, my study offers a number of examples of how the experiences of exile shaped the creativity of Joyce's mature works, and I hope that these examples serve as catalysts for other readers to extend their own understanding.

2

Dubliners

The First Glimpse of Ireland from Abroad

The time had come for him to set out on his journey westward.

The passage from "The Dead" that appears as the epigraph to this chapter may seem to get the process backwards. When Joyce left Ireland in 1904, he went progressively farther east, ending in Pola, which he called "a naval Siberia," physically and psychologically remote from everything Irish. Nonetheless, as it did with Gabriel Conroy, Ireland remained a central feature of Joyce's psyche for as long as he was away from it.

Of course, like any other exile's, Joyce's consciousness was significantly influenced by the very specific attitudes, events, and environments informing his life outside Ireland. Nonetheless, as noted in the introduction, his response to displacement from his native land was quite similar to most other exiles.' Time and again, the exile's attitude toward the country left behind will be grounded in sentiments of rancor and/or nostalgia. As shown in the previous chapter, Joyce, from the time he left Ireland, saw himself as an exile, and the common experiences of all people traumatically displaced from their homeland affected him and had an immediate and lasting impact on his artistic output: in the way he contextualized his fiction, in the perspective that he applied to the construction of its ambiance, and in the characterization of the figures who inhabited it.

As we have seen, early in his life Joyce embraced a sense of uniqueness and a feeling of marginalization that stand as preliminary stages of any fully realized exilic perspective. In correspondence written over the summer of 1904, Joyce vigorously expressed this predisposition to the feelings of exile. In the final months before he left Ireland, when he began working on early versions of the *Dubliners* stories, the exilic sense of rancor already seemed to be shaping his narratives. As the intensity of these feelings increased, they became a goad that propelled Joyce out of his native land in 1904.[1] Once abroad, the experience of having to live as an exile strengthened that perception and also stimulated feelings of nostalgia that were not previously in evidence. From 1904 right up until 1939 when he completed *Finnegans Wake*, some form of an exilic voice was a constant presence in his writings.

There is ample evidence throughout his first published work of fiction, *Dubliners*, that the complex and conflicting exilic attitudes were fully integrated into his process of composition. Joyce began writing early versions of some of the stories before leaving Ireland. Work on the collection continued with additional stories and ongoing revisions over the next eight to ten years.

A good deal of material in his letters and in the recollections of friends shows that the anger common to the exilic experience inflected his writing, though that is not always the term used to describe those feelings. Many passages written in this vein have been quoted for decades as support for critical analyses that emphasize the rancor one finds in his writing. In the previous chapter I quoted a diatribe against Ireland and Irish culture in a 23 June 1906 letter to the man who would eventually publish *Dubliners*, Grant Richards. The sentiments Joyce expressed are worth revisiting. It is important to keep in mind that he was writing to an editor reluctant to bring out a work tinged with so much bitterness toward Ireland. Joyce's tone combines self-righteousness and exasperation as he offers a very complex assessment of his position and outlines the aims of his writing:

> It is not my fault that the odour of ashpits and old weeds and offal hangs round my stories. I seriously believe that you will retard the course of civilization in Ireland by preventing the Irish people from having one good look at themselves in my nicely polished looking-glass. (*Letters* I.63–64)

While the passion animating these lines cannot be ignored, one needs to exercise care in assessing exactly what emotions are being expressed and what motivations lie behind them. The apparently unmitigated anger at all things Irish embedded in Joyce's statement has seemed self-evident to several generations of critics. At the same time, that sweeping generalization reduces a complex emotional situation to a pedestrian stereotypical reaction. Drawing the simple conclusion that Joyce's words demonstrate an unqualified rejection of every aspect of the world he left in Dublin takes a complicated individual and sums him up as an angry and unreflective malcontent. The complexity one finds in Joyce's nature and in his writings prescribes equally complex responses. This does not mean that one should ignore the role that rancor plays in his nature and his art, but it most decidedly does advocate seeing it as part of a complex array of feelings within the author's consciousness.

The quoted passage certainly reflects a willingness, one might even say an eagerness, to criticize the flaws inherent in the Irish character. However, identifying that attitude alone as the force behind his sentiments does not sufficiently explain the range of emotions and expressions of intent compressed into this brief but emphatic defense of his writing. A careful reader who assesses the same potential for complexity in his letters that one readily finds in his work will discover the same polyphonic resonances here that one encounters throughout the canon. It is no great leap to acknowledge the possibility that the mirror metaphor highlights the intention of reflecting the entire spectrum of features characterizing the Irish nature, not simply its flaws, and evidence from accounts of his personal life suggests that the impulse Joyce felt to celebrate positive aspects of the Irish nature was as strong as his need to critique its negative features.

A letter to his brother Stanislaus, written three months after the one quoted above, takes a markedly different tone. Joyce frankly acknowledges omissions in his short stories' descriptions of the spiritual, emotional, and psychological traits that distinguish his fellow countrymen. Further, he implies an obligation to redress that imbalance with a more tempered view of his native land.

> Sometimes thinking of Ireland it seems to me that I have been unnecessarily harsh. I have reproduced (in *Dubliners* at least) none of the attraction of the city for I have never felt at my ease in any city since I left it except Paris. I have not reproduced its ingenuous insularity and its hospitality. The latter 'virtue' so far as I can see does not exist elsewhere in Europe. I have not been just to its beauty: for it is more beautiful naturally in my opinion than what I have seen of England, Switzerland, France, Austria or Italy. (*Letters* II.166)

In lines as deeply felt if not as graphically articulated as those in his letter to Grant Richards, Joyce shows himself finely attuned to the amenable features of Irish life. Sympathy and admiration suffuse this description as much as do anger and disdain in other assessments of the Irish ethos.

Joyce certainly was aware of his contradictory feelings toward Ireland and the Irish and of his seeming powerlessness to change them. The letter goes on to say: "And yet I know how useless these reflections are. For were I to rewrite the book . . . I am sure I should find again what you call the Holy Ghost sitting in the ink-bottle and the perverse devil of my literary conscience sitting on the hump of my pen." However, "the perverse devil" did not always succeed in dominating descriptions of the Irish milieu.

Over the course of his literary career, Joyce would continue to offer alternative perspectives of his native land, though as he grew older the criticism, whether through resignation or melioration, tended to be less emphatic. I do not mean to suggest that a mellower attitude arose in Joyce's works. Rather, beginning with the representations of Ireland as he wrote and rewrote the stories in *Dubliners*, his narratives created an equilibrium where rancor and nostalgia existed hypostatically in a both/and interpretive environment. A full understanding of these works, then, requires simultaneous comprehension of these contrasting attitudes shaping Joyce's creative efforts.[2]

From this perspective it is only logical to make a connection with the physical displacement that Joyce was enduring in his life abroad. That is to say, the conflicted feelings laid out in the letters were informed and amplified by the conditions inherent in the exile experience. With this in mind, a simple syllogism offers the clearest outline of how to proceed. Rather than assuming that a single, polarized view shapes Joyce's writings, the reader seeking the fullest possible understanding of that work needs the fullest possible understanding of the cultural, emotional, and spiritual context from which it emerged. That in turn demands a commitment to comprehending his responses to the exilic experience.

By the time Joyce, at twenty-five years of age, wrote "The Dead," the last story for *Dubliners*, the complex oscillation of nostalgic and rancorous representations of Irish life had become deeply ingrained in his narrative.[3] Certainly manifestations of this duality are most evident in the final story, but the disposition to view Dublin from multiple points of view grew increasingly evident over the course of the collection.

As with so many received opinions on Joyce's work, for better or worse, one finds evidence of this view originating in Richard Ellmann's biography, *James Joyce*. It is clearly presented in a segment titled "The Backgrounds of 'The Dead.'" There Ellmann comments on Gabriel Conroy's after-dinner speech. In a style that he seems to prefer whenever he moves from biography to criticism, Ellmann hints at more than he actually asserts. Nonetheless, despite the rhetoric, his intentions are clear, for he characterizes "The Dead" as "Joyce's oblique way, in language that mocked his own, of beginning the task of making amends."[4]

A much more detailed and extremely thoughtful assessment of "The Dead," also arguing for seeing it as counterpoint to the other stories in the collection, appears in an essay by Florence Walzl.[5] There, in a much more direct and thorough fashion, Walzl focuses on the tone of the final story and sees it as markedly different from the others. Although, as noted later in this chapter, I do not completely agree with all of Walzl's conclusions regarding *Dubliners*, it would be difficult to overestimate the profound contribution her work has made to our understanding of it.

Other critics have echoed the views of Ellmann and Walzl. By dint of this repetition, it has become a critical commonplace that "The Dead" is primarily a story written to counterbalance the harshness of those preceding it. However, that approach sets up the kind of neat dichotomy that often fails to encompass the full interpretive possibilities of a Joycean narrative, and I would like to explore alternative possibilities for understanding made possible by the exilic perspective.

Let me begin with a few remarks about the limitations of Ellmann's view of "The Dead" as written primarily as a mea culpa for previous criticisms of Ireland. In light of recent scholarship, one might find a number of reasons for challenging that approach, but the simplest refutation comes from the chronology of composition. Joyce's writing for the collection did not end with the completion of the first draft of "The Dead" in 1907. He continued to revise many of his stories.[6] The timing of those efforts makes it logical to assume that whatever attitudes informed the composition of "The Dead"—including the duality of nostalgia and rancor—were subsequently present and influential as Joyce formed the final versions of the other stories. Thus across the collection, one sees how Joyce established the pattern of his fiction with its oscillating perspectives of the Irish ethos that he would continue to explore through *Finnegans Wake*. Over the course of his artistic career, Joyce's subject never varied. He could not stop writing about Dublin, and he could only completely express his feelings by oscillating between perspectives of sentimentality and bitterness.[7]

Before continuing, let me underscore the two posited assumptions upon which my assessment of representations of this complex attitude depends: the basic duality of the exile experience exists from the beginning of the composition process, and the subtlety of its expression in the narrative increases with the growing sophistication of Joyce's writing. Signs of this evolving process emerge early in Joyce's writing, and grow more intense and more complex with each successive work. It is made immediately evident through an examination of the various stages of composition of the first story in *Dubliners*, "The Sisters."

This short story, though the first to be composed, has all of the intensity and intricacy of later works in the collection. It grew in the complexity of its perspectives and emotional tenor over the decade-long period between its first rendering and its final form when the entire collection was published in 1914. The initial version of "The Sisters" appeared on two pages of the 13 August 1904 issue of the *Irish Homestead*, a little less than two months before Joyce would leave Ireland to begin his exile. From Joyce's description of the story and of his plans for further work—found in a letter written to a former college classmate, Constantine Curran, a month before "The Sisters" first appeared—one can see it as already part of a larger project, at that point organized around a distinctly hostile view of his native city: "I am writing a series of epicleti—ten—for a paper. I have written one. I call the series *Dubliners* to betray the soul of that hemiplegia or paralysis which many consider a city" (*Letters* I.55).

As with examinations of Joyce's 23 June 1906 letter to Grant Richards, many critics have followed a narrow course in assessing this statement. They have presumed that Joyce restricted the compositional pattern of his stories for *Dubliners* to follow a rigid adherence to this early plan. Their supposition of Joyce's unshakable commitment to goals delineated at the beginning of his writing process provides a neat summation of the emotional scope of the stories. However, and this is a point I feel the need to emphasize time and again, given the complexity that stands as a hallmark of Joyce's fiction from its earliest representations, the prudent reader will entertain the possibility that his dissection of the paralysis of Dublin could produce a narrative structure reflecting a much more diverse range of attitudes that go well beyond a blanket revulsion for the community. At the very least, the ambiguity of the term *epicleti*, an apparent Latin transliteration of a Greek word, should signal to the prudent reader that even at this early stage there were any number of possible ways of seeing Joyce's writing.[8]

In fact, an overview of the stages of composition through which the first story passed offers solid evidence supporting the latter view. As I will show, intermediate versions of "The Sisters" present an accrued sense of the story becoming increasingly emotionally diffuse. Further, the final rendition in the collection first published in 1914 represents far more ambivalent and in some instances far more overtly sentimental positions than the passage from Joyce's letter quoted above would lead readers to assume. Indeed, the changes introduced over that ten-year period attest to a significant expansion and a marked refinement of its narrative arc, and attentiveness to this change gives one a much fuller sense of the interpretive potential of all of the stories.[9]

I readily acknowledge that my reading runs counter to any number of previous interpretations. Critics have shown little interest in seeing the slightest duality in the story's narrative voice, and it is useful, before offering an alternative reading, to see how this traditional response has developed. Florence Walzl, with her typical scrupulous care, has traced the thematic evolution of "The Sisters" through its various manifestations—first as a short story in the *Irish Homestead*, then as what she calls an intermediary revision in 1905, then in its 1912 version made ready for the possible publication by the Maunsel printing house which never came about, and finally in the form found in the collection brought out by Grant Richards in 1914.[10] Walzl's approach follows the pattern of close reading at which she excelled. She fixes her critical attention on issues long acknowledged as central to the story—like the words "paralysis," "gnomon," and "simony" that appear on the first page—and in a patient exposition of each establishes their influence on one's comprehension of the work. Her analysis here, as elsewhere, serves as a powerful illustration of the insights that accrue when a careful reader with a clearly articulated perspective focuses close attention on the fundamental thematic structure of a work.

Concurrently, one can discern within such readings the limitations that can grow out of the fundamental assumptions upon which they are based. Walzl's explication of the central issues of "The Sisters" and her assessments of the creative changes that Joyce imposed reinforce received opinions rather than breaking new ground. The difficulty, ironically, stems from one of Walzl's undisputed strengths: a thorough knowledge of the relevant scholarship preceding her work. Walzl's keen sense of the critical tradition surrounding "The Sisters" inclined her toward interpretations reinforcing findings that other readers had previously articulated.

This is not to dismiss her effort as the derivative work of someone simply parroting conventional wisdom, for Walzl's own scholarship is anything but that. Rather, it demonstrates to me the strength of received opinion, shaping as it does the views of a very insightful and a highly conscientious critic.[11]

L. J. Morrissey, in a subsequent examination of the various drafts of "The Sisters," acknowledges but does not develop the possibilities for discerning diverse attitudes within the story. Morrissey offers a detailed and thoughtful syntactic assessment of the changes that took place over the course of Joyce's revisions of the story.[12] His approach to the work is strikingly different from Walzl's. He foregrounds a formal interest in Joyce's writing, implicitly following a methodology that blends the ideas of Roland Barthes with those of narratologists like Gérard Genette, and thereby highlights a stylistic shift in the story's discourse that heightens its ambiguity and legitimizes for readers greater creative latitude in understanding it. At the same time, Morrissey's efforts emphasize elaboration of received views over reassessment, and ultimately, like Walzl's study, this essay does not challenge traditional interpretations.

Commonly, readers have perceived Joyce's work from his earliest writings to his final efforts as tracing the increasingly sophisticated development of a writer maturing in his craft. This perception may apply to his stylistic ability. However, signs of the uninhibited imaginative diversity and the polyphonically discursive discourses associated with *Ulysses* and *Finnegans Wake* can be found in his work from the start.

Nowhere is this more apparent than in the multiple, diverse feelings that informed Joyce's views on Ireland. Although Joyce's narratives never ignore the often numbing harshness encountered in urban life, they also linger over moments that highlight the humanity and humaneness found in the ethos of the Dublin that Joyce knew. Thus, multiplicity rather than singularity always serves as the more useful approach to understanding him.

Attentiveness to this approach yields immediate benefits in reading "The Sisters" from the perspective of exile. Nostalgia and rancor, operating simultaneously throughout the discourse, emerge coincidentally with Joyce's move to the Continent. One can see the coolness and detachment of the *Irish Homestead* story evolving into the more nuanced and emotional engagement with the complexities of childhood, friendship, and death that characterize the final version.

In the first rendering, for example, the boy's narration assumes a matter-of-fact tone as he gazes each night on the window of the room where he knows the priest is dying.

> Three nights in succession I had found myself in Great Britain-street at that hour, as if by Providence. Three nights also I had raised my eyes to the lighted square and speculated. I seemed to understand that it would occur at night. But in spite of the Providence that had led my feet, and in spite of the reverent curiosity of my eyes, I had discovered nothing.[13]

Curiosity and chance rather than any stronger force motivate the boy's peregrinations, and his speculations convey a detached attitude toward an event identified only by a vague pronoun that avoids naming the painful, inevitable event—death—that would bring his observations to a conclusion. "I seemed to understand that it would occur at night."

By the time that Joyce writes the final version of that scene, it presents a more complex, more humane, and more emotionally involved response with its intimations, muted but there nonetheless, of fear and concern as the boy thinks of the priest's demise.

> There was no hope for him this time: it was the third stroke. Night after night I had passed the house (it was vacation time) and studied the lighted square of window: and night after night I had found it lighted in the same way, faintly and evenly. If he was dead, I thought, I would see the reflection of candles on the darkened blind. (*D* 3)

In a deft stylistic move, Joyce sustains the still unsophisticated point of view that captures the consciousness of a young boy while infusing the passage with greater psychological complexity through the acknowledgment of competing emotions. The introduction of the term "hope," expressed as an absence and surrounded by the passive voice, interjects a tone of sympathy not previously articulated. At the same time, it underscores the immense loss and pain waiting at the end of the vigil. Further, the reconfigured description—"night after night"—of the boy's return to his post in front of the house draws out the process by making the time more ambiguous and attenuating the period of engagement. In a few lines the description incorporates pain and sympathy into an experience that propels the boy toward a harsher, more mature view of the world.

Likewise, in its first rendition, the story truncates and simplifies emotion in a way that subsequent writing eschews. The boy of the *Irish Homestead* version acknowledges learning of the priest's death by simply noting his prescience, with no apparent emotion associated with the moment, "I found myself a prophet."[14] The passage does already have the wonderful, self-reflexive irony that will be a feature of the next thirty-five years of Joyce's writing. However, in this case it underscores the distance between narrative voice and narration. As we will see, the exilic experience progressively shrinks that distance.

In its final form the passage conveys a more intense and conflicted emotional state. It suggests, to my mind, the voice of the exile, acquired over the years, that has now grown familiar with both/and experiences. It has the boy withholding his feelings initially, fighting to hide his reactions from Old Cotter, and by extension from the reader, when the death is first announced. Later, while falling asleep, the boy allows himself to confront the news of the priest's passing. He struggles to articulate the complex and at times contradictory emotions that haunt his imagination:

> In the dark of my room I imagined that I saw again the heavy grey face of the paralytic. I drew the blankets over my head and tried to think of Christmas. But the grey face still followed me. It murmured; and I understood that it desired to confess something. I felt my soul receding into some pleasant and vicious region; and there again I found it waiting for me. (*D* 5).

With a few phrases, Joyce humanizes the reflection on death. He reminds readers that they are hearing the impressions of a child confronted, perhaps for the first time, with one of life's harshest realities—its finitude. Joyce's revisions transform the original cold, aloof tone of resignation into the confused and conflicted attitudes we often experience when coming to grips with another's passing. The fact of the priest's death remains stark, but the emphasis has shifted to explore the emerging humanity of a child coping with realities of the adult world.

Revisions of other passages in the short story reinforce the impression of an evolution from the near unresponsive emotional tone of early versions into a much more sophisticated representation of complex, albeit childish, feelings in subsequent renditions. In the *Irish Homestead* story, for example, the boy expresses little more than mild surprise that the priest looked much older than the age listed on the card announcing the death, and then he starts to reminisce about visits with the priest. In the final version, reading the card so flusters the boy that he feels he cannot enter the house where the priest's sisters still reside. Instead, he begins to think of previous meetings in an effort to blunt the reality that the card proclaims.

Examples like this accrue as one compares any number of passages from the first and the final version. In the story published in 1914 in *Dubliners*, the sustained tone of melancholy and sadness suffuse the discourse, but no matter the degree of pain and suffering, the descriptions never degenerate into tawdriness or brutality. Rather, this narrative shows what will become increasingly evident over the course of the collection: As Joyce—the maturing exilic writer—measures Dublin with his critical eye, he increasingly balances sharp criticisms of institutional intolerance and cultural insensitivity with idyllic descriptions of cherished experiences, so that a degree of sympathy and a measure of respect balance the harshness of the portrayals of many individuals and events.

It remains important to stress that such gestures do not blunt his impulse to criticize the flaws he feels are inherent in the Irish world that he describes in such meticulous detail. Indeed, the small-minded parochialism that provoked such bitterness in his letter to Richards becomes more evident in the final rendition of the story. Mr. Cotter has changed from a mildly annoying figure who has learned of the priest's death before the boy did to an insidious, Polonius-like "Tiresome old red-nosed imbecile" (*D* 10) who asserts an emphatic if vague sense of corruption in the priest's nature and so insinuates a criticism of the boy's aunt and uncle for allowing the child to associate with Father Flynn: "I wouldn't like children of mine, he said, to have too much to say to a man like that" (*D* 10). The fully evolved Cotter now employs half-sentences and knowing looks to get his meaning across without taking full responsibility for what he utters:

> —No, I wouldn't say he was exactly . . . but there was something queer . . . there was something uncanny about him. I'll tell you my opinion . . .
>
> —I have my own theory about it, he said. I think it was one of those . . . peculiar cases. . . . But it's hard to say. (*D* 3–4, ellipses in original)

At the same time that he so deftly presents small-minded slanders, Joyce also celebrates the decency to be found in ordinary exchanges. At the dinner table, one sees the boy's aunt challenging Cotter to explain his insinuations, rather than allowing them to fester uncontested, and forcing him to respond in circumlocutions:

> —How do you mean, Mr Cotter? asked my aunt.
> —What I mean is, said old Cotter, it's bad for children.
>
> —But why do you think it's not good for children, Mr Cotter? she asked.
> —It's bad for children, said old Cotter, because their minds are so impressionable. When children see things like that, you know, it has an effect . . . (*D* 4–5)

With the aunt's questions transforming the reader's impressions of old Cotter's remarks from leering innuendo into sputtering bluster, Joyce's narrative shows an alternative to the mean-spirited gossiping within the Irish temperament.

The aunt's gentle but insistent assertion of human decency carries over into a description of the events of the next day. She takes the boy to the house he was too timid to enter alone to make a visit to comfort the sisters. During the course of the conversation, it becomes clear that, for all the aunt's clichéd expressions of formulaic sympathy, she is nonetheless making a sincere and humane effort to alleviate the grief that the sisters are experiencing. "—Ah, well, he's gone to a better world" (*D* 8). The point is not whether she performs this task skillfully but rather that in performing it at all she rebuts assumptions that Dubliners are numb to empathetic feelings. Even the seemingly throwaway references to the kindnesses of the priest's friend Father O'Rourke, a character not mentioned in the first version, draw attention to an active human concern countering the sense of paralysis that many readers see gripping the story (*D* 9–10).

Perhaps the most striking interpretive possibilities that are illuminated by the point of view that I advocate, however, come from the narrative's representations of the Flynn sisters, who despite the priest's dismissive misogyny have treated him with great love and have given him tender care.[15] They pose a conundrum since, though ostensively the title characters, they seem rather minor figures, and some of the most esteemed critics of *Dubliners* have found little in their portrayals to challenge their brother's dismissal. Florence Walzl, for example, offers this assessment of their significance:

> As in the prose epiphanies Joyce was writing at this period, realistic actions and descriptions convey the moral significance. Father Flynn, a representative of the clergy, is unable to sustain the duties of his office. The sisters as representatives of the laity, pious and poor, ignorant or deaf, sustain him at great sacrifice to themselves.[16]

Walzl goes on to posit that these characterizations underscore Joyce's criticism of Ireland and the Irish.[17] Although she may be correct in her delineation of the women's failings, I think it reasonable also to recognize the positive effects of their behavior, delineated if not elaborated, in the story. While poverty and ignorance are hardly virtues, the self-sacrifice and devotion of the sisters make them as deserving an object of approbation as of scorn. Indeed, in a 6 September 1906 letter to his brother Stanislaus written around the time he was revising "The Sisters," Joyce expressed a regard for just this type of woman:

> it seems to me my influence on male friends is provocative. They find it hard to understand me, and difficult to get on with me even when they seem well-equipped for these tasks. On the other hand two ill-equipped women, to wit, Aunt Josephine and Nora, seem to be able to get at my point of view, and if they do not get on with me as well as they might they certainly manage to preserve a certain loyalty which is very commendable and pleasing. (*Letters* II.157)[18]

One might infer from the tone of Joyce's letter that the condescending attitude expressed in the text of "The Sisters" may be as much a bias of the author as anything else. Nonetheless, as was the case with Nora's and Aunt Josephine's relations with Joyce, the sisters' devotion to their brother cannot be questioned. Indeed, it may well be his condition as a spiritual exile, cut off from his pastoral duties and now dependent upon these women for psychological and emotional sustenance, that led Joyce to the grudging appreciation he expresses to Stanislaus for the women in his life. Though that revelation could not have influenced his choice for the title of the first story in his collection, selected well before he left Dublin, it may very well have reconfigured the way the he came to see it.

The initial composition of "The Sisters" took place in July 1904, and Joyce completed revisions on it in July 1906.[19] This is the period during which Joyce made his commitment to exile and began to form a life on the Continent. Comparison of the initial and final drafts shows that the shift in style is quite notable, and becomes more understandable if one keeps in mind that exilic emotions—nostalgia and rancor—were already playing a part in the composition process from Joyce's earliest fiction. Though admittedly many factors contribute to the fabric of the discourses in his writings, attentiveness to the growing complexity of Joyce's attitudes toward Ireland will give readers a more sophisticated sense of the attitudes at work throughout the narratives and in turn lead to subtler interpretations.

Along these lines, it is important to realize that new feelings did not efface old ones. Signs of positive recollections of the Irish ethos overlay but do not obscure the harsh criticisms of the Dublin environment evident in every story. In their fashion, they serve the important function of challenging approaches to the text that take a single, exclusionary point of view, ignoring the complexity of Joyce's own nature. Indeed, examples reflecting the author's pleasure in his recollections of certain Dublin moments punctuate the collection.

The mundane process of accompanying his aunt on her shopping, for instance, has the unnamed boy in "Araby" presenting, perhaps unconsciously, a poignantly lyrical account of the diverse sights and activities of a Dublin Street:

> On Saturday evenings when my aunt went marketing I had to go to carry some of the parcels. We walked through the flaring streets, jostled by drunken men and bargaining women, amid the curses of labourers, the shrill litanies of shop-boys who stood on guard by the barrels of pigs' cheeks, the nasal chanting of street-singers, who sang a *come-all-you* about O'Donovan Rossa, or a ballad about the troubles in our native land. (*D* 21–22)

The boy's description, as one might expect in the impressions of a child, goes too far, for he says in the next line:

> These noises converged in a single sensation of life for me: I imagined that I bore my chalice safely through a throng of foes. Her [Mangan's sister's] name sprang to my lips at moments in strange prayers and praises which I myself did not understand. (*D* 22).

The irony of the final lines may seem irresistible, but an erudite reader will keep the entire passage in mind and balance the diverse impressions it presents. This is a gritty urban scene of energy and diversion. There is a harshness to it that might seem to pose a sardonic rebuttal to the romanticism that overtakes the narrator. No description of a modern city street could escape that edginess. Yet one can also find exuberance there, a celebration of Dublin's nervous, raucous energy. We need to be attentive to recognize it, but seeing it will make us less quick to dismiss the sentiments of the young narrator.

The consistent necessary feature of any sophisticated reading of Joyce's works, no matter what the perspective or methodology, is complexity. Without a sense of the possibility for positive feelings as one of the elements that exile has inculcated in the author, such an interpretation would stretch credulity. Ignoring the duality of sentiments shaping a writer's backward glance at his homeland condemns one to the received wisdom of viewing every description as a condemnation. That view is simply too reductive to do full justice to Joyce's prose.

Clearly, I am not trying to suggest a reading that idealizes the city or the citizens whom Joyce depicts. The harsh responses he makes in his writings to a myriad of features emblematic of Dublin cannot be ignored or denied. In the same vein, the narrative shows no mercy in representing certain types that seem both perfectly ridiculous and perfectly at home in the city. Jimmy Doyle, for example, at the center of "After the Race," remains a vacuous young man with too much money from start to finish. In the context of the collection, that view is an exception for its single-minded and unmitigated criticism.[20]

The story had appeared in the *Irish Homestead* shortly after Joyce left Dublin for the Continent, and to some degree its structure is dictated by the fact that it grew out of an actual interview with the French race car driver Henri Fournier that Joyce did for the *Irish Times* in the spring of 1903. In an August 1906 letter (*Letters* II.151) Joyce speaks of revising the story. However, there is little evidence that he did.

Other negative representations, even one as extreme as the brutish behavior of the feckless alcoholic clerk Farrington in "Counterparts," offer at the very least a duality in the figure seemingly set up for ridicule and disdain. In fact, the title of the story begs a comparison of Farrington with his employer, the bullying Mr. Alleyne, particularly in the final lines of the story, when Farrington seizes the feeblest of excuses for beating his son in a thinly disguised effort to suppress a sense of his own inadequacies. However, the comparison evokes both the oppressor and the oppressed, and even here there is more than immediately is evident from a single interpretive approach.

A suggestion of greater possibilities can be found in an anecdote unearthed by Vivian Igoe, offering a delightful insight into the choice of names in this story. Henry Allyene, as manager and chairman of the Dublin and Chapelizod Distillery Company, employed John Joyce as secretary of the company. When John Joyce discovered that Alleyne was defrauding the company, Alleyne disappeared and Joyce's father lost his job.[21] Of course, it may be nothing more than Joyce using his fiction as a weapon against real enemies of himself and his family, as he did in *Ulysses* when he felt wronged by the British authorities in Zurich. But it is as likely that Joyce was underscoring a parallel by suggesting that even the loutish Farrington deserves as much sympathy as we extend to poor Tom who incurred his father's anger by letting the fire go out.

This approach is not an attempt to ignore or even to blunt the harsh feelings toward Ireland and the Irish that Joyce demonstrates in any number of instances. However, I do most emphatically urge more than a single perspective. Reference to the exilic experience usefully recalls the complexity of Joyce's nature and the impact of that experience on his art. A range of feelings moved him, and the sophisticated reader will attend to them all.

That is not to say that one should expect identical emotional emphasis between nostalgia and rancor in every story, for the exilic experience contributes to rather than dictates the process of composition for the author. Nonetheless, the impact of the collection on readers changes appreciably if one sees bitterness and sympathy coexisting in Joyce's backward glances at Ireland long before he undertook the gesture of recompense that many critics associate with "The Dead." A closer look at a few stories will illustrate my point.

"A Little Cloud" offers a sardonic view of an inverted assessment of the exilic experience. On first reading it might seem to lay out a strong argument for the freedom conferred on the exile, but readers aware of Joyce's own life overseas will find the self-aggrandizing Ignatius Gallagher's account of life abroad, fictional in every sense of the word, very much at odds with it. This knowledge, by extension, might lead us to more diverse readings of the exile and of the one who stayed behind.

Numerous reasons exist to disparage and perhaps even to pity Little Chandler, the nondescript clerk at the center of the story. Unlike his friend Gallagher, who has left Ireland to make a career as a journalist in London, Chandler, circumscribed by his steady job and temperate habits, has remained in Dublin only to be berated by his wife in the final paragraphs for his ineffectuality as a father and husband. Nonetheless, one can grant those facts without turning Chandler's existence into a melodramatic catastrophe. Gallagher is a coarse, insensitive individual whose accounts of his life in London and Paris seem far less ideal and most probably less successful than he intimates. Certainly the story satirizes Chandler's naïve romanticism, his sense of loss at not living the Byronic existence, and his inability to take satisfaction from the normal life he leads.

> —You'll put your head in the sack, repeated Little Chandler stoutly, like everyone else, if you can find the girl.
> He had slightly emphasised his tone and he was aware that he had betrayed himself; but though the colour had heightened in his cheek he did not flinch from his friend's gaze. Ignatius Gallaher watched him for a few moments and then said:
> —If ever it occurs you may bet your bottom dollar there'll be no mooning and spooning about it. I mean to marry money. She'll have a good fat account at the bank or she won't do for me.
> Little Chandler shook his head.
> —Why, man alive, said Ignatius Gallaher vehemently, do you know what it is? I've only to say the word and tomorrow I can have the woman and the cash. You don't believe it? Well, I know it. There are hundreds—what am I saying?—thousands of rich Germans and Jews, rotten with money, that'd only be too glad. . . . You wait a while, my boy. See if I don't play my cards properly. When I go about a thing I mean business, I tell you. You just wait. (*D* 66–67, ellipsis in original)

Gallaher's cynical view of married life stands as little more than an extension, albeit with a great deal more coarseness, of Lenehan's dream of domestic salvation in "Two Gallants" (*D* 46). The very crudeness of it, the empty, materialistic cynicism that appears as the only foundation for Gallaher's life, undermines any presumption, at least on the reader's part, regarding the desirability of the exilic experience. In the end both his hyperbolic accounts of adventures abroad and Chandler's self-pitying and overstated response to his domestic upheavals come across not as the summation of a great tragedy but as gentle rebukes for a sentimentalist who cannot see the tawdriness in Gallagher's description of his life abroad and the foolishness in Little Chandler for admiring it.

"A Painful Case" takes a much more emotionally intense look at male-female relations than what we see in any of the previous stories, dealing as it does with the excruciating consequences of absence rather than with the overwhelming sense of presence. It might initially seem to echo, from a more mature perspective, the theme of unrequited love explored earlier in "Araby." However, an important distinction obtains. "A Painful Case," unlike the tale of preadolescent fascination that takes pleasure in the loss of something that never truly existed, develops its pathos in the unspoken, delayed recognition of the rupture that occurred.

At the same time, one need not see either as unreservedly bitter recollections. The boy in "Araby" feels foolish at the end of his experience in much the way we all have felt at our first encounter with love.

> Gazing up into the darkness I saw myself as a creature driven and derided by vanity: and my eyes burned with anguish and anger. (*D* 26)

Despite the overblown rhetoric, his response does not signal defeat, much less paralysis. Rather it underscores the vitality of being able to experience emotion.

One may grant that Mr. Duffy can in some respect be pegged as a tragic figure who misses the opportunity of love, yet at the same time acknowledge that the very description of the desolation he now feels, articulated in the last few sentences of the story, attests to his having broken the cycle of paralysis.

> He began to doubt the reality of what memory told him. He halted under a tree and allowed the rhythm to die away. He could not feel her near him in the darkness nor her voice touch his ear. He waited for some minutes, listening. He could hear nothing: the night was perfectly silent. He listened again: perfectly silent. He felt that he was alone. (*D* 99)

Duffy's final condition is one of mourning, certainly. The pain he experiences, like the pain of Mrs. Sinico patronizingly misrepresented by the headline announcing her death, has a searing, desperate quality, but there is also an inherent vitality in it. The conclusion of "Araby" and of "A Painful Case" each shows a central character in a similar condition of isolation, but the disparate tones that differentiate these experiences underscore the idea that the complexity of human response extends far beyond an immobilizing apathy. Without diminishing the poignancy found in the former story, the latter adds a sense of gravity to the loss, an awareness that the kind of relationship idealized by the boy in "Araby" may be not an unattained ideal but rather one that never truly existed. Indeed, both contribute to the way we grasp how Gabriel Conroy in "The Dead" can end his story with a new understanding of love.

The exilic point of view shows us this possibility of augmenting our reading. The idea that the author can extend a measure of genuine affection for both the unnamed boy and Mr. Duffy gives complexity to the emotional complexion of the collection. The harsh view that scourges the follies of Dubliners is from the start mitigated by an undertone of tenderness for them.

Shaking the assumption that all but the last of the *Dubliners* stories grew out of a single-minded impulse to pillory Irish society can radically alter what we feel we have encountered. Seeing new options for understanding heretofore thematically monolithic stories enriches and diversifies our experiences with the collection. "Ivy Day in the Committee Room," for example, may seem at first glance a narrowly focused, sardonic representation of the fatuousness of underemployed men adept at ignoring their own shortcomings. Certainly that is a powerful thread in a story that traces the venality of ward-heeler politics and that highlights the pettiness of men who view the process of electioneering with pragmatic resignation. It ends with the poem commemorating the death of Charles Stewart Parnell that Joe Hynes recites. Hynes's composition has all the trappings of maudlin sentimentality that one might expect from a man unpracticed in writing verse and in the grip of strong emotion.

At the same time, despite the understandable tendency of readers to condemn the venality of the layabouts at the center of the story—Mr. Henchy, old Jack, Mr. O'Connor, and Crofton—attentiveness to the oscillation inspired by nostalgia and rancor can lead to observations that argue against a too easy dismissal of the unabashedly sincere Hynes. While Joe's composition certainly does not match in power or subtlety what one finds in the verses of Yeats celebrating the same subject, its awkwardness does not reach a level that would make it an object of ridicule. On the other hand, if the narrative sought to convey its awkwardness as an amateur rendering shaped by raw emotion rather than innate talent, there would be no need to give the full version of Hynes's tribute to Parnell. Its sentimentality is quite obvious after the first few lines:

> The Death of Parnell
> 6th October 1891
> He cleared his throat once or twice and then began to recite:
>
> He is dead. Our Uncrowned King is dead.
> O, Erin, mourn with grief and woe
> For he lies dead whom the fell gang
> Of modern hypocrites laid low. (*D* 114)

The poem goes on for ten more stanzas, taking the reader beyond satire to actual consideration of the work. Admittedly, additional lines do not improve the quality of the poem, but they do suggest that the narrative is taking it seriously.

Those familiar with Joyce's biography will know that as a young child he wrote a now lost poem on the same subject, "Et Tu, Healy."[22] Combining the irony and possible nostalgia that Joyce felt at recalling a poem from his childhood, most probably one of the first he composed, strongly encourages a less categorical dismissal of it and of its fictional author. It underscores for us the point that to scorn Hynes for his good-hearted sentimentality would be to align ourselves with the cynical creatures whose temporary loyalties have been purchased with a dozen bottles of stout and whose low-energy mendacity impels them to excoriate whichever man has just left. Instead, one finds in the momentary reverence evoked by Joe's sentiments a softening recollection that serves to counteract the deadening stasis gripping the other men in the room.

A sense that nostalgia and rancor coexist throughout the collection offers enhanced interpretive choices even when one does not discern the overt presence of either attitude. More to the point, acknowledging the perspective of the exile does a great deal to disrupt traditional linear responses that otherwise might become default readings. Neither sentimentality nor bitterness need inevitably provoke an ironic understanding of the scene in which it appears. Instead, once one identifies manifestations of the exilic impulse in particular stories, it becomes evident in others that openness to diverse points of view provides similar opportunities for complex judgments.

This can be particularly useful in highlighting the narrative's divergence from typical or even stereotypical attitudes about groups, issues, or situations. It is all too easy, for example, on first reading to dismiss Mrs. Mooney in "The Boarding House" as little more than a depiction of self-interested female cunning or Mrs. Kearney in "The Mother" as simply a harsh representation of an insensitive, self-absorbed, and overly aggressive woman. Such assessments, however, commit to the same exclusionary, prescriptive attitude that I have steadily criticized as limiting one's understanding of other stories.

A very different perspective emerges when one judges that behavior from the point of view of mothers and daughters. In both stories the women operate from a disadvantaged position that demands a deft sense of social dynamics, and in both instances their daughters move in even more uncertain spheres of power. In describing Polly Mooney's pliant acquiescence to her mother's unvoiced hope that Polly secure a husband, Joyce traces an arc of behavior analogous to that laid out for Kathleen Kearney by her mother, reflecting a determination to succeed in a world where men seem to have all the power. Both stories show imperfect mothers and daughters, but that says no more than what is true of us all. If one focuses on Mrs. Mooney experiencing a dubious victory and Mrs. Kearney enduring an ambivalent defeat, that truncates interpretive potential. A richer response explores the full implications of the dynamics of the mother-daughter relations.[23]

With "Grace" Joyce returns to the theme of the irresponsible father and husband, whose condition is exacerbated by heavy drinking, that he explored earlier in "Counterparts." One can certainly see Tom Kernan's literal fall at the beginning of the story as having ironic Edenic echoes of the consequences of recklessness and self-indulgence. Likewise, his return to a state of grace at the end, through his participation in a highly secularized version of religious liturgy, imposes a mechanical resolution that under scrutiny emerges as extremely problematic.

The alternative approach to the story, derived from our sense of the oscillating views of the exile, suggests a more complex consideration of the central feature of Catholic faith at which Joyce both laughs and celebrates: forgiveness, a complex concept in its own right and one, to the great relief of many Catholics, that does not require perfect contrition. In fact Catholic dogma, acknowledging human imperfection, extends forgiveness to all who genuinely seek it without exhaustive scrutiny of their motives.

The men who gather in Kernan's sickroom, as bumptious and ingenuous as they may seem to contemporary readers, take enormous comfort from the belief that they can avail themselves of a gift that remains precious even in our jaded society: the opportunity for exculpation.[24]

This does not inoculate them against criticism, for Joyce's short story is merciless in its representation of their simplistic and largely self-interested approaches to belief, exemplified by the inaccurate, pious certitudes of Martin Cunningham and the others on various points of religious practice. At the same time, Joyce's narrative extends to them the ability to feel the sense of beginning again, an optimistic condition any of us would relish.

As noted earlier in this chapter, a great many readers have already found in "The Dead" persuasive evidence that Joyce remained true to his desire to use it to counterbalance, or at least blunt, some of the criticism for Ireland and for Irish life inherent in his earlier stories. I hope I have shown, whether or not he realized this goal, that such sentiments toward melioration were already present in many of the other works in the collection and that his sense of his status as an exile contributed in no small part to a disposition to balance contradictory sentiments in representations of much of the world of Dublin about which he wrote. In closing, I do feel it worthwhile to quote from the final lines of this last story to underscore just how much Joyce celebrated and simultaneously castigated his native land with a lyrical evocation of its poignant beauty:

> The time had come for him to set out on his journey westward. Yes, the newspapers were right: snow was general all over Ireland. It was falling on every part of the dark central plain, on the treeless hills, falling softly upon the Bog of Allen and, farther westward, softly falling into the dark mutinous Shannon waves. It was falling, too, upon every part of the lonely churchyard on the hill where Michael Furey lay buried. It lay thickly drifted on the crooked crosses and headstones, on the spears of the little gate, on the barren thorns. His soul swooned slowly as he heard the snow falling faintly through the universe and faintly falling, like the descent of their last end, upon all the living and the dead. (*D* 194)

Without doubt, one can trace the outline of a cold, unfeeling universe in this description. At the same time, one also cannot ignore the plaintive tenderness of Gabriel's recollections. After earlier rejecting Miss Ivors's invitation to visit the Aran Islands in the summer, he now relents and moves in his mind over the territory that leads there. Gabriel sees it realistically and affectionately, and its contemplation leads to a profound emotion and to a sense of community with Ireland that he would not acknowledge earlier. Joyce, the exile, writes with tenderness and courage. He represents the harshness in the land he has left, but he also draws out the beauty that has him returning to it with every creative gesture.

In all of these instances, I have not sought to deny Joyce's sometimes searing criticism of Dublin and its citizens. What I have aimed at is a recognition of the impact of exile on his recollection of his native country. Though there is as much rancor in these early stories as in my grandfather's view of Ireland, there is an appreciation that dilutes the bitterness and reminds us of the nostalgia felt by so many other exiles.

3

Stephen Dedalus's Lifelong Exile

The shortest way to Tara was via Holyhead.

The word "exile" appears only once in *A Portrait of the Artist as a Young Man*. Near the end of the novel, in the classic gesture of the disenchanted modernist, Stephen Dedalus articulates the feelings of separation, marginalization, and loss that have been suggested with a building intensity over the course of the narrative.[1] The passage to which I refer forms part of a longer, wide-ranging conversation with his friend Cranly that serves as a summary of the beliefs and attitudes that Stephen has come to see as the defining features of his consciousness. It also provides a detailed account of the associations, traditions, and beliefs to which he no longer feels a loyalty or even an attachment.

The portion of the discourse that I specifically wish to examine here opens with Stephen's defiant rejection of the primary institutions that have been shaping his sense of the world during his childhood and adolescence and that have been demanding his unquestioning fealty. He speaks his views bluntly to his friend Cranly—

> You have asked me what I would do and what I would not do. I will tell you what I will do and what I will not do. I will not serve that in which I no longer believe whether it call itself my home, my fatherland or my church:

—then goes on to sketch, in clear and direct language, a plan for the recasting of the system of values governing his life, his scheme for establishing his maturity and achieving his independence through self-reliance and ingenuity:

> and I will try to express myself in some mode of life or art as freely as I can and as wholly as I can, using for my defence the only arms I allow myself to use, silence, exile and cunning. (*P* 218)

On first reading, this comes across simply as a straightforward and courageous, if fairly predictable, statement of how he intends to live. It presents a bold, if naïvely constructed, declaration of Stephen's determination to confront a world whose views threaten to smother his own.

However, under scrutiny, the aims put forward in that declaration become more complex, bifurcated as one detects marked shifts in tone and disposition about halfway through the statement. The opening lines, proclaiming Stephen's intention to rebel against conventional constrictions, come across with unambiguous boldness. Stephen quickly follows with an articulation of his strategy for implementing this resolve that highlights stillness, withdrawal, and craftiness. This introduces a marked emotional and psychological shift, injecting a certain ambivalence into a heretofore brashly assertive tone. The closer one looks, the more it seems that Stephen's strategy for asserting his independence has an odd passivity, closer to submissiveness than to defiance, which threatens to undercut the initial boldness with its tepid conclusion.[2]

Once one becomes aware of the tension created by this juxtaposition of gestures toward activity with those moving toward passivity, the problem of how to reconcile the anomalous elements takes on a good degree of significance. However, for those who have been noting bifurcated feelings throughout the narrative, its resolution becomes fairly straightforward.

Understanding Stephen's statement demands that readers show openness to oscillating, nonlinear perspectives that would immediately stand out as a challenge to familiar conventions for reading, were it not the case that such a pattern of interpretation is exactly what the narrative has been fostering from its opening lines. This fluctuating condition is simply presented more overtly here. This instance emphasizing the disruptiveness of the interpretive approach that produces the fullest engagement with the text also makes overt a thematic disposition that runs throughout the entire novel: the impulse in Stephen toward separation from the world that surrounds him. In the passage quoted above, the inclusion of physical displacement in Stephen's strategy for resistance is only a logical extension of the attitudes growing in him toward the social context from which he has emerged.

It requires no great intuitive leap to see how an awareness of Joyce's own background will clarify the way Stephen seeks to challenge his world. Drawing analogies between the actual boyhood of James Joyce and the fictional accounts of Stephen Dedalus's maturation has been a common practice since the first biography of the author—Herbert Gorman's *James Joyce: His First Forty Years*—popularized that approach nine decades ago.[3] I do not want to minimize the problems that arise when readers draw too fine comparisons between the two representations. However, the social, cultural, and psychological forces shaping an author's imaginative context always play a role in shaping creative products. It is my contention that the formative events in Joyce's life during the novel's composition, specifically Joyce's separation from Ireland, brought an extratextual perspective to bear on the writing process, and awareness of that condition can lead readers to important insights into Stephen's views.

The invocation of the theme of exile late in *A Portrait of the Artist as a Young Man* calls attention to the way perceptions change radically when they have been cut off from direct contact with the familiar environment of the homeland. It reminds us of exile's disruptive effect on linear thinking. As already noted, examples of sharp mood swings between sentimentality and resentment can be found throughout Joyce's letters once he left Ireland in 1904. Sensitivity to this impact on his process of composition allows us to adopt an interpretive perspective that I believe greatly enhances our understanding of Stephen's process of maturation. For the careful reader, that insight applies not just in the passage above from the final chapter but over the course of the narrative of *A Portrait of the Artist as a Young Man.*

Despite the argument offered in the preceding chapters on the impact that exile had on Joyce's process of composition, basing an understanding of *A Portrait of the Artist as a Young Man* on the application of issues relating to exile may seem a quixotic approach to a novel with a central character who, over the course of the narration, never goes farther from Dublin than a trip to Cork with his father. However, as one finds generally throughout Joyce's adult correspondence and specifically in the 6 September 1906 letter to Stanislaus (*Letters* II.156–58), from at least 1904 onward the emotions of exile informed Joyce's consciousness and by extension necessarily helped to shape the novel he wrote.

Indeed, Stephen's melodramatic renunciation of Ireland and Irish institutions in his conversation with Cranly is only the final instance of examples running throughout *A Portrait of the Artist as a Young Man* of Joyce's application of the rancorous and nostalgic points of view of the exile to enforce on Stephen a marginalized status. The book emphasizes themes of isolation and loss that correspond in a significant way to Joyce's own exilic experiences. A logical extension of this premise of association, then, leads us to see that a subtext focusing on separation and loss shapes the reader's sense of Stephen's world as much as or more than do overt descriptions of the physical markers of the Dublin streets, buildings, and monuments that surround him.

Evidence of the influence of an exilic point of view appears as soon as one begins reading. References to displacement and marginality are embedded beneath the reassuring familiarity of the novel's formulaic opening lines. The seemingly straightforward expository marker of the first words of the narrative, "Once upon a time," paradoxically reinforce a traditional storytelling form and simultaneously begin the process of disrupting the reader's confidence in the assumption that a simple linear movement toward meaning governs the logic of Joyce's discourse.

The novel's opening phrase seemingly announces a familiar narrative form with its equally familiar patterns of reading—the fairy tale genre—by the use of a tagline that has become a permanent fixture at the start of every such story. However, familiarity should not be equated with prescriptiveness, and the conventional linear ways of engaging the genre have become, in the minds of any number of prominent scholars of fairy tales, far less dependable methods of exposition. Within the past few decades critics from Bruno Bettelheim to Jack Zipes have shown that a polymorphous quality lies at the center of the fairy-tale tradition. They, and colleagues building on their findings, have done a great deal to overturn conventions of reading that made the interpretation of fairy tales little more than a formulaic process.[4]

Once one acknowledges mutability tied to what many previously presumed to be a static narrative form, it becomes relatively easy to see how the discourse of Joyce's novel evokes multiple impressions in nontraditional ways. Making the event singular—"Once"—while detaching it from any precise chronological progression undermines a sense of specificity even as it asserts the singularity of the event. Similarly, "upon a time" identifies what follows as written according to the strictly delineated and highly prescriptive fairy-tale genre, yet the formulaic assertion simultaneously refuses to assign a precise chronological moment to the experience.

This both/and quality overturns linearity and calls to mind the subversive, conflicted impulses that only lately we have come to see associated with that genre.

As the opening passage in Joyce's novel unfolds, it invites the reader's awareness of the metatextuality infused into the discourse. Its plurality is highlighted by the narrative's invocation of a traditional discourse and simultaneously diminished by its inconsistent imitation of the genre it evokes. Acknowledging this plurality leads one toward contradiction of the assumptions associated with conventional narrative patterns.

From this perspective one readily sees that the passage cannot abide for very long the fairy tale's deferral of resolution which assures readers only at the end of the story that the central characters come to a condition allowing them to live "happily ever after." Instead, Joyce's prose immediately asserts a positive sense of the world he describes: "Once upon a time and a very good time it was" (*P* 5). This proleptic assurance of happiness, which on first reading appears to be simply a superfluous stylistic flourish, in fact sets the pattern of hyper-idealization that punctuates the narrative and shades Stephen's consciousness in key passages throughout the novel. The phrase establishes a need to project the seamless, sentimentalized vision of a nostalgic representation of emotional tranquility, even as its disruption of the fairy tale formula injects a lack of certitude regarding the accuracy of the statement.

Once one sees how incertitude has been introduced, it becomes apparent how subsequent sentences go on to assert contrary impulses even more directly. As the narrative lays out an idyllic picture of childhood happiness, it simultaneously introduces a measure of disorientation and uneasiness through nuanced linguistic evasions, in the process obscuring the source of the account with a series of stuttering pronoun iterations.

> His father told him that story: his father looked at him through a glass: he had a hairy face.
>
> He was baby tuckoo. The moocow came down the road where Betty Byrne lived: she sold lemon platt. (*P* 5)

As in the previous example, first reading gives the impression of seamless continuity, but that is directly traceable to the reader's inclination to efface disruptive moments by eliding them into a single, linear experience. That, however, does not stand up to close scrutiny.

Within the very short space of the first compound sentence quoted above, the possessive pronouns pile up in staccato repetition: "His . . . him . . . his . . . him . . ." They all unambiguously relate to the young boy, but that clarity becomes obscured when the final pronoun, "he," abruptly calls for a shift in reference with the invocation of the "hairy face." Barring a sudden, miraculous onset of puberty, the reader needs to find another antecedent. It is readily there in the noun "father" at the head of the sentence. We make the connection effortlessly and, unless we have a pedantic streak, ignore the grammatical hiccough. It's easy to do, but it runs counter to the mindset we need when engaging the prose of an author as careful with words as James Joyce.

Hugh Kenner's often repeated assertion that one of the primary things that reading *Ulysses* does is to teach us how to read *Ulysses* is at least as applicable to the narrative of *A Portrait of the Artist as a Young Man*.[5] In all of Joyce's prose, one needs to remain open to new epistemologies, because Joyce is self-consciously writing in ways different from any that preceded him. The opening of this novel is one such teaching moment.

The point in noting this shift in pronoun antecedent is not to show that the author has momentarily lost grammatical control of the discourse, but rather to demonstrate how he wonderfully mimics the solipsistic narrative voice of a little boy. In a single deft stroke, Joyce captures the self-absorbed consciousness of the child who assumes we understand the world, and his shifting perspective of it, exactly as he does. It is a minor moment of interpretive adjustment that will go unremarked by most readers, but it introduces the pattern of rapid alternation within the narrative point of view that will follow. Like the dynamic systems highly sensitive to initial conditions studied in chaos theory, slight shifts in narrative mood can produce significant consequences in Joyce's discourse, and throughout *A Portrait of the Artist as a Young Man* such shifts brought about by the exilic experience will exert a strong effect on the narrative as it unfolds.

The next paragraph in Joyce's novel, though on the surface a model of clarity, in fact reinforces that calculated ambiguity through a gesture ostensively meant to dispel it. The phrase "He was baby tuckoo" creates a chain of associations that can enforce a much broader reading of the text than what the discourse can support. Because of our habits of associative understanding when we read, the direct assertion of identity quickly leads to elaborations and connections of which the reader can often remain unaware. It tempts anyone who already knows the name of the novel's main character to make the leap that imagines the central character as the narrator and that sees the child to which the sentence refers as Stephen. This assumption inexorably leads to the conclusion that the father referenced in the passage must be Stephen's and that Simon Dedalus had "a hairy face."

While such an interpretation neatly fits the context of the passage, that connection is in fact nothing more than conjecture. Close analysis will show that the only certitude at which one can arrive is that the young male at the center of this account is called "baby tuckoo." Once again the narrative uses pronouns to avoid clarity. We readers step in to see the antecedent of "He" as Stephen Dedalus and of "his father" as Simon. These are assumptions most of us make unconsciously, for they sustain the linear unity that we generally take as an attribute inherent to the story.

My point is not that it is incorrect to posit that baby tuckoo and the man with the hairy face should be linked to the duo of Stephen and Simon Dedalus. What this selection does show, however, is the degree to which Joyce's narrative overtly involves the reading in the completion of meaning. I emphasize the word "overtly" since one can make the argument that any text involves the reader in the completion of meaning.

Every reading vivifies the words on the printed page through individual, subjective apprehension that creates the unified impression that stands as our reading experience. For engaging Joyce's works as fully as possible, an understanding of their metatextuality, their intention to foreground the act of creating meaning, stands as a crucial epistemological function. In a very emphatic fashion, identification of meaning in Joyce's writing comes out of the external imposition of an order that privileges a particular way of reading while often suppressing alternative approaches. I am endeavoring here, in examining *A Portrait of the Artist as a Young Man* and by extension all of Joyce's fiction, to offer insights that accommodate that extratextuality while avoiding the prescriptiveness that comes from full commitment to a single point of view.

I want to emphasize how these efforts to parse the options for interpretation go beyond linguistic quibbles, so let me highlight the provisionality of identity within the opening passage of the novel and how any resolution of that provisionality commits readers to a very specific way of understanding all that will follow in the narrative. The clearest illustration of this comes from taking up a fundamental question of origins often overlooked in initial readings of the opening: What voice speaks to us?

For many, that question of source does not even arise, and if it does, readers more often than not will quickly come to an answer. Nonetheless, closer scrutiny will call into question whatever conclusion one reaches, for the source of the account is by no means definite. In fact there are a range of choices that one can make regarding the initial narrator.

There are two distinct parts to the opening section of *A Portrait of the Artist as a Young Man*: the story of baby tuckoo ("Once upon a time") and the commentary on it ("His father told him that story"). As in all of Joyce's fiction, initial impressions can contribute to comprehending their significance, but a full understanding comes only with engagement of the underlying complexities of the discourse. On first apprehension of the opening, it is logical to assume that two distinct voices are speaking—the man with the hairy face recounting the story and baby tuckoo contextualizing it. Further consideration makes other sources for the discourse seem equally possible. It is quite logical to see the whole passage as an account being related by baby tuckoo, who imitates his father's voice telling the story and then contextualizes it. On the other hand, it is equally reasonable to say that it is the unnamed narrator who imitates the father's voice and then, in exposition, identifies the son. The narrative does not give primacy to one position over the others. Rather, it leaves open the choice of which of the points of view best suits the reader's understanding of the passage.

This sets the epistemological pattern for everything that follows. Once one acknowledges that the opening discourse supports multiple explanations of source with equal logical confidence, these simultaneously functioning alternative points of view make the conventional, exclusionary linear interpretive approach counterproductive, or at the very least inhibitive of a full understanding. One sees this amply illustrated in the next few paragraphs.

> He was baby tuckoo. The moocow came down the road where Betty Byrne lived: she sold lemon platt.
> *O, the wild rose blossoms*
> *On the little green place.*
> He sang that song. That was his song.

> *O, the geen wothe botheth.*
> When you wet the bed first it is warm then it gets cold. His mother put on the oilsheet. That had a queer smell. (*P* 5)

In the staccato representations of this passage, voice and perspective careen about through a montage of baby tuckoo's experiences, underscoring his possessiveness of the world by the reconfiguration of the passage on the rose.[6] One can certainly bracket those experiences by adopting a specific voice taking the dominant perspective. However, a view that tolerates multiplicity will come much closer to the perspective of a toddler coming to grips with the diverse and as yet uncategorized experiences that make up his world.

(A distinguishing feature of each of the novel's chapters is its ability to recount events in language appropriate to Stephen Dedalus's level of maturation at any given point. This in effect offers an extended impression similar to that created by free indirect discourse: we read the narrative in language that evokes our sense of the central character without having markers that link the discourse solely to Stephen's consciousness.)

Thus we see, after a brief lyrical introduction of baby tuckoo's idiosyncratic rendition of a familiar song, the text confronting us with prosaic, unpleasant reminders of the fundamental features of a toddler's life: "When you wet the bed first it is warm then it gets cold. His mother put on the oilsheet. That had a queer smell." Understatement and deflection seem to be the dominant tones of these accounts, first with a measure of sentimentality softening the experiences recounted and then, in the case of the bed, with just a touch of anxiety that tinges its consequence. Overall, we witness the effect of detachment and selectivity creating fragmented and conflicted recollections of a world now past. That in itself, however, does not fully encompass the options offered for creating meaning.

A tone that captures the fluctuating senses of optimism and vulnerability will evoke the oscillating feelings of a child still striving to comprehend the rudimentary conditions that shape the world that he finds himself inhabiting. In that vein, the reader's attentiveness to the impact of nostalgia and rancor on the boy's perceptions of ordinary events helps to clarify the basis for Stephen's early disposition toward duality, his impulsive and restless curiosity that has him always reimagining and reevaluating events. Though never overtly identified to the reader as exilic impulses, these feelings of disconnection and of distance have already begun to inform Stephen's sense of the world.

> The Vances lived in number seven. They had a different father and mother. They were Eileen's father and mother. When they were grown up he was going to marry Eileen.
> He hid under the table. His mother said:
> —O, Stephen will apologise.
> Dante said:
> —O, if not, the eagles will come and pull out his eyes.
> *Pull out his eyes,*
> *Apologise,*
> *Apologise,*
> *Pull out his eyes.*
>
> *Apologise,*
> *Pull out his eyes,*
> *Pull out his eyes,*
> *Apologise.* (*P* 5–6)

Disoriented perceptions and clashing emotions dominate the passage. However, that does not mean that it unfolds without a unifying logic that can shape the reader's sense of the discourse. Indeed, this selection perfectly captures the oscillation of a child's attention from one idea and one emotion to another.

A charming naïveté punctuates the first four sentences. They describe in shorthand fashion the domestic situation of the Vances as compared with that of Stephen's family, acknowledging different parents while presuming that no other variances obtain. Through the simply constructed declarative sentences, the narrative establishes the boy's sense of unsophisticated order of the construction of this world and conveys the seemingly undisturbed rhythm of the life that Stephen experiences.

The abrupt displacement of the idyllic opening tone—"He hid under the table"—reminds us of the provisionality of any of the boy's observations. The passage goes on to establish the tenuousness of such a view through the callous, retributive chant that follows. In blunt, assertive language it introduces menace, vulnerability, and disruption into what the boy has heretofore characterized as a pleasant, ordered world. These oscillating perspectives sum up Stephen's incomplete comprehension of the world around him and the inadvisability of relying on any single feeling as sufficient explanation for that world.

Form follows function as well. The shift in style from prose to verse graphically signals a sharp change in tone. Even there, however, the discourse refuses to fall into a single predictable, linear causal pattern. The emphatic tone emerging from the declarative sentence in the final lines of the exposition gives way to the incantatory lines, which initially threaten and then soften their tone through lyrical repetition. Familiarity turns the retributive menace of adult authority into a less ominous and more formulaic threat and ultimately perhaps even into the mockery of a young boy's mimicking voice. In the process the raw threat of physical violence metamorphoses into expressive carnival.

Ambiguity is a crucial feature here, as it is in all of Joyce's fiction, and the key to the fullest understanding of this approach lies in an interpretive methodology that accommodates rather than resolves ambiguity. I have outlined this approach in earlier critical studies.[7] Here I want to elaborate on the way exile experiences gave a very specific orientation to that inclination toward ambiguity.

As with the story told to baby tuckoo, the creative intensity of the transgression passage comes out of the shifting perspectives and uncertain sources of the discourse. The opening lines take a tone like Stephen's, though it may be a narrator imitating that point of view. The next few sentences are clearly identified as coming first from May Dedalus and then from Dante Riordan. However, rather than clarifying the perspective of the discourse, this sequence of narrators raises the possibility of the lyrical section that follows originating from any one or combination of the three voices.

We may simply be hearing Dante, reemphasizing in a melodious refrain her threat to punish Stephen for his unnamed offense. Likewise, it could be Mrs. Dedalus adding her support to the threat. In a slightly more complex wrinkle, this singsong summation of Dante's intimidating prediction may be the creation of a defiant Stephen, safely established under the table, mimicking her menace and mocking her impotence to carry it out. Or it simply could be the narrative voice again at work, echoing the lines of an incident from the past with no attempt at attribution.

In keeping with the duality of the exilic approach, the passage becomes even richer if we sustain the possibility of all narrators. This captures the significance of each of the diverse attitudes of the moment, allowing polyphony to displace the hegemony of a single voice. As the episode unfolds, the divergent possibilities for its source become increasingly evident, and the need to delineate the details of the events described or to identify the particular figures recounting them becomes progressively less important.

The shift of attention to the performative features coloring the account brings a reorientation in interpretive values. Incident and actors are no longer as important as the emotional color of the selection. The reader is still called upon to impose a resolution by putting what is said in context, but our growing awareness of competing impulses and of an ongoing disorientation in the narrative undermines the validity of linking that resolution to a seemingly objective and relentlessly linear account of facts. Rather, we begin here to discern the underlying aim of the narrative that runs throughout the novel: to trace the elliptical evolution of the complex emotional relationship between the central character and the world he perceives as he grows to manhood.

Joyce employs disarmingly simple language to open *A Portrait of the Artist as a Young Man*. He presents a discourse that unfolds with apparent directness and simplicity, but on closer examination its meaning becomes increasingly opaque and diffuse. In this understated fashion, the narrative introduces the idea of uncertainty that will lie just below the surface at any point in the novel. To my mind, this emphasis stands as a logical, though not uncomplicated, stage in Joyce's creative development.

By the time Joyce began writing *A Portrait of the Artist as a Young Man* around 1907, he was living abroad with Nora and their two children, yet his personal life hardly reflected the rhythms of conventional domesticity. In addition to almost constant financial concerns, there was an ongoing sense of separation directly related to living abroad. All this influenced the construction of his novel.

As evident from the examination in the last chapter of the composition of *Dubliners*, the conflicted emotions characterizing the experience of exile had already disposed Joyce to see Ireland from multiple, contrasting points of view. His attitudes, fluctuating between sentimentality and bitterness, are subtly manifested even in accounts of the most quotidian moments of Stephen Dedalus's childhood, and they make a cumulative impression on our efforts at interpretation. Over the course of the novel, these attitudes, manifested both in the demeanors of various characters and in the perspectives of the narrative voice, become increasingly assertive and take on accumulated significance in the way one comprehends the nature of Stephen Dedalus. For the fullest understanding of the narrative they need our attention from their first manifestations.[8]

This observation runs counter to the assumption that Stephen's maturation followed an undeviating path of steadily increasing alienation from Irish cultural institutions. Instead it evokes the tendency of chaotic systems, already noted, to respond to slight deviations in a significant way, but only after numerous iterations.[9] The disparity between the understandings that come from a sense of Stephen's oscillating attitudes toward Ireland and Irish culture and the received ideas about the linear progression of Stephen's views increases as the narrative progresses. In consequence, as is the case with readings of the stories in *Dubliners,* if one accepts the influence of exilic attitudes, one needs to be open to a very different understanding of the novel than those suggested by previous interpretations.

The creative disposition toward multiplicity that comes out of the exilic point of view neatly subverts the apparent commitment to linearity suggested by the sequential development of a narrative chronicling Stephen Dedalus's life from toddler to young adult. In the process, it highlights the need for multiple points of view to approach a full understanding of the novel: one aspect of maturation shows a steady chronological progression from infancy to adulthood, while another traces an elliptical emotional development that produces recurrent impulses toward engagement and disassociation with the world around it.[10]

Through all this, Stephen's feelings and beliefs demonstrate consistent and simultaneous commitments to and revulsions for core conceptions, evolving, at a glacierlike pace over the twenty or so years encompassed by the narrative, to a position that finally separates him from the social institutions—family, church, and state—that seek to direct his life and the lives of his contemporaries in the community. This progress animates both the ongoing engagement and the measured dissolution inflecting most of his experiences. These changes might seem capricious or haphazard without a clear sense of large forces motivating them.

Here is where an awareness of the exilic mentality enhances our understanding of both Joyce's process of composition and his representation of Stephen's unique mental condition. The central character of *A Portrait of the Artist as a Young Man* is not simply the archetypal artistic rebel who instinctively, from earliest moments of sentience, opposes all that he encounters in the bourgeois world that surrounds him. Of course, numerous readers have seen Stephen in that fashion, for the familiar representation of the conventional bildungsroman protagonist is quite consistent with readings conditioned by lifelong habituation to a Cartesian, exclusionary, cause-and-effect way of seeing. However, that does not accommodate the fact that Joyce animates and distinguishes the main figure in his narrative by challenging readers to sustain alternating views of Stephen's nature.

An awareness of the exilic experience, with all its complexity, makes this approach easier to comprehend and to pursue. The exilic perspective allows one to see emphasis moving from the event to the emotions, ranging across the spectrum from bitterness to sentimentality, that it has produced. Joyce writes with unique insight and sensitivity about Stephen as a reluctant outsider in his hometown of Dublin because Joyce had become that exilic outsider as he composed *A Portrait of the Artist as a Young Man* in his adopted town of Trieste. Illustrations of the influence of this exilic state recur from the earliest pages. Understanding the discourse that unfolds in the next section of the novel—an abrupt jump to Clongowes Wood College where the young Stephen has recently begun classes—becomes much easier if one grasps the alternation of harsh and wistful feelings, which provides a clearer comprehension of the complex attitudes that shape the young boy's consciousness.

Its opening sets the tone with a description of a football game on the college playing field, presented as an unpleasant experience that the protagonist seeks to avoid by keeping "on the fringe of his line, out of sight of his prefect, out of the reach of the rude feet, feigning to run now and then" (*P* 6). The narrative then leads Stephen to direct recollection of two of his classmates who have alternately fascinated and intimidated him: "Roddy Kickham was a decent fellow but Nasty Roche was a stink" (*P* 6). This in turn brings to mind thoughts of his family. The montage of his recollections of coming to Clongowes Wood and bidding farewell to his parents reflects the attendant feelings of exile that might seem melodramatic if we did not know of Joyce's circumstances and disposition:

> His mother had told him not to speak with the rough boys in the college. Nice mother! The first day in the hall of the castle when

> she had said good-bye she had put up her veil double to her nose to kiss him: and her nose and eyes were red. But he had pretended not to see that she was going to cry. She was a nice mother but she was not so nice when she cried. And his father had given him two fiveshilling pieces for pocket money. And his father had told him if he wanted anything to write home to him and, whatever he did, never to peach on a fellow. (*P* 7)

The lines sound childish, befitting the language of a young boy away from home for the first time, but it is the sentiment not the simplicity of the language that should hold our attention.

Despite the rather abrupt jump from thinking about bullying and solicitous classmates to dreamy remembrances of the day his parents brought him to Clongowes Wood College, a consistency in feelings links the passages. Stephen, unconsciously or not, is beginning to respond as an exile, cut off from the nurturing world of the opening pages. The dual notions of rancor and nostalgia are already beginning to shape Stephen's response to Clongowes and to affect the way that he remembers his home and his family—often producing conflicted views of previously stable relationships. His mother is "nice" until she becomes overly emotional. His father is generous but also stern in advocating group loyalty. All this comes as Stephen stands apart from and remains intimidated by the rough play of his classmates. In a more overt and perhaps more vulnerable fashion, Stephen echoes the bitterness and sentimentality that often color the exile's sense of the world that has been lost and impressions of the world now inhabited.

This growing disposition in Joyce's process of composition toward integrating the perspective of the exile-like feelings continues and becomes even more insistent in the daydreams Stephen has while recuperating in the sick ward of the college. While they neatly capture the childish solipsism that would be common to all young boys away from home for the first time, they also project an intense vulnerability that singles out Stephen as more than just a homesick boy.[11]

After composing an imaginary letter to his mother announcing his illness, Stephen falls into a reverie that turns on his sense of separation. At the same time, even while imaging his death, it exudes a profound enjoyment in the contemplation of the pomp and ceremony that would surround it:

> How far away they [his parents] were! There was cold sunlight outside the window. He wondered if he would die. You could die just the same on a sunny day. He might die before his mother came. Then he would have a dead mass in the chapel like the way the fellows had told him it was when Little had died. All the fellows would be at the mass, dressed in black, all with sad faces. Wells too would be there but no fellow would look at him. The rector would be there in a cope of black and gold and there would be tall yellow candles on the altar and round the catafalque. And they would carry the coffin out of the chapel slowly and he would be buried in the little graveyard of the community off the main avenue of limes. And Wells would be sorry then for what he had done. And the bell would toll slowly. (*P* 20)

Imagining death, the most extreme form of exile, leads Stephen to a complex if melodramatic projection of its impact. There is without doubt a somber, even dour, tone in his daydream full of self-pity, but there is also a deep sentimental pleasure in the imagery created by these feelings. Indeed, Stephen takes unapologetically exaggerated pleasure in the sorrow of his classmates over his demise, and he caps it with a vindictive satisfaction at the idea that Wells will be ostracized. It is good to see all this as founded in a larger sensibility, so that one does not too quickly dismiss it as the reverie of a moment.

On the one hand, it is easy to imagine any young boy feeling this way. There is clearly resentment of the bully, intense bitterness toward Wells as the personification of the forces that give him pain. There is also a childish satisfaction in the mourning that emphasizes the stylized grieving of his classmates that creates an idealized vision of their lost classmate.

At the same time, the passage, like so many in Joyce's writings, has a seductive charm that can lead to premature interpretation. It wonderfully captures the extravagant fantasies of retribution familiar to any child who has been bullied. Nonetheless, to see these musings as nothing more than childish wish-fulfillment takes a reductive interpretive course. A much fuller sense of the emotional condition and complexity of the boy comes to the foreground when we entertain the possibility that the pain and pleasure that Stephen experiences to no little degree grows out of the unvoiced exilic attitude that he has unconsciously come to adopt as part of his nature. It shapes the overall experience of being sent away to

Clongowes because he has been, at least in his own mind, cast out of the world that nurtured him. The brutish Wells is simply a catalyst for the expression of these feelings.

Recognizing this exilic disposition does not limit one's understanding of Stephen's nature. Recognizing him as a literal or even metaphoric exile is not the equivalent of interpretive pigeonholing. Rather, it acknowledges broad forces that shaped the author's creative consciousness. An expanded perspective does not overturn initial perceptions of what Stephen is thinking. The lines remain no less self-dramatizing and self-pitying—"He wondered if he would die. . . . He might die before his mother came"—after one makes the connection with the outcast mentality. However, these statements do seem less cloying and naïve when perceived as coming from the diverse effects of separation: feelings approaching bitterness ("Wells too would be there but no fellow would look at him") and nostalgia ("All the fellows would be at the mass, dressed in black, all with sad faces"). In the process, Stephen demonstrates here an emotional complexity that will increasingly distinguish his way of seeing things over the course of the novel.

Because the tone of Stephen's lament follows that of so many other resentful, alienated young people in literature, for a full understanding of his nature it is important to distinguish his feelings from the starkly different sense of isolation that motivates, for example, Holden Caulfield in *The Catcher in the Rye*. In *A Portrait of the Artist as a Young Man* we are not presented with the musings of an angry, isolated loner. Quite the contrary, we see a boy with complex, conflicted relations with the society in which he finds himself. In the passage just quoted and in subsequent sections running throughout the novel, Stephen maintains the symbiotic links to the persons and institutions from which he feels separated—physically, emotionally, or spiritually—that so crucially distinguish the exilic experience from parallel conditions. He continues to define himself in relation to the family, religion, and nation to which he simultaneously feels less and less affiliation. Thus, in the infirmary, Stephen's feelings can retain poignancy even with his maudlin expressions of sentiment because exilic-like desires for unification and vindication animate and meliorate the bitterness that also occupies his consciousness.

Keeping in mind that conflicted relation of self to environment helps explain, in scenes like the Christmas dinner argument over the place of Parnell in Irish politics, the attitudes sparking the range of contradictory emotions that color Stephen's impressions and to a degree those of the characters who play central roles in the argument as well.[12] While in that scene awareness of separation remains more immanent than present, even expressed in this understated fashion it underscores for readers the ever-present possibility of traumatic separation. The violent quarrel over Parnell that eventually breaks out between Dante Riordan, Simon Dedalus, and Mr. Casey may very well embody on an individual scale issues dividing the nation, but it also highlights a highly personal trauma that marks the struggle for identity in a claustrophobic environment and that haunts Stephen throughout the narrative. In a more general fashion, the entire episode reinforces the reader's conception of the sentimentality and bitterness informed by an immanent sense of disruption, more pervasive than the episodically specific conflict that stands as its emblematic representation, which is beginning to influence the atmosphere of the novel.

This broader sense of the possibility of fracture and disassociation is demonstrated early in the segment in a passage that draws together the sentimentality of the moment and introduces an ominous hint that the violence that will shortly erupt is not an aberration but a condition habitually in tension with the sense of tranquility of an idealized childhood:

> Why did Mr Barrett in Clongowes call his pandybat a turkey? It was not like a turkey. But Clongowes was far away: and the warm heavy smell of turkey and ham and celery rose from the plates and dishes and the great fire was banked high and red in the grate and the green ivy and red holly made you feel so happy and when dinner was ended the big plumpudding would be carried in, studded with peeled almonds and sprigs of holly, with bluish fire running around it and a little green flag flying from the top. (*P* 25)

The paragraph, with its description of an opulence in the Dedalus family life that will disappear progressively in successive chapters, captures the awe and delight of a young boy at "his first Christmas dinner" (*P* 26), but it enforces a much more complex worldview as well. The exilic mentality that is forming in Joyce's consciousness leads him to balance pleasure against bitterness in descriptions of Irish life. More specifically, contrasting this pleasant reverie with the cataclysmic political argument that follows gives the scene a greater significance even as it blunts the force of heightened emotions. Just as a disposition toward nostalgia has exaggerated Stephen's sense of the holiday atmosphere, his vulnerability to rancor distorts the significance of the argument over Parnell. These are feelings that will continue to build as the narrative unfolds.

In passages like this, so similar to the description of the table at the Morkan sisters' dinner party, Joyce both celebrates and ironizes Irish custom and culture.

> He waited outside the drawing-room door until the waltz should finish, listening to the skirts that swept against it and the shuffling of feet. He was still discomposed by the girl's bitter and sudden retort. It had cast a gloom over him which he tried to dispel by arranging his cuffs and the bows of his tie. Then he took from his waistcoat pocket a little paper and glanced at the headings he had made for his speech. He was undecided about the lines from Robert Browning for he feared they would be above the heads of his hearers. Some quotation that they would recognise from Shakespeare or from the Melodies would be better. The indelicate clacking of the men's heels and the shuffling of their soles reminded him that their grade of culture differed from his. He would only make himself ridiculous by quoting poetry to them which they could not understand. (*D* 155)

In "The Dead" exilic feelings arise more slowly than they do in *A Portrait of the Artist as a Young Man*, due in part at least to the difference in genre. Also, the nostalgia felt by Gretta, and to a degree Molly Ivors, ultimately offers a redemptive promise for Gabriel, a more mature and ultimately a more self-aware exile. No such meliorating force will blunt the harshness of the argument about to erupt in front of Stephen. Though he is the product of an older Joyce, Stephen remains in every way a much younger character, with a much more naïve sense of the world, than Gabriel Conroy. Nonetheless, we understand both scenes far better when we sustain this duality embedded in an exile's sense of his world.

Alternating patterns of euphoria and revulsion appear throughout the narrative of *A Portrait of the Artist as a Young Man*, enlivening seemingly prosaic description and underscoring the complexity of the perspectives both of the author and of his central character. I do not propose to examine every instance. However, a survey of a series of key examples of the exilic impact on the remainder of the novel will enforce the point I seek to make.

At the opening of chapter 2 we can identify feelings of sweet and painful disassociation informing Stephen's engagement with the world around him, beginning with a description of the liminal period between Stephen's leaving Clongowes Wood and entering Belvedere:

> Aubrey and Stephen had a common milkman and often they drove out in the milkcar to Carrickmines where the cows were at grass. While the men were milking the boys would take turns in riding the tractable mare round the field. But when autumn came the cows were driven home from the grass: and the first sight of the filthy cowyard at Stradbrook with its foul green puddles and clots of liquid dung and steaming brantroughs sickened Stephen's heart. The cattle which had seemed so beautiful in the country on sunny days revolted him and he could not even look at the milk they yielded. (*P* 55)

The narrative, in alternately describing feelings of childish exuberance and unabashed disgust, wonderfully evokes not simply the young boy's growing awareness of the relation between self and environment; it also brings out the author's sophisticated sense that the evolution of a child's consciousness follows a nonlinear path, tracing instead a looping, elliptical journey of emotional development. In a similar manner, in a section immediately preceding this passage, the narrative elaborates on Stephen's fascination with a well-known fictional exile, Edmond Dantès, the hero of Alexandre Dumas's *The Count of Monte Cristo*. In a wistful, imaginative gesture Stephen projects Dantès's world onto his own: "Outside Blackrock, on the road that led to the mountains, stood a small whitewashed house in the garden of which grew many rosebushes: and in this house, he told himself, another Mercedes lived" (*P* 54). Stephen goes on to interject himself into the narrative, so that he might echo the line by which Dantès offers a stinging rebuke to his former love: "Madam, I never eat muscatel grapes" (*P* 55). This adoption of melodramatic hyperbole to describe his own sense of isolation now that he has left Clongowes Wood College gently reminds us of both his precociousness and his naïveté.

The consequences of such inclinations in Stephen, however, go beyond the narrative voicing ironic reflections on the boy's emerging consciousness. The opening of chapter 2 announces that Stephen has become an economic exile. "In a vague way he understood that his father was in trouble and this was the reason why he himself had not been sent back to Clongowes" (*P* 56). It marks the first stage of what will be the family's protracted decline from a middle class to an impoverished lifestyle. The sense of otherness and marginality that have inflected Stephen's life since chapter 1 when he stood on the edge of the football line at Clongowes grows in intensity in subsequent episodes. "The noise of children at play annoyed him and their silly voices made him feel, even more keenly than he had felt at Clongowes, that he was different from others" (*P* 56).

While a sense of isolation may be common for a child, particularly one as precocious as Stephen, the actual source of that feeling is noteworthy here. Stephen's classmates do not shun him. Rather, he expresses an inclination toward self-exile that will grow over the course of the narrative. Keeping this in mind during readings of subsequent chapters of the novel will enhance one's sense of Stephen's evolving nature.

With increasing emphasis on this position of separateness, the narrative traces recurring instances of Stephen's self-perception as a social exile. In each case, understanding the source of his ambivalence enriches reader awareness of the experience of the separation. The idea of alternation is crucial for following this development.

Chapter 2 provides numerous instances of this. During Stephen's time at Belvedere he seemingly returns to the familiar setting of a Jesuit school. In fact it provides him with ample opportunities to reinforce the condition of exile. The chapter shows Stephen fully integrated into school life, but time and again examples appear of his detachment from it.

The exchanges between Stephen and Heron, both immediate and recollected (*P* 66–73), bring this state of affairs to the foreground. As the acknowledged class leaders, the two boys stand at the center of life at the school, yet their engagement with that environment could not be more different. Heron exudes a smug self-centeredness that takes his own status for granted. Stephen, on the other hand, never forgets his dual roles as both insider and outsider. Though he occupies a central place among his classmates, as he did at Clongowes after complaining of Father Dolan's unfair treatment, Stephen cannot lose a sense of vulnerability that the unjust punishment at the priest's hands initially inspired. Even as he and Heron exchange witty remarks about the foibles of the Belvedere faculty, Stephen's mind turns to recollecting the brutal bullying he endured when he first came to the college

> —Behave yourself! cried Heron, cutting at Stephen's legs with his cane.
>
> It was the signal for their onset. Nash pinioned his arms behind

> while Boland seized a long cabbage stump which was lying in the gutter. Struggling and kicking under the cuts of the cane and the blows of the knotty stump Stephen was borne back against a barbed wire fence.
>
> At last after a fury of plunges he wrenched himself free. His tormentors set off towards Jones's Road, laughing and jeering at him, while he, half blinded with tears, stumbled on, clenching his fists madly and sobbing. (*P* 71–72)

As with many of the events recounted in chapter 1, the incident of bullying will be familiar to any child. In this regard, it will hardly seem worthy of note. However, in the larger context of the unique nature evolving in Stephen, it reinforces and highlights the distinct significance of even the most ordinary and predictable events in the boy's life.

The duality of exile, producing both a longing for something that may never have existed and a bitterness over separation from that nonexistent ideal, increasingly inflects Stephen's conception of the world around him. Heron and his friends beat Stephen because he espouses different aesthetic values from theirs, preferring the poetry of Byron to that of Tennyson. For both Stephen and his antagonists, the particular predilection in fact is of little significance. More to the point, Stephen is already constructing a world of his own reinforced with values that he will steadfastly defend against the views of others, and he is suffering the outrage that others feel toward his defiance of conformity.

Further, Stephen has gained a sense of the advantage held by the solitary artist. He has developed an awareness of the power of language that takes him out of the world circumscribed by the perception and imagination of someone like Heron. When confronted by Heron with the possibility that Stephen has a girlfriend not heretofore acknowledged publicly, Stephen, who as noted above has previously endured a beating from Heron and his cronies for refusing to conform to their demands, now responds in a subtler, more effective fashion:

> Stephen's moment of anger had already passed. He was neither flattered nor confused but simply wished the banter to end. He scarcely resented what had seemed to him at first a silly indelicateness for he knew that the adventure in his mind stood in no danger from their words: and his face mirrored his rival's smile.

> —Admit! repeated Heron, striking him again with his cane across the calf of the leg.
> The stroke was playful but not so lightly given as the first one had been. Stephen felt the skin tingle and glow slightly and almost painlessly; and bowing submissively, as if to meet his companion's jesting mood, began to recite the *Confiteor*. (*P* 68)

While the situation echoes the incident in which he was beaten, the dynamics have shifted appreciably. Stephen uses his wit, his sense of Heron's need to seem sophisticated, and the detachment he feels to control the situation. Deflection, not defiance, triumphs, and in the process Stephen preserves his sense of separation far more successfully than in the previous confrontation.

Paradoxically, that does not make him empathetic to similar feelings. The trip to Cork with his father, who is traveling there to sell off the last of the family property, reinforces the shame that another's nostalgia can produce.

> He listened without sympathy to his father's evocation of Cork and of scenes of his youth, a tale broken by sighs or draughts from his pocket flask whenever the image of some dead friend appeared in it or whenever the evoker remembered suddenly the purpose of his actual visit. Stephen heard but could feel no pity. (*P* 76)

In a further demonstration of the inconsistencies that are all too common in human nature, this judgment of his father does nothing to blunt the same impulse in Stephen. Indeed, the profligacy he subsequently displays in squandering his thirty-guinea exhibition prize shows an urge as strong as his father's to reconfigure the world, if only temporarily.

> How foolish his aim had been! He had tried to build a breakwater of order and elegance against the sordid tide of life without him and to dam up, by rules of conduct and active interests and new filial relations, the powerful recurrence of the tides within him. Useless. From without as from within the waters had flowed over his barriers: their tides began once more to jostle fiercely above the crumbled mole. (*P* 86)

The narrative not only sums up the profligacy of Stephen, but it does so in a tone that catches the state of mind of the young protagonist and his paradoxical self-centered idealism, the florid metaphoric excess that one would expect of a young aspiring author.

The third chapter is centered on the annual retreat that the boys at Belvedere attend. It takes the most inclusive of Church ceremonies, a communal movement toward spiritual renewal and an event that occupies an annual place on the Belvedere calendar (and indeed remains a fairly common practice in Catholic schools), to illustrate Stephen's contrasting views from the periphery. The familiar form of the pre–Vatican II retreat, standardized almost as scrupulously as the rituals for the celebration of the Church's sacraments, aims to promote reconciliation and amalgamation.[13] Stephen subverts these intentions of inclusiveness; instead he uses the retreat to set himself apart and to make his experiences far different from those of his classmates.

The subjugation of the individual's ego to the participation in communal worship that the retreat seeks to produce in fact is lost on Stephen, who can only imagine what is passing before him in a self-involved fashion: "Every word of it was for him. Against his sin, foul and secret, the whole wrath of God was aimed" (*P* 101). While Mr. Tate and Vincent Heron joke about the severity of the retreat sermons and then chat idly about bicycling to Malahide, Stephen feels a profound, albeit self-involved, sense of spiritual awakening: "He had not died. God had spared him still. . . . There was still time." (*P* 109–10)

At the same time, despite Stephen's sense of separation, the retreat promotes the urge for some form of acceptance, manifest through sentimental reveries that mingle his secular appetites for Emma Clery with pious devotion to the Blessed Virgin as he imagines Mary saying:

> —Take hands, Stephen and Emma. It is a beautiful evening now in heaven. You have erred but you are always my children. It is one heart that loves another heart. Take hands together, my dear children, and you will be happy together and your hearts will love each other. (*P* 102)

There may be a temptation for readers simply to dismiss this scene as a satirically juxtaposed portrait of piety and sexual desire, but one needs to recall the centrality to Stephen of the images and rituals of Irish life, alternately idealized and demonized, that run throughout the book.

If we take a patronizing view of Stephen's reaction to the powerful forces of the retreat, we risk imposing a reductive explanation on his behavior.

This is where the duality of the exilic perspective offers an important tool to facilitate a fuller understanding of Stephen's nature, with the both/and elements of nostalgia and rancor continually asserting themselves.

Throughout the novel, Stephen has exercised a hypersensitive and highly romanticized perception of the world around him, from the opening chapter where we see a description of locals who live in the village adjacent to Clongowes—

> Through Clane they drove, cheering and cheered. The peasant women stood at the halfdoors, the men stood here and there. The lovely smell there was in the wintry air: the smell of Clane: rain and wintry air and turf smouldering and corduroy. (*P* 17)

—to the final segment when Stephen ascribes a mystical, fatal power to the Irish peasantry:

> John Alphonsus Mulrennan has just returned from the west of Ireland (European and Asiatic papers please copy). He told us he met an old man there in a mountain cabin. Old man had red eyes and short pipe. . . . I fear him. I fear his redrimmed horny eyes. It is with him I must struggle all through this night till day come, till he or I lie dead. (P 223)

These alternating sentimental and harsh views come from the exilic vacillations between contrasting attitudes toward a past that may have no basis in reality, and we cannot have a full comprehension of Stephen's consciousness without acknowledging them. His self-centered orientation is not an end but the reflection of the identity that is growing upon him as he matures: he is of and out of Ireland, and that duality produces polarities in his perceptions that he never fully understands, much less masters.

The descriptions that open chapter 4—elaborations on the pleasure and the revulsion that Stephen feels over the acts of mortification that he has undertaken as a consequence of the spiritual renewal (albeit a highly subjective and even idiosyncratic regeneration) that he derived from the Belvedere retreat—coincide neatly with the oscillating points of view that come out of defining himself as an exile. As an aspiring ascetic who takes penance and self-denial to an extreme, Stephen sets himself apart from those who surround him. He is not simply seeking spiritual perfection through acts of penance. He strives to separate himself. This behavior shows his subsequent rejection of the Society of Jesus and his embrace of the imaginative life as grounded in more than artistic aspirations.

> The voice of the director urging upon him the proud claims of the church and the mystery and power of the priestly office repeated itself idly in his memory. His soul was not there to hear and greet it and he knew now that the exhortation he had listed to had already fallen into an idle formal tale. He would never swing the thurible before the tabernacle as priest. His destiny was to be elusive of social or religious orders. The wisdom of the priest's appeal did not touch him to the quick. He was destined to learn his own wisdom apart from others or to learn the wisdom of others himself wandering among the snares of the world. (*P* 141–42)

These are not simply the solipsistic sentiments of a surly adolescent suspicious of any authority. They are the views of one already unconsciously committed to the life of an exile. To become a member of the Society of Jesus would be to enter a community (the term that the Jesuits themselves favor) of like-minded adherents to the Spiritual Exercises of the order's founder, St. Ignatius of Loyola, and to renounce the position of privileged isolation he has occupied. The imaginative life, on the other hand, allows a link to the world while sustaining independence. It is the both/and condition of the exile artist that Stephen embraces.

The final scene of the chapter, with the birdgirl, underscores this view. His rapturous encounter, in which he recognizes the artist's power to capture and reproduce beauty, is an epiphanic moment. However, unlike the Epiphany of Zachary, celebrated by the Catholic Church, Stephen's illumination comes in a moment of solitude, separate from the young woman wading in the surf who inspires it.

Along the same lines, the spiritual, social, emotional, and cultural withdrawals that take place in chapter 5 while Stephen is at University College Dublin continue the movement toward separation from the Irish milieu that he has been refining since he was baby tuckoo. University life frees Stephen from much of the discipline that characterized his previous schooling. In response, he more openly asserts individuality by articulating formal dissolutions of his ties with the social forces shaping the world around him.

Ireland—"the old sow that eats her farrow" (*P* 179), as Stephen describes his country in a conversation with his nationalist friend Davin—is the easiest institution from which to separate, at least physically. From the Christmas dinner onward, Stephen has not shown the attachment to national identity that he has toward other features of Irish life. Nonetheless, his dismissal of Ireland establishes a paradigm for dealing with other social institutions: overt rejection while remaining under the influence of recollections and emotions.

Catholicism commands a more personal, a broader, and a more concrete attachment, and it remains another condition that Stephen needs to both sustain and overcome. Hugh Kenner, in commenting on Stephen's rejection of the Church, famously noted that Stephen's cry is "non serviam" and not "non credo."[14] In fact, Stephen needs to believe in God, or at least in the God represented by the Church's teachings, if his gesture of defiance is to have any significance. This makes perfect sense from the exilic point of view, for one cannot conceive of an exile without evoking the country from which that person is exiled. The symbiotic relationship must be sustained to nurture the exilic identity that Stephen is cultivating. Catholic liturgy will remain a rich metaphoric resource in his art, just as Catholic authority will assert itself continually as a force against which he must strain. Like any longtime nemesis, the Church takes on a comfortable antagonism for Stephen.

Family, particularly embodied in his mother, stands as the most problematic institution for Stephen to escape in his efforts to achieve independence. The selfless love that May Dedalus offers and that in fact has sustained Stephen throughout the narrative is something he does not wish to deny, even as he feels the need for separation. His mother's passive resistance comes close to matching his own "silence, exile, and cunning," and it is only through a deft substitution that he finds the lever to enforce his escape. May Dedalus's concern that her son make his Easter Duty—receiving, upon pain of mortal sin, the sacraments of Penance and the Holy Eucharist sometime between Ash Wednesday and the Feast of Pentecost—allows Stephen to reject his mother by rejecting the Church. It also enables him to use the same religious imagery that animates his mother's concern for him, centered upon the effect of transgressions on the soul, to defend his view and to defy the efforts of an otherwise extremely cynical Cranly to persuade him otherwise, even when Cranly appeals to the impulse most attractive to Stephen, uniqueness.

> —Whatever else is unsure in this stinking dunghill of a world a mother's love is not. Your mother brings you into the world, carries you first in her body. What do we know about what she feels? But whatever she feels, it, at least, must be real. It must be. What are our ideas or ambitions? Play. Ideas! Why, that bloody bleating goat Temple has ideas. MacCann has ideas too. Every jackass going the roads thinks he has ideas. (*P* 213)

Ultimately, all such exchanges illuminate Stephen's exilic impulse and intensify the reader's sense of why at the end of *A Portrait of the Artist as a Young Man* he feels he must leave.

> Amen. So be it. Welcome, O life! I go to encounter for the millionth time the reality of experience and to forge in the smithy of my soul the uncreated conscience of my race. (*P* 224)[15]

The nostalgia and rancor he has developed in response to the world he inhabits are now the central forces guiding perception. However, their intensity is too great to offer a comprehendible view of Ireland as long as Stephen remains there. Only distance will bring clarity.

Noting these feelings in Stephen does more for the reader than clarify the narrative of *A Portrait of the Artist as a Young Man*. It gives one a more precise sense of the range of forces shaping Joyce's creative process. That insight, in turn, disposes the reader to see a richer representation of the characters in *Exiles*, *Ulysses*, and *Finnegans Wake*, giving one a sense of the wide-range feelings of alienation and despair that inflect not just the central characters of Joyce's subsequent works but most of the individuals who populate them.

4

Re-Viewing Richard

Nostalgia and Rancor in *Exiles*

It is a terribly hard thing to do, Mr. Rowan, to give oneself freely and wholly—and be happy.

Those with a passing knowledge of Joyce's canon might expect to see, in a study exploring the theme of exile in that author's writings, some space devoted to an examination of the only work in his canon that contains the word "exile" in the title. At the same time, those more familiar with Joyce's only surviving play and its rather melodramatic efforts to imitate Ibsen's works might expect it merited little more than a passing reference. Few who have commented on it see *Exiles* as having an aesthetic impact comparable to any of Joyce's fiction, and this perceived disparity makes discussion of it difficult.

I do not feel those initial impressions are entirely justified, and the way the play has generally been encountered can offer some explanation for the willingness of many readers to dismiss it. One often approaches *Exiles* only after an immersion in Joyce's fiction and not infrequently aware of the low esteem in which the work is held. Turning to the play becomes a task, like reading *Stephen Hero* or some of Joyce's occasional writings, undertaken more out of scholarly conscientiousness than any other impulse. The expectations created by the artistic achievements of *Dubliners*, *A Portrait of the Artist as a Young Man*, *Ulysses*, and *Finnegans Wake* can tempt one to dismiss the play as a failed effort in a genre that even Joyce could not quite master.[1]

John MacNicholas, who has written more on *Exiles* than any other critic, bluntly sums up these views ranging from disappointment to hostility in the terse statement "It is generally agreed, perhaps especially among

Joyceans, that *Exiles* is a bad play, opaque to both reader and viewer."[2] As one would expect from a reader who has devoted so much time to the play, MacNicholas does not share this opinion, and he uses empirical evidence—surveying more than a half century of responses to performances of the play and finding most to be favorable—to challenge this assumption of blanket disapproval. Nonetheless, despite his generally positive assessment of *Exiles*, MacNicholas acknowledges that the drama has elements that create antipathy in others. "Perhaps," he speculates, "literary critics have had difficulty liking the play because Richard Rowan himself is so unlikeable."[3]

Most of those who are familiar with *Exiles* will readily agree that the difficulty of feeling any empathy with Richard stands as a significant obstacle for a great many of us seeking to like the play. The opening scene, featuring an exchange between Richard and Beatrice Justice that grows increasingly awkward as it unfolds, offers ample evidence to confirm just how difficult it can be for even the most tolerant of readers or viewers to develop positive feelings for Richard:

RICHARD

I had begun to think you would never come back. It is twelve days since you were here.

BEATRICE

I thought of that too. But I have come.

RICHARD

Have you thought over what I told you when you were here last?

BEATRICE

Very much.

RICHARD

You must have known it before. Did you? [*She does not answer.*] Do you blame me?

BEATRICE

No.

RICHARD

Do you think I have acted towards you—badly? No? Or towards anyone?

BEATRICE

[*Looks at him with a sad puzzled expression.*] I have asked myself that question.

RICHARD

And the answer?

BEATRICE

I could not answer it. (*E* 16)

It is not simply the instances here of circumlocutions, portentousness, and prickliness that incite repulsion for Richard and leave people ready to dismiss the entire play as inferior to Joyce's fiction. There is vagueness in all that he says, an overriding disposition suggesting a deeper meaning without apparently offering a guide to discerning it.

That impulse to dismiss Richard's representations as unfinished or insufficient, however, ignores important generic differences dictating the framing of drama as opposed to the protocols shaping the construction of Joyce's other writings. Of particular significance is the way that narrative voice informs our impressions of Joyce's fiction. The absence of any similar stylistic guide in *Exiles,* and in almost all drama, requires adjustments in our interpretive approach to the play.

Indeed, the construction of the dialogue of Joyce's drama deprives the characters in *Exiles* of the ironic distance that the narrative voice adds with such telling effect in Joyce's fiction. While one can find many of the most off-putting features of Richard Rowan's nature replicated and even expanded in the direct discourse of Stephen Dedalus, the narrative structures supporting the discourses of *A Portrait of the Artist as a Young Man* and *Ulysses* regularly use elaboration, digression, and irony to soften or at least diffuse our responses to harsher elements of Stephen's character revealed in his locutions. In *Exiles* Richard's character remains unmediated by indirect discourse, and reading his nature requires an approach distinctly different from that applied to his fiction.

Approaches to the play that attempt to apply the same interpretive perspective that one uses on Joyce's fiction inevitably will distort one's comprehension of a work in a markedly dissimilar genre. Several critics have already called attention to the problems that arise when a single epistemology is applied in an undifferentiated fashion to all of Joyce's writings, although their views have not always been given the attention they deserve. Kirsten Shepherd-Barr, for example, makes an excellent point in refusing to accept a blanket judgment that reads the drama as if it were an inferior representation of Joyce's fiction. Instead, she argues that a clear comprehension of the play depends upon a very different approach, particularly in acknowledging its conformity to a dramatic tradition that specifically eschews irony.[4] Miranda Hickman, discussing *Chamber Music*, *Exiles*, and *Giacomo Joyce*, also highlights the importance of making such distinctions.

> It is above all the passion for Joycean irony that has shunted these works to the margins. . . . At this moment, however, it would be well to resist the tendency to regret the lack of signature irony in these so-called minor texts and attempt . . . to accept these texts on their own terms, as worthy of critical treatment in their own right. Their placement in the framework of Joyce criticism has often distorted them, pulled them ellipsoid in efforts to make them in some way serve or match the terms of other works. In general, evaluation of these texts according to the criteria of judgment derived from the 'major' works has occluded other dimensions of them that deserve consideration.[5]

Even beyond the important point about irony, there are broader implications in what these critics are saying that need to be explored. The achievements of Joyce's fiction will be part of the consciousness of any reader, and it is not realistic to propose that one ignore them. At the same time, as Hickman suggests, this awareness of the fiction does not preclude a flexible approach to the play.

Recent studies of *Exiles* have taken up the challenge to make more writerly responses to the text, in Roland Barthes's use of the term,[6] by expanding our sense of specific features. In most instances, this has entailed readers offering more sophisticated assessments of the natures of the central characters.[7] In others, critics have sought to broaden awareness of the social dynamics of the play. Vicki Mahaffey, for instance, has explored the implications of different characters' expressions of love as a means to understand the play.[8] Nick De Marco, on the other hand, has emphasized a more thematic approach, assessing the play's efforts "to establish a new moral order."[9] Still others, like Zack Bowen, Sandra Pearce, and Brandon Kershner, have explored the influence of specific elements in familiar social institutions—the sacraments of the Catholic Church or the politics of University College Dublin—in shaping individuals in the play.[10]

In a 28 February 1905 letter to his brother Stanislaus (*Letters* II.83–84), Joyce's self-characterization "as a voluntary exile" and his acknowledgment of the concept's impact on his early writing provide, as I argue throughout this study, a useful orientation for approaching all his works. Specifically, throughout Joyce's canon the dominant exilic emotions to which I have been referring—rancor and nostalgia—infused his creative attitudes, and nowhere are they more evident than in the views expressed by Richard Rowan in the play *Exiles*.

The play's early and frequent references to Richard's life abroad alert us to his disposition, even after returning to Dublin, to adopt the point of view of the outsider, while an awareness of the exile condition makes us sensitive to how that perspective is manifested.[11] In the readings that follow I hope to enhance our understanding of the emotional landscape of the play through an assessment that both keenly reflects and sharply contrasts the feelings that inflect Joyce's retrospective arrangement of Irish life.

A clear indication that rancor and nostalgia influenced his creative perspective appears in one of Joyce's notes for *Exiles* appearing among those collected at the end of the published version of the play. There, by expressly linking a well-known biblical passage to the title of his play, Joyce underscores the contrasting views that animate his sense of the feelings of exile:

> Why the title *Exiles*? A nation exacts a penance from those who dared to leave her payable on their return. The elder brother in the fable of the Prodigal Son is Robert Hand. The father took the side of the prodigal. This is probably not the way of the world—certainly not in Ireland: but Jesus' Kingdom was not of this world nor was or is his wisdom. (*E* 149)

Although Joyce's notes emphasize the bitterness associated with the homecoming of an exile, the story of the Prodigal Son is more than the account of a dramatic return to one's homeland. At its heart, the parable highlights the nostalgic view of home that propels the young man to act. Indeed, the prodigal idealizes life in his family's household to the point of envying the lot of its servants. "How many of my father's servants have food to spare, and here I am starving to death! I will set out and go back to my father" (Luke 15:17–18). By linking Richard to the prodigal son, Joyce alerts us to the need for readers to be aware of the impulse toward nostalgia, not overtly evident in Richard's dialogues yet common to many exiles, which serves as at least a partial explanation for his return.

At the same time, the author's notes assert the unlikelihood of the prodigal's story playing out in the same happy fashion in Ireland—"A nation exacts a penance from those who . . . leave." Thus we see evidence of the harsh recollections that Joyce has brought to his own representations of exile. Like any draft material, these lines capture a transitory stage of the creative process, but they also draw attention to an ongoing point of view, and an awareness of it will enhance readers' interpretations.

When he wrote those notes for *Exiles*, Joyce had already been living outside Ireland for a decade. It seems no great strain on credulity to see in the play's representations of Richard's attitudes toward his homecoming indications of Joyce's evolving concept of exile. Both sequentially and psychologically, Richard's character marks a midpoint in the transition from the Stephen Dedalus about to leave Ireland at the close of *A Portrait of the Artist as a Young Man*—determined to "fly by" the "nets . . . of nationality, language, religion" (*P* 179)—to the young man who stands out as the recently returned exile in *Ulysses*, seeking some, though not complete, accommodation with the world in which he has reimmersed himself: "Dublin. I have much, much to learn" (*U* 7.915).

Richard Rowan does not articulate his views about escape from Ireland, nor about the challenge of reintegrating into the life of his country, as directly as does Stephen, yet readers will have a more sophisticated sense of Richard's character by attending to his exilic impulse manifest in the subtle but unmistakable oscillation between hostility and affection toward Ireland. Richard's exchange with Beatrice about her secret engagement to Robert Hand, for example, can seem less malicious (despite the stage direction to the contrary) if one considers that nostalgia might to some degree inform his recollections.

RICHARD

Yet that separated me from you. I was a third person, I felt. Your names were always spoken together, Robert and Beatrice, as long as I can remember. It seemed to me, to everyone . . .

BEATRICE

We are first cousins. It is not strange that we were often together.

RICHARD

He told me of your secret engagement with him. He had no secrets from me; I suppose you know that.

BEATRICE

> [*Uneasily.*] What happened—between us—is so long ago. I was a child.
>
> RICHARD
>
> [*Smiles maliciously.*] A child? Are you sure? It was in the garden of his mother's house. No? [*He points towards the garden.*] Over there. You plighted your troth, as they say, with a kiss. And you gave him your garter. Is it allowed to mention that?
>
> BEATRICE
>
> [*With some reserve.*] If you think it worthy of mention.
>
> RICHARD
>
> I think you have not forgotten it. [*Clasping his hands quietly.*] I do not understand it. I thought, too, that after I had gone . . . Did my going make you suffer?
>
> BEATRICE
>
> I always knew you would go some day. I did not suffer; only I was changed. (*E* 20–22, ellipses in original)

While there is an undeniable measure of insensitivity, a calculated thoughtlessness, informing Richard's words, there is also an eagerness to recall times in Ireland that were happy for him. In this instance, the argument that he brings up the past because recollecting it gives him pleasure has as much validity as the explanation that he does so because such references give Beatrice pain. There is ample evidence in the play to show that Richard is cold, self-centered, and tactless, but these traits alone do not justify seeing him as a sadist.

However, while personal revelations and the charged interactions that grow out of them seem to lie at the heart of the play, in fact the tensions arising between individuals and their efforts to negotiate the conventions frame the action. Family ties, complicated by the exilic experience, particularly inform Richard's sense of self.

When speaking to Beatrice about his mother, Richard embodies the rancor of the exilic condition. He freely, and with a good measure of self-pity, articulates the feeling of persecution by forces that take on a significance larger than any individual. His recollections elevate her from a person to a powerful social agent responsible for expelling him from his native country.

> She drove me away. On account of her I lived years in exile and poverty too, or near it. I never accepted the doles she sent me through

> the bank. I waited, too, not for her death but for some understanding of me, her own son, her own flesh and blood, that never came. (*E* 24)

Without an awareness of the universalizing attitudes of exile that reconfigure the sources of his suffering, speeches like this—and there are a number of others exuding the same tone running throughout the play—can come across simply as overwrought melodrama. When mediated by a sense of the acrimony growing out of his exile, Richard's account of his mother underscores the deep, ongoing, and genuine pain that separation has caused.

It also helps explain the stark deviation from Joyce's own experiences. Evidence from the letters shows that Joyce's mother Mary did not welcome her son's decision to leave Ireland, and yet, once Joyce committed himself to that course of action, his mother made a great many sacrifices to see that the family could support him, if only in a very meager fashion (*Letters* II.20–23, 29–30, 32–33, 36–37). Additionally, according to Richard Ellmann, she exerted a pronounced effort to understand his artistic views by reading Ibsen. Admittedly, this example illustrates how Ellmann can be a shaky prop to any argument. He claims in his biography that Mary Joyce read Ibsen to please her son, "and she stood the test surprisingly well." Unfortunately, in what has proved to be an all too frequent habit of Ellmann's, he uses fiction to substantiate fact, citing in a footnote passages from *Stephen Hero* to support this assumption.[12]

Nonetheless, the very ambiguity of the source for this incident highlights the concept of duality that I advocate. Whether or not one accepts the circumstantial evidence suggesting that Mary Joyce made a mother's effort to understand the intellectual and artistic forces influencing her son is of secondary importance to understanding the proposition that, as an exile himself, Joyce consciously or not brought his own sense of the condition into the events of the play. In fact, in *Exiles* Joyce heightens the rancor and nostalgia informing Richard's experience by denying him the very things that sustained the young Joyce's first sojourn abroad. Providing emotional wounds for his fictional character underscores Richard's nature as an exile.

Likewise, the exilic impulse for elaboration and emendation of the actual events and circumstances of one's life leads Joyce to a representation of Richard's father as a far more benevolent paternal figure than the profligate John Joyce. Richard suggests that his father's will made him financially independent: "[My mother] could not alter the terms of my father's will nor live forever." In the next breath, Richard recounts his father's death, in a story that appropriates the experiences of John Joyce when his father died:

> I was a boy of fourteen. He called me to his bedside. He knew I wanted to go to the theatre to hear *Carmen*. He told my mother to give me a shilling. I kissed him and went. When I came home he was dead. Those were his last thoughts as far as I know. (*E* 25)[13]

In life, John Joyce did not conveniently die in 1915 leaving his eldest son financially secure. Rather Joyce père lived for seventeen more years, and he continued to deplete the family's already meager resources, with little regard for anyone but himself.[14]

As was the case in the representation of Richard's mother, Joyce uses his drama to reconfigure his biography. This time the recollections are informed by nostalgia, but however tempting it may be to explore the psychological implications of the saintlike quality of Richard's father contrasting with Joyce's, the actual irresponsibility of John Joyce is simply an interesting side note. Of greater importance is the playwright's commitment to presenting Richard as a man who returns to Ireland with complex, conflicted feelings for the country and the people that he left years earlier. This emotional ambivalence expands our sense of him well beyond the prickly, aloof demeanor he projects in many of his exchanges with others, and it suggests a vulnerability in his nature that might otherwise go unremarked. Joyce was aware of a range of attitudes that Ireland could provoke, and his work attests that he was sensitive to all without feeling the need to resolve the ensuing ambivalence. With this in mind, one can see the starkness of melodrama giving way to the complexities of a modernist view.[15]

It seems evident to me that the feelings embedded in the play come up as a direct consequence of the goals of the exile. Richard Rowan left Ireland not simply to break away from his family. He left, in the words of Edward Said quoted in this study's introduction, "the safety of familiar territory," and this in turn leads to what Victor Bergin calls "the melancholy tension of separation from our origins."[16] Keeping these conditions in mind helps explain the often wooden, detached attitude he assumes in his exchanges with others. Because the world Richard left no longer exists, returning to Ireland cannot restore a sense of safety or remove melancholy tensions. Quite the contrary, the disjunction in perceptions attests to the futility of aspirations for a full recovery for any exile.

Acknowledging the tenacity, even perhaps the perpetuity, of Richard's exilic experiences changes the way we see any aspect of his nature. The exile's detachment from his homeland offers insights that help one understand the most troubling issue of the play: Richard's passivity or perhaps even his complicity in attempts by Robert to seduce Bertha.

Because Richard says frankly at the end of the play, "I am wounded, Bertha" (*E* 112) as they are considering the state of their relationship, it seems logical to see the injury as psychosexual and as a consequence of Richard's reaction to whatever happened between his wife and his friend the night before. That assumption, however, only perpetuates inclinations toward a melodramatic reading and ignores the more significant struggle that engaged Richard well before Robert's efforts to seduce Bertha: the conflict of the contrasting feelings that characterized his sense of self in relation to Ireland.

Richard's dispassionate response to Robert's behavior and his agitated denunciation of the secrecy surrounding it exasperates Bertha and creates interpretive puzzles for readers.

BERTHA

[*Crosses towards the lounge and stands near him.*] Are you jealous?

RICHARD

[*As before.*] No.

BERTHA

[*Quietly.*] You are, Dick.

BERTHA

[*Looking at him.*] What are you going to do?

RICHARD

[*Shortly.*] Follow him. Find him. Tell him. [*Calmly.*] A few words will do. Thief and fool.

BERTHA

[*Flings the slip on the couch.*] I see it all!

RICHARD

[*Turning.*] Eh!

BERTHA

[*Hotly.*] The work of a devil.

RICHARD

He?

BERTHA

[*Turning on him.*] No, you! The work of a devil to turn him against me as you tried to turn my own child against me. Only you did not succeed.

RICHARD

[*Appealing.*] Bertha, believe me, dear! It is not jealousy. You have complete liberty to do as you wish—you and he. But not in this way. He will not despise you. You don't wish to deceive me or to pretend to deceive me with him, do you? (*E* 49–53)

This is not the way one expects a character, acting as either the injured husband or the sadomasochistic voyeur, to behave, for the sentiments expressed here eschew both outrage and indifference. Instead, Richard embraces a more complicated, even self-contradictory, reaction that challenges our understanding of what he feels and why he is so disposed.

Joyce's notes offer oblique hints at how to go about interpreting Richard's response:

> Since the publication of the lost pages of *Madame Bovary* the centre of sympathy appears to have been esthetically shifted from the lover or fancyman to the husband or cuckold. This displacement is also rendered more stable by the gradual growth of a collective practical realism due to changed economic conditions in the mass of the people who are called to hear and feel a work of art relating to their lives. This change is utilised in *Exiles* although the union of Richard and Bertha is irregular to the extent that the spiritual revolt of Richard which would be strange and ill-welcomed otherwise can enter into combat with Robert's decrepit prudence with some chance of fighting before the public a drawn battle. (*E* 150)

Though convoluted, the language that Joyce employs in his notes makes an important point: the integration of the middle class into the theater audience has reconfigured the aesthetic values to which the playwright must be attuned—"the gradual growth of a collective practical realism due to changed economic conditions in the mass of the people who are called to hear and feel a work of art relating to their lives." Those middle-class attitudes still valorize the general concept of marriage, despite the irregularity of Richard and Bertha's union, to the point of tolerating "the spiritual revolt of Richard which would be strange and ill-welcomed otherwise." Joyce's point as I see it is that the audience can accept Richard's struggles not because he endeavors to enforce sexual proprietorship but rather because he wishes to emphasize his idealistic if idiosyncratic view of marriage.

Eros is the chimera that threatens a full understanding of the dynamics of the human relationships emphasized throughout the play. The seemingly justifiable perception, for instance, that Richard is complicit in his wife's possible adultery leads some to highlight the sexual nature of the exchange quoted above in a fashion that, intentionally or not, distracts attention from the larger issue that he articulates. Richard insists on freedom of choice and on the independence of human action to a degree that suggests mania. In fact, one can plausibly argue that his reaction suggests the heightened sensitivity of a man governed alternately by highly charged antipathetic feelings. Richard is a man of conflicted feelings, and that attitude comes, in part at least, from the trauma he has experienced through his separation from Ireland.

It is the rancor and nostalgia of the exilic condition that most clearly inform Richard's attitudes toward Bertha. In a terse and gnomic fashion, he acknowledges to Robert Hand his own apprehension of the complexity of his domestic relationship: "Many ideas strike a man who has lived nine years with a woman" (*E* 50). It is no great logical leap to see that the alternating tenderness and hostility apparent in his exchanges with Bertha and Robert are come from a disposition shaped by separation from an Ireland to which he can never return. In each case sympathy and bitterness inform his perspectives in a fashion that makes his nature at once more simple and more complex than that of a man whose actions are motivated by the desire to manipulate others. Indeed, the text abounds in examples of his nostalgic and rancorous response to Robert and Bertha's relationship:

> Robert, not like this. For us two, no. Years, a whole life, of friendship. Think a moment. Since childhood, boyhood . . . No, no. Not in such a way—like thieves—at night. [*Glancing about him.*] And in

> such a place. No, Robert, that is not for people like us. (*E* 61, ellipsis in original)

> You may be his and mine. I will trust you, Bertha, and him too, I must. I cannot hate him since his arms have been around you. You have drawn us nearer together. There is something wiser than wisdom in your heart. Who am I that I should call myself master of your heart or of any woman's? Bertha, love him, be his, give yourself to him if you desire—or if you can. (*E* 96)

Earlier Bertha remembered "those long letters" (*E* 68) that Richard wrote to Beatrice. Late in the play Bertha again brings up the subject saying bluntly that these letters caused Richard to return to Ireland.

> BERTHA
>
> [*Almost cheerfully.*] It looks as if it was you, Miss Justice, who brought my husband back to Ireland.
>
> BEATRICE
>
> I, Mrs. Rowan?
>
> BERTHA
>
> Yes, you. By your letters to him and then by speaking to your cousin as you said just now. Do you not think that you are the person who brought him back?
>
> BEATRICE
>
> [*Blushing suddenly.*] No. I could not think that (*E* 124).

The scene is direct and painful, but while she may have a point, Bertha also oversimplifies her husband's motivation. His correspondence with Beatrice stands as an exile's effort to keep a nostalgic connection, helping to sustain a link to the Ireland left behind a decade earlier, a world more relevant to him than the Ireland he encounters on his return. For this reason the anger that he expresses over Robert's behavior, the cynicism he shows for the university administrators offering employment, and his recurring disdain for elements of Irish society that he encounters all reflect a disappointment that the world that confronts him bears little resemblance to his recollections of the world he left a decade before.[17]

Consequently, although Richard has returned to Ireland, exile remains a dominant concern. With skillful indirection, Joyce uses Robert Hand's newspaper article about Richard to move the play toward its conclusion with a definitive account of that condition:

> Not the least vital of the problems which confront our country is the problem of her attitude towards those of her children who, having left her in her hour of need, have been called back to her now on the eve of her longawaited victory, to her whom in loneliness and exile they have at last learned to love. In exile, we have said, but here we must distinguish. There is an economic and there is a spiritual exile. There are those who left her to seek the bread by which men live and there are others, nay, her most favoured children, who left her to seek in other lands that food of the spirit by which a nation of human beings is sustained in life. Those who recall the intellectual life of Dublin of a decade since will have many memories of Mr. Rowan. Something of that fierce indignation which lacerated the heart . . . (*E* 128–29)

Robert's article makes the same point articulated earlier in this chapter. Spiritual exiles who left their homelands because of a dearth of imaginative sustenance are influenced by an absence no less formidable or threatening than that confronting economic exiles. At the same time, the newspaper column has a problematic duality quickly acknowledged by the characters. Beatrice characterizes it as the work of "a friend who understands you," while Richard calls attention to the blunt criticism of the opening, "those who left her in her hour of need" (*E* 129).

Robert's mixed tone and Richard's ambivalent reaction, however, only serve to intensify the significance of the passage. The thin-skinned Richard says nothing about the characterization of the exilic attitude toward Ireland as the country that "in loneliness and exile they have . . . learned to love" (*E* 129), and his silent acquiescence provides an important indication of what is going on in the play. These lines suggest that even in return the exilic condition remains.

Richard has held himself aloof throughout the play. He has steadfastly refused to become a participant in the immediate action because he remains a spiritual exile, cut off from direct engagement with Irish life and recollecting it alternately through perspectives of nostalgia and rancor. The features of exile show his attitude encompassing much more complex feelings than simply those of someone who dismisses his country of origin.

Robert Hand has seen the rancor in Richard's nature. He remarks on it during their first meeting, referencing a line from the English version of the epitaph that Jonathan Swift composed for himself: "You have that fierce indignation which lacerated the heart of Swift" (*E* 51–52). He repeats it in the article mentioned above (*E* 129), suggesting that Richard, for all his "fierce indignation," retains such great affection for the Ireland that he remembers.[18] This does not erase the hard view that Richard offers time and again, but it does balance it.

Let me close my discussion of the play by reiterating the broad implications of the central assumption of my analysis of *Exiles*: my sense that the title of the play refers to the active consequences of experiences rather than to static labels of diverse people. Richard Rowan has endured a series of spiritual displacements, and his return to Dublin, paradoxically, marks not a reversal of that trend but rather yet another instance of it. Recognizing this movement, seeing Richard as an ongoing exile—still cut off from the social institutions that define his consciousness and still feeling rancor and nostalgia as a consequence—greatly enhances my understanding of him throughout the play. In a similar fashion, the "spiritual exile" experienced by Joyce manifests itself in his process of composition of the other characters, highlighting in them a series of psychological displacements. Seeing the lives of Richard, Robert, Bertha, and Beatrice reflected through separations brings to the foreground previously overlooked motivations for their complex and at times seemingly contradictory responses to the world around them.

As with other Joyce works under consideration in this study, it is important to acknowledge that recognizing this exilic condition does not mean embracing a template for a programmatic reading of Richard and the other characters. That would simply replicate the impulse for narrow readings of the play criticized earlier. Perceiving the exilic impulse opens readings to a greater range of responses and enriches each reencounter with the work with the opportunity for a slightly different perspective. By underscoring the idea that the multiplicity one finds in Joyce's fiction exists in his play as well, one accepts not only that no single analysis can hope to exhaust possibilities for understanding but also that recurring engagements will produce continuing imaginative rewards.

5

Ulysses

Exiles on Main Street

I'm tired of all them rocks in the sea, he said, and boats and ships. Salt junk all the time.

Throughout the narrative of *Ulysses*, in a fashion more subtle but just as insistent as that which one finds in the discourse of *A Portrait of the Artist as a Young Man*, Joyce's writing accumulates examples that reiterate the inadequacy of social establishments like the family, the Church, and the nation for individuals seeking guidelines for defining their sense of self. In the pattern of all modernist/postmodernist novels, these institutions no longer delineate paths for fulfillment.[1] Rather, they lay traps that circumscribe individuality with sterile prohibitions meant to prop up an artificial moral system.[2]

By the time Joyce began *Ulysses*, the articulation of modernist sensibilities was part of the contemporary literary atmosphere, and some might argue that at the very least an incipient postmodernism had also begun to appear. Whichever point of view one adopts, modernism and postmodernism subscribe to similar views that had become integral to Joyce's artistic vision, and their influence only intensified during the course of the novel's composition.[3] *A Portrait of the Artist as a Young Man* had already established Joyce's deep connection with sensibilities openly challenging contemporary social institutions. As he continued to write, and to live abroad, the disposition to reject societal norms, and the dominant emotions of the exilic experience, nurtured a complex perspective that allowed him to describe Dublin from multiple points of view without himself becoming encumbered by the parallactic thinking that so puzzles Bloom and, in Barbara Stevens Huesel's view, gives a number of characters a false sense of their world.[4]

Certainly the narrative of *Ulysses* works strenuously to move readers away from the assumptions of a literary tradition that endorsed conventional expectations and traditional communal loyalties. Instead, it extends the interpretive challenges found in the work of Flaubert and other mid- to late nineteenth-century writers, highlighting the corrosiveness of the social environment in which individuals in the novel are immersed. Bloom's critical summation, in the Lotus Eaters chapter, of the psychological impact of a key element of pre–Vatican II Catholic religious rituals on the congregation—"Good idea the Latin. Stupefies them first" (*U* 5.350–51)—bluntly and cynically dismisses liturgy as an empty, mechanical, obfuscating practice aimed at manipulation rather than at enlightenment. It also captures in emblematic fashion what modernists perceived as the broad aims of all social institutions: numbing discernment and promoting acquiescence.

Examples of similar derisive summations of other Irish institutions abound in the narrative. The nameless narrator in the Cyclops chapter neatly skewers the bombastic Irish chauvinism of the Citizen, and by extension all nationalistic sentiments, as pure hypocrisy by focusing on the contrast between portentous oratory and mendacious behavior:

> All wind and piss like a tanyard cat. Cows in Connacht have long horns. As much as his bloody life is worth to go down and address his tall talk to the assembled multitude in Shanagolden where he daren't show his nose with the Molly Maguires looking for him to let daylight through him for grabbing the holding of an evicted tenant. (*U* 12.1311–16)

The reiteration of the idea, sometimes offered sardonically and sometimes in a matter-of-fact tone, that communal institutions serve only to undermine the integrity of an individual's nature in short order becomes a familiar theme in the discourse. By the time the reader comes to the Eumaeus chapter, there can be little surprise when Stephen Dedalus, in answer to Bloom's question on why he left his father's house, characterizes the dysfunctional quality of family life in no more than three dismissive words—"To seek misfortune" (*U* 16.253)—punning on the title of an English fairy tale, *How Jack Went to Seek His Fortune*, to lampoon what was even then a clichéd sentiment.

In this insistent refrain, characters express a dissolution of confidence in the social institutions that for generations commanded the loyalty and respect that allowed them to shape Irish values and assumptions. It leads readers to see many individuals as operating, consciously or not, outside the protocols of the systems defining the world around them. Those who do work within the social institutions stand out as ignorant blowhards like Garrett Deasy with his letter to the press that he must ask someone else to publish:

> —That reminds me, Mr Deasy said. You can do me a favour, Mr Dedalus, with some of your literary friends. I have a letter here for the press. Sit down a moment. I have just to copy the end. (*U* 2.289–91)

Or they appear as bloated, high-handed functionaries like the priest in Hades whom Bloom criticizes for his domineering attitude and ill-concealed intolerance as he works mechanically through the funeral service for Paddy Dignam:

> Father Coffey. I knew his name was like a coffin. Dominenamine. Bully about the muzzle he looks. Bosses the show. Muscular christian. Woe betide anyone that looks crooked at him: priest. Thou are Peter. Burst sideways like a sheep in clover Dedalus says he will. With a belly on him like a poisoned pup. Most amusing expressions that man finds. Hhhn: burst sideways. (*U* 6.595–600)

Or they take on the role of self-centered domestic tyrants like Theodore Purefoy, a man whose abuse is insidious and unrelenting as he impregnates his wife in tedious succession with no apparent thought to the consequences. Again, it is Bloom who considers the situation with unsentimental frankness: "Mina Purefoy swollen belly on a bed groaning to have a child tugged out of her. One born every second somewhere" (*U* 8.479–81).

This interpretation, underscoring the insistence in the discourse that individuals have grown alienated from contemporary society, has by now become a critical commonplace applied for decades by readers of modernist and postmodernist fiction. However, if one does no more than gloss the narrative as simply claiming that social institutions have lost their legitimacy, without examining the consequences of that change, one fails to come to a full understanding of the condition being described in the novel. The emphasis of this study on the consequences of the exilic experience takes the next necessary step to lay out how this alienation translates into the way individuals in the novel see the world.[5]

Much as he did in the opening of *A Portrait of the Artist as a Young Man*, from the start of *Ulysses* Joyce's narrative gradually introduces the idea that most of the characters in the novel are informed by feelings of the exile. Initially it seems that they suffer from nothing more complicated than a form of solipsism. In that vein, the process of delineating their natures and needs begins with Mulligan's booming disquisition on his sense of place in the universe. Seemingly as much through love of the sound of his own voice as for any other reason, Mulligan mockingly attempts to describe an idealized family-like ethos, with him and Stephen taking up roles of aesthetic luminaries too advanced for Ireland:

> —My name is absurd too: Malachi Mulligan, two dactyls. But it has a Hellenic ring, hasn't it? Tripping and sunny like the buck himself. We must go to Athens. Will you come if I can get the aunt to fork out twenty quid? (*U* 1.41–43)

Stephen, profoundly self-absorbed in his own right, has little patience with another's self-aggrandizing daydreaming. He ignores Mulligan's invitation and instead counters with an oblique allusion to a much more pragmatic domestic concern: the disruptions caused by their English houseguest. "How long is Haines going to stay in this tower?" (*U* 1.49). So far, we see little more than a representation of the self-centered world of two glib young men, but the narrative quickly expands its perspective to contextualize them, and what follows unfolds in a broader and more elaborately delineated world.

In a seamless acknowledgment of Stephen's discontent, the chameleon-like Mulligan shows his adaptive dexterity as he shifts the discourse to fit more neatly the emotional tenor. Displaying both a willingness to jump from one topic to another and a sensitivity to the need to keep Stephen's loyalty, Mulligan opines: "God, isn't he dreadful? . . . A ponderous Saxon. He thinks you're not a gentleman. God, these bloody English. Bursting with money and indigestion. Because he comes from Oxford. You know, Dedalus, you have the real Oxford manner. He can't make you out" (*U* 1.51–54). However, before this newly expressed concern can begin to take effect, Mulligan allows a patronizing dismissiveness to creep into his tone with a question that sounds like a mother addressing a petulant child: "Were you in a funk?" (*U* 1.59). The pseudo-domesticity and insincere concern of these flippant remarks suggests that Mulligan's gesture toward nurturing and support has no more efficacy than that offered by the traditional family.

Indeed, Mulligan's disquisition outlines the central threat to individuality that, somewhat paradoxically, comes as a result of the absence of meaningful family relations. The ever so subtle dismissal of Stephen's feelings, the trivialization of his emotional engagement with the pseudo-family in the Martello Tower, is more than a move by Mulligan in the struggle for domestic dominance. It forms part of Mulligan's larger carefully choreographed effort at marginalization to brand Stephen, through his exercising individuality, as an outsider and to place him, emotionally and spiritually, beyond the boundaries of the community.

In the process this exchange reflects, albeit expressed in a more sophisticated fashion, the rhetorical struggles between Richard Rowan and Robert Hand in *Exiles*. Stephen, like Richard before him, has found himself occupying a liminal position that neither frees him from a desire for integration nor disposes him toward the necessary accommodation. Mulligan, on the other hand, proves to be very much like Robert. He can pretend to set himself apart from society while he in fact conforms to its dictates in every meaningful way.

These distinctions between the social roles assumed by or forced on these young men become even more apparent as the exchange unfolds. Mulligan, as the voice of social normalcy, more and more assertively both in this chapter and then throughout the narrative assigns to Stephen the position of outsider, shifting the topic from Haines's disrupting their night's sleep with a gratuitous observation on the class distinctions that Stephen must endure. "And to think of your having to beg from these swine. I'm the only one that knows what you are" (*U* 1.160–61). The remark, though seemingly only mildly offensive in its patronizing tone, marks the beginning of an escalating series of observations that, under the guise of benevolence, underscore Stephen's isolation:

> Why don't you trust me more? What have you up your nose against me? Is it Haines? If he makes any noise here I'll bring down Seymour and we'll give him a ragging worse than they gave Clive Kempthorpe. (*U* 1.161–65)

The sinuous aggressiveness of Mulligan's rhetoric represents quite effectively the formidable yet mutable ethos dominating the harsh and treacherous world surrounding the returned exile. Although Mulligan seems to begin by consoling Stephen and then goes on to form a pact with him against Haines, in fact a careful look at what Mulligan says shows him to be hard at work marginalizing his putative friend: reminding Stephen of his status as an outsider, suggesting his isolation due to a lack of trust, and most insidiously enforcing the power of the group to bully the individual. It is not necessary to demonstrate that Mulligan sees Stephen as a kind of exile for this perspective to have validity. One need only be aware that Joyce, as an exilic writer, now has a heightened sense of the experience of alienation, and his unique perspective of it intensifies for a thoughtful reader the representation of Stephen and other marginalized figures.

By the same token, it is not important to discern whether Stephen sees himself as an exile, for whether he does so consciously or not, he takes up traits common to the exilic experience. Stephen demonstrates his own inclination toward isolation through his wariness of Mulligan's friendship and his subsequent unwillingness to be drawn into complicity with Mulligan's efforts to manipulate the situation. The novel is quick to show Stephen's distance as a matter of choice, a determined separation that springs out of suspicion and self-interest.

As the narrative makes clear early on in their exchange, Stephen has a keen sense of Mulligan's competitiveness and no illusions about the nature of their so-called friendship. "He fears the lancet of my art as I fear that of his" (*U* 1.152). That insight gives readers an immediate and permanent understanding of Stephen's perception of his place in the world of the novel. As long as Mulligan and his like dictate the social order, Stephen can neither risk nor tolerate being part of it, even if others choose to readmit him. (These are the same issues facing Richard Rowan in *Exiles*, and Richard's response prepares us for Stephen's.) In the end, his response to Haines's presence in the tower is more a demonstration of resignation to the unalterable conditions that surround him than any indication that he feels integrated into this world. "Let him stay, Stephen said. There's nothing wrong with him except at night" (*U* 1.177–78).

The reader can, of course, choose to understand what transpires as little more than a demonstration of the sort of rivalry that often arises when bright young men find themselves at close quarters. That approach, however, would have more purchase in a world where values were lucid and mutually agreed upon. In the (post)modern world of *Ulysses*, this jockeying for place takes on a much greater significance than the desire for preference within a clear, stable, and widely recognized social structure.

In fact, that view does not obtain here. Almost all of the individuals in Joyce's novel—from the central figures to minor characters—operate outside the restraints of any conventional communal order. Though ostensively part of a larger group, they actually behave independently and at best pay no more than lip service to the concept of membership in a community. Under close scrutiny, the existence of community comes into question when there seems to be no stable group operating in contrast to the isolated individuals who populate the narrative.

The zero-sum quality of their endeavors becomes evident early on to readers attuned to this ruthless individuality. In the Dublin of *Ulysses*, an individual creates a distinctive identity only at the expense of others. One does not exchange isolation for community but rather enhances oneself by the diminution of the possibility for community. Think of the postcard sent to Denis Breen with the cryptic message that further agitates Breen's unbalanced mind and sends him on a wild goose chase all around Dublin looking for legal recourse. Early on, Bloom speculates on the source.

> U.p: up. I'll take my oath that's Alf Bergan or Richie Goulding. Wrote it for a lark in the Scotch house I bet anything. Round to Menton's office. His oyster eyes staring at the postcard. Be a feast for the gods. (*U* 8.320–22)

Though seemingly done by individuals for the amusement of a group, Bloom sees it as gratuitous nastiness. With an awareness of the pervasiveness of the exilic mentality of isolation, the motivation becomes clearer and more complex. The social orders that seem to be regulating behavior of individuals in the narrative are actually nonexistent creations of alternately nostalgic and rancorous imaginations. They are evoked by a "*retrospective arrangement*" (*U* 6.150), to use Tom Kernan's catchphrase, but they never in fact shape behavior.

This illustration gives one a more meaningful sense of the self-aggrandizing gestures of so many of the characters. As the narrative quickly makes clear, this gesture pervades the text. Whether referencing John Henry Menton's treatment of Bloom in the Hades episode (*U* 6.1015–33), Mulligan's disparagement of Stephen to Haines in the Wandering Rocks episode (*U* 10.1058–92), or Boylan's dismissal of the "unregarded" Lydia Douce after her performance with her garter (*U* 11.460–65), one character is continually seeking to put another *sous rature*, viewing that person as both present and absent.[6]

At the same time, and here is where exilic duality exerts itself, individuals also feel the need to maintain a kind of referentiality. For example, unlike Stephen, Mulligan has not overtly embraced isolation and so still seeks to sustain a sense of community, on his own terms of course. Thus, when reminded of his flippancy in describing Stephen's bereavement—saying to his mother who inquires after the identity of a visitor, "*it's only Dedalus whose mother is beastly dead*" (*U* 1.198–99)—Buck sputters, cajoles, reasons, and then offers a half-hearted apology that acknowledges the offense in terms suggesting the violation of social conventions.

> You crossed her last wish in death and yet you sulk with me because I don't whinge like some hired mute from Lalouette's. Absurd! I suppose I did say it. I didn't mean to offend the memory of your mother." (*U* 1.212–15)

Stephen's reaction makes clear to readers that his response to being surrounded by a society of exiles is starkly different from that of his antagonist. Mulligan has as sharp a social sense as does Stephen, but he chooses the safety that accrues from maintaining the fiction of allegiance to a community. Stephen shows not only his self-perceived place as an outsider but his determination to embrace openly the self-reflexivity of that role. He creates, through his sense of dignity, both a foundation upon which to exist on his own and a shield for his sense of self, as is evident in his response to Mulligan's flippant apology for his announcement of the death of May Dedalus.

> —I am not thinking of the offence to my mother.
> —Of what then? Buck Mulligan asked.
> —Of the offence to me, Stephen answered. (*U* 1.218–20)

By keeping in mind the tradition of exile that has permeated Joyce's earlier fiction, we readers can see the complexity of Stephen's behavior, and we can understand more fully the depth of the alienation that he feels. This is because we understand the despair that comes from knowing the impossibility of the existence of a condition other than exile. Stephen sees himself as being categorized as a marginal figure of little or no consequence in a society that stands as a community in name only. Mulligan's off-the-cuff dismissal stings so sharply because by its very casualness it underscores not just the immediate condition of isolation that any individual might endure for a time but the inevitable and unrelieved separation that surrounds every character in this environment.

By extension, Stephen's response reflects not simply the tender feelings of a grieving son quick to take exception at the merest slight but the more complex attitude of someone who has gone beyond conventional stages of grieving, appropriating the experience and refocusing it completely on the self. Just as his dress affects a Hamlet-like representation, his attitude has encompassed a Hamlet-like disposition. He is no longer a part of the world that surrounds him, for he feels that world, in a unified sense, no longer exists. At the same time, he maintains nostalgic links to conventions that have now become symbols of an unrecoverable past.

In this fashion, his contentiousness with Mulligan demonstrates more than a simple case of struggling for an advantageous position in the social hierarchy that is evolving between competitive acquaintances. Like the prototypical exile, Stephen is an individual endeavoring to define himself outside of but according to a world to which he no longer belongs, a world that from the postmodernist perspective no longer definitively and exclusively exists. His rancorous views come out of a determination that continually reviews the circumstances of his separation with a harsh interpretation of the elements that propelled him into his current condition.

Clarifying this liminal coexistence to readers who still subscribe to belief in an ordered, inclusive social structure in which a place exists for everyone can prove to be challenging. Stephen does not fit into a linear category in his relationship with Ireland, so to see him—from the point of view of alternating dualities either striving for reconciliation with or unswervingly hostile to Irish culture—oversimplifies conditions. Moved by both rancor and nostalgia, he creates an amalgam of the feelings that draw him to Ireland with those that repel him. Often these seem to work simultaneously within his consciousness.

This both/and condition is as difficult for other figures in the novel to comprehend as it may be for readers. Stephen attempts to present an explanation of these diffused, conflicted attitudes when he speaks to the Englishman Haines. In the process, he shows the impossibility of conveying a clear impression of these circumstances to a person who complacently assumes he knows the structure of the community that surrounds him, even when he is a foreigner in that community. Haines's unshakable faith in the linear, either/or world makes Stephen's dualities nearly incomprehensible.

In a preview of the unsuccessful attempts at instruction that will open the next chapter, Stephen endeavors to lay out the formative influences on his situation through a series of straightforward metaphors. In the process, it becomes quickly apparent to the observant reader that the roots of his marginalization lie much deeper than a figure committed to the status quo will grasp.

> —I am a servant of two masters, Stephen said, an English and an Italian.
> —Italian? Haines said.
> A crazy queen, old and jealous. Kneel down before me.
> —And a third, Stephen said, there is who wants me for odd jobs.
> —Italian? Haines said again. What do you mean?
> —The imperial British state, Stephen answered, his colour rising, and the holy Roman catholic and apostolic church. (*U* 1.638–44)

The synecdochic references and the quick gloss that Stephen offers to explain them do little to enlighten the dim-witted Haines. Nonetheless, they introduce us to a familiar pattern of interpretive instruction that runs throughout the novel. The abbreviated allusion to Jesus's statement in Matthew 6:24—"No man can serve two masters. Either you will hate the one and love the other, or you will be devoted to one and despise the other. You cannot serve God and Mammon"—creates more perplexities than it resolves. Experienced readers will suppose that Stephen has no wish to serve either master, yet the fact that he chose a quotation that presumes a commitment to one or the other should invite further consideration.

Stephen's hostility to social institutions remains evident throughout the narrative. Passages like this, on the other hand, indicate that he also feels a sense of loss. The either/or certitude that comes from serving a master has no place in his exilic worldview, but his biblical allusiveness suggests a lingering fondness for this now absent condition.

The laughable qualities of the exchange remain intact even as one acknowledges the deeper referentiality. Just as the narrative is filled with pseudo-Odysseus figures to show us alternative forms of behavior, this scene of attempted enlightenment produces a humorous example of how not to engage the narrative. Haines takes up the analogous role of pseudo-reader. In that function, he makes the mistakes and demonstrates the confusion that the narrative does not want us to fall into. His fatuous incomprehension discourages us from following a similar analytic course.

The significance of the passage goes beyond a moment of comic relief. Haines exemplifies the anti-reader, the individual who has no concept of how to engage Joyce's narrative, because of his unwillingness and inability to take a detached view of the environment and the characters surrounding him. This gesture demonstrates the antithesis of the exile mentality. Haines has no capacity for distancing himself from the subjects of his observations, and so cannot imagine an alternative construction to the one immediately before him. Haines fails to discern the connections that Stephen is making, much less the irony implied in the statement, because the very perspective is foreign to him. In the process, he illustrates what this absence of the other—the lack of recognition so total as to deny alternative existence—does to attempts at understanding.

His anti-exilic disposition can hardly surprise one. With an unquestioning faith in social institutions, as well as a deep commitment to English colonialism, Haines cannot conceive of himself as an outsider. Indeed, given the reassuring reductive, prescriptive sense that he imposes on the world around him, the point of view of the outsider, the other, would unquestionably pose a threat to him. Further, his dull-witted response to Stephen shows that he lacks the capacity to challenge the status quo and so cannot grasp the subtleties of the proposition. (He is certainly not nearly as intellectually dexterous as either Stephen or Buck). As one of the few individuals in the novel lacking any sense of the exilic perspective, he has no conception of what Stephen is experiencing, and his buffoonish misprisions serve as a cautionary tale for those who would follow too closely traditional perspectives for understanding.

That's not to say that most of those who engage *Ulysses* are likely to fall into this temptation. Readers, particularly those familiar with Joyce's other writing, have had ample exposure to the fluctuating attitudes of complex characters. Throughout *Dubliners* one encounters a range of individuals with complex points of view which open for us diverse interpretive possibilities, and in *A Portrait of the Artist as a Young Man* Stephen's behavior has given us a crash course in engaging natures with multiple perspectives. In *Ulysses* these representations continue on with a broader scope and a greater depth.

Over the course of the novel Stephen embodies that sense of alienation that goes well beyond ordinary social awkwardness or aloofness. There is a duality that reflects heightened awareness of isolation even as it also presents a keen sensitivity to all that surrounds him. As he says at the close of *A Portrait of the Artist as a Young Man*—"I go to encounter for the millionth time the reality of experience and to forge in the smithy of my soul the uncreated conscience of my race" (*P* 224).

By the time the narrative of *Ulysses* begins, his awareness of threats inherent in the structure of society has grown and become more sophisticated. That perspective is important for readers to remember and understand. For despite all the unpleasantness that he experiences from the snobbishness, bullying, and insensitivity summed up in characters like Haines and Mulligan, throughout the novel it is institutions, not individuals, that actively threaten to inhibit his spiritual growth and to suppress his creative development.

Paradoxically, as becomes increasingly obvious over the course of the narrative, he has gained a keen sense of his dependence on the world from which he has emerged. As Stephen notes in Aeolus, before he begins his Parable of the Plums, "Dublin. I have much, much to learn" (*U* 7.915). No matter what he has become, he will always be "A child Conmee saved from pandies" (*U* 9.211), and part of his maturation process is the recognition that his art will grow out of his past. While that point has already been examined, a fuller perspective evolves from a sense of the exilic influence on Stephen.[7] This retrospective arrangement stands out not as a factual, impersonal invocation of an objective past but rather as a selective recollection that has been tinged by both the rancor and the nostalgia that have infused Stephen's time abroad, as well as that of his creator.

Thus the difference that obtains between readers' perceptions of Stephen's nature in *A Portrait of the Artist as a Young Man* and the comprehension of what unfolds in *Ulysses* lies in their awareness of the growing impact of the condition of exile as its influence, now appreciably increased since the period chronicled in *A Portrait of the Artist as a Young Man*, intensifies the ambiguity of his current position and heightens the complexity of any resolution. At the close of the earlier novel, one finds Stephen on the brink of a departure that seems, more than anything else, like an escape from the isolation he has been suffering. In *Ulysses* Stephen now has achieved the insight of the exile who knows the price that one pays by being cut off from the cultural context in which one has come to understand the world. He is now both of and out of Ireland, and for much of the day he struggles to find a resolution for that uneasy dynamic.

For Stephen, isolation stands as the most prominent feature defining one's relation to one's environment. Once the reader grows aware of that disposition, this same condition becomes increasingly evident in many of the other characters in the novel, and the reader needs to understand its connection with the exilic experience to understand the dynamics of character development throughout the text. Indeed, isolation stands out less as a feature of an individual's nature and more as a constant of the environment. Like the meteorological climate, it surrounds everyone.

For this reason, isolation can have significance for the reader only when combined with a sense of each character's affiliation with a community. This is true even when individual reconciliation or reuniting with the group is early on seen as an unreachable goal. Thus, in the Telemachus chapter one sees an unexpected desire for recognition from a stranger, and resentment when it is withheld, when the old milk woman stops at the tower for her morning delivery: "Stephen listened in scornful silence. She bows her old head to a voice that speaks to her loudly, her bonesetter, her medicineman: me she slights" (*U* 1.418–19).

Such sensitivity to the old woman's disregard may seem odd given the aloofness Stephen has already displayed toward Mulligan's overtures and will soon show to Haines. In fact, from an exilic point of view, the woman's regard holds greater significance for Stephen than Haines's or Mulligan's. Not all readers may wish to see her as an evocation of the Shan Van Vocht (the poor old woman), a common personification of Ireland. However, she certainly stands as a sharper representation of the Irish temperament than does Haines or Mulligan. Her disinterest sharply emphasizes the exile's awareness of his lack of connection with his native land.

At the same time, the patronizing tone taken by both Haines and Mulligan sets the woman apart. This makes her personification of Ireland all the more poignant: as the representative of the country, she stands nonetheless as isolated as any of its other citizens.

Attentiveness to isolation from the dominant cultural background can make the exile vulnerable in ways that one would not foresee. Just as Stephen felt the conflicted sentiments of longing and resentment when he was ignored by the milk woman, he is sensitive to the snubs of the Protestant class, embodied in both the headmaster of Mr. Deasy's school and the schoolboys he is attempting to teach in the opening pages of the Nestor chapter.

> All laughed. Mirthless high malicious laughter. Armstrong looked round at his classmates, silly glee in profile. In a moment they will laugh more loudly, aware of my lack of rule and of the fees their papas pay.
>
> Some laughed again: mirthless but with meaning. Two in the back bench whispered. Yes. They knew: had never learned nor ever been innocent. All. With envy he watched their faces: Edith, Ethel, Gerty, Lily. Their likes: their breaths, too, sweetened with tea and jam, their bracelets tittering in the struggle. (*U* 2.27–38)

The account that unfolds of Stephen's clumsy efforts to take up the role of pedagogue can lead the reader to a simplistic misprision of Stephen's feelings for Cyril Sargent, the dull boy kept behind to copy his sums. Stephen's own words invite readers to discern a genuine empathy for the young boy. "Like him was I" (*U* 2.168). However, as one observes Stephen trying to tutor the insecure and doltish young boy and goes on to recall images from *A Portrait of the Artist as a Young Man* of the younger Stephen at Clongowes Wood and Belvedere, the comparison seems increasingly forced. Stephen was a bright student. Sargent is not. Stephen was popular with his classmates. Sargent is not. Stephen, who first confronted the rector of Clongowes and then challenged teachers at Belvedere, had boldness. Sargent does not. What Stephen in fact comprehends, despite the differences in attitude and abilities, is a shared sense of isolation. Circumstances create a parallel, and the nostalgic impulse of the exile creates a bond that facts do not fully justify.

The seeming fellow feeling voiced by Stephen is a projection of his own nostalgia that grows out of exilic desire. One sees this in Stephen's extended musing on Sargent's mother.

> Ugly and futile: lean neck and thick hair and a stain of ink, a snail's bed. Yet someone had loved him, borne him in her arms and in her heart. But for her the race of the world would have trampled him underfoot, a squashed boneless snail. She had loved his weak watery blood drained from her own. Was that then real? The only true thing in life? (*U* 2.139–43)

The last lines link the paragraph to Stephen as they call to mind the words of Cranly in *A Portrait of the Artist as a Young Man*, admonishing Stephen for insensitivity in dismissing May Dedalus's concerns for her son's soul. "Whatever else is unsure in this stinking dunghill of a world a mother's love is not" (*P* 213). What we see in this passage is Stephen, who has been feeling guilt all morning recollecting his behavior toward his mother, briefly sentimentalizing Sargent. He then deftly, if subconsciously, elides speculations about the mother of the boy in front of him with reminiscences of his own familial experiences.

Exilic attitudes are equally useful in clarifying the motivating forces behind Stephen's obvious disdain for the blustery Garrett Deasy, the schoolmaster who piously preaches austerity and unselfconsciously jumbles the details of prominent incidents in Irish history. Over the course of the conversation between the two men, Deasy's demeanor never really exceeds that of a harmless, if bigoted, blowhard. Nonetheless, his outspoken prejudices and narrow-minded pieties stir feelings of resentment that will be expanded in later chapters because they evoke a sense of Irishness that the exile has come to resent.

These impulses, however, only suggest the degree to which the nature of Stephen's relationship with Irish society has evolved. On the beach in Proteus, Stephen's reflections present the most detailed and complex summary of how the exilic mentality shapes his perceptions. There, for the first time in the narrative, readers come to a full sense of the diverse effects of the multiple perspectives shaping his sense of the world he now inhabits.

The chapter begins as an examination of ontology shading into a survey of epistemologies: "Ineluctable modality of the visible: at least that if no more, thought through my eyes" (*U* 3.1–2). In short order, the sentences that follow highlight Stephen's pedantic inclinations—though not for the first or last time in the narrative—as they offer a roll call of eminent philosophers from the Classical period to the Enlightenment.

Stephen quickly turns the hermeneutic examination unfolding within this internal monologue into a more focused scrutiny of himself and his nature. While the disquisition shows the same intellectual curiosity that one sees in his presentation of an aesthetic theory to Lynch in chapter 5 of *A Portrait of the Artist as a Young Man*, it also foregrounds a newfound ability to look at himself critically, through his ironical inversion of the details of Christ's conception from the Nicene Creed to cover his own:

"Wombed in sin darkness I was too, made not begotten. By them, the man with my voice and my eyes and a ghostwoman with ashes on her breath. They clasped and sundered, did the coupler's will. From before the ages He willed me and now may not will me away or ever" (*U* 3.45–48).

The biblical reference that allows him to introduce a topic that both repels and fascinates him is both poignant and sardonic. It firmly establishes the development of a very new nature beyond that seen in *A Portrait of the Artist as a Young Man*. In a few lines, Stephen offers a complex and touching view of his nature through what might seem to some a surprising testament of faith in a Divine plan. Nonetheless, with the idea of exilic nostalgia in mind, Stephen's ruminations over the course of the chapter become far less puzzling.

The empty beach provides the opportunity for solitary reflection, and in that state the feelings of rancor and nostalgia quickly reassert themselves. Stephen is walking along Sandymount Strand, animating the moment with alternately mildly pleasant and mildly harsh recollections: the imagined visit to Aunt Sally's and Uncle Richie's (*U* 3.61–98), the pretentious preening of an aspiring writer (*U* 3.136–46), his life in Paris (*U* 3.174–99), images of ancient Dublin (*U* 3.300–309), and the extended meditation on the two tinkers he sees (*U* 3.354–436) fill the chapter. What seem like random thoughts as he trudges along the beach can coalesce into a litany of experiences that formed the boundaries of his consciousness and that now take on a more precisely delineated significance for the reader keeping the sentiments of the exilic mentality in mind. From his new perspective, they represent the complicated process by which he has laid claim to his Irish identity.

However, the clearest sense of the impact of the exilic experience on Stephen comes not from memories of his solitary life abroad but from the young man's recollection of his meeting with the expatriate Kevin Egan and of his consequent knowledge of Egan's life in Paris. Although the passage is long, it bears testimony to the assertions about Stephen presented above:

> Noon slumbers. Kevin Egan rolls gunpowder cigarettes through fingers smeared with printer's ink, sipping his green fairy as Patrice his white. About us gobblers fork spiced beans down their gullets. *Un demi setier!* A jet of coffee steam from the burnished caldron. She serves me at his beck. *Ilestirlandais. Hollandais? Non fromage.*

Deuxirlandais, nous, Irlande, vous savez? Ah, oui! She thought you wanted a cheese *hollandais*. Your postprandial, do you know that word? Postprandial. There was a fellow I knew once in Barcelona, queer fellow, used to call it his postprandial. Well: *slainte!* Around the slabbed tables the tangle of wined breaths and grumbling gorges. His breath hangs over our saucestained plates, the green fairy's fang thrusting between his lips. Of Ireland, the Dalcassians, of hopes, conspiracies, of Arthur Griffith now, A E, pimander, good shepherd of men. To yoke me as his yokefellow, our crimes our common cause. You're your father's son. I know the voice. His fustian shirt, sanguineflowered, trembles its Spanish tassels at his secrets. M. Drumont, famous journalist, Drumont, know what he called queen Victoria? Old hag with the yellow teeth. *Vieille ogresse* with the *dents jaunes*. Maud Gonne, beautiful woman, *la Patrie*, M. Millevoye, Félix Faure, know how he died? Licentious men. The *froeken, bonne à tout faire*, who rubs male nakedness in the bath at Upsala. *Moi faire*, she said, *tous les messieurs*. Not this *monsieur*, I said. Most licentious custom. Bath a most private thing. I wouldn't let my brother, not even my own brother, most lascivious thing. Green eyes, I see you. Fang, I feel. Lascivious people.

The blue fuse burns deadly between hands and burns clear. Loose tobaccoshreds catch fire: a flame and acrid smoke light our corner. Raw facebones under his peep of day boy's hat. How the head centre got away, authentic version. Got up as a young bride, man, veil, orangeblossoms, drove out the road to Malahide. Did, faith. Of lost leaders, the betrayed, wild escapes. Disguises, clutched at, gone, not here.

Spurned lover. I was a strapping young gossoon at that time, I tell you. I'll show you my likeness one day. I was, faith. Lover, for her love he prowled with colonel Richard Burke, tanist of his sept, under the walls of Clerkenwell and, crouching, saw a flame of vengeance hurl them upward in the fog. Shattered glass and toppling masonry. In gay Paree he hides, Egan of Paris, unsought by any save by me. Making his day's stations, the dingy printingcase, his three taverns, the Montmartre lair he sleeps short night in, *rue de la Goutte-d'Or*, damascened with flyblown faces of the gone. Loveless, landless, wifeless. She is quite nicey comfy without her outcast man, madame in *rue Gît-le-Coeur*, canary and two buck lodgers. Peachy cheeks, a

> zebra skirt, frisky as a young thing's. Spurned and undespairing. Tell Pat you saw me, won't you? I wanted to get poor Pat a job one time. *Mon fils*, soldier of France. I taught him to sing *The boys of Kilkenny are stout roaring blades*. Know that old lay? I taught Patrice that. Old Kilkenny: saint Canice, Strongbow's castle on the Nore. Goes like this. *O, O*. He takes me, Napper Tandy, by the hand.
>
> *O, O the boys of*
> *Kilkenny . . .*
>
> Weak wasting hand on mine. They have forgotten Kevin Egan, not he them. Remembering thee, O Sion. (*U* 3.216–34, ellipsis in original)

The painful existence endured by Kevin Egan, as it is evoked through Stephen's memory, provides a clear guide for seeing the characters in Joyce's novel from a perspective that goes beyond nihilistic rejection. It underscores how a sense of exile leaves an indelible mark on the psyche, and produces complicated reactions. Extrapolating from Kevin Egan to see Dubliners as internal exiles will give the reader a more sophisticated view of the complex relations of an individual with the environment of the novel.

This is not to say that Stephen relishes his isolation. Just as he has sought the esteem of the milk woman, of his students, and even of Garrett Deasy, near the end of the Aeolus chapter he works to the best of his ability to emulate his father's skills as a raconteur to secure the esteem of Myles Crawford and Professor MacHugh. He relates to them his urban vignette, "A Pisgah Sight of Palestine or the Parable of the Plums"—itself a nicely balanced combination of sentimental and rancorous views of a slice of life in Dublin—as a way of gaining attention, esteem, and acceptance from the same group of men who have warmly welcomed his father. It is probably an extemporaneous performance: inspired by the two women he saw earlier on Sandymount Strand (*U* 3.29–37), he creates his own story on the spot.

Stephen, the exile, however, lacks the skill and confidence of a practiced entertainer like Simon Dedalus and cannot shake the perspective of an outsider. The abrupt and inconclusive ending of Stephen's story, in the best modernist fashion and thus reminding us of the oscillation always at work in the narrative, underscores his distinctness and leaves his listeners somewhat uneasy and clearly at a loss as to how to respond—"Finished? Myles Crawford said. So long as they do no worse" (*U* 7.1031).

Stephen continues the pattern of trying to please while maintaining a level of distance in subsequent chapters. In Scylla and Charybdis, as he entertains the Dublin literati in the National Library, the contrasting tones of his interior and exterior monologues seem less insincere when exilic motivations come into play. He wants both to court the favor of these men and to express disdain for them because the sentiments of nostalgia and rancor oscillate within him. "Between the Saxon smile and yankee yawp. The devil and the deep sea" (*U* 9.139–40). By the end of the disquisition, it has become obvious that he cannot, as Mulligan suggests, "do the Yeats touch" (*U* 9.1160–61), because he lacks Yeats's monocular view of the world.

The duality of these feelings makes a linear approach to understanding Stephen untenable. The disruption of linearity continues with increasing assertiveness until it becomes undeniable in the Oxen of the Sun chapter where, at the Holles Street Hospital, we have a painful example of Stephen's obvious need for recognition and acceptance. There he struggles for recognition, contending against the clamoring for attention from the other solipsists in the group and pretending, in one instance of his desperate need for acclaim from others, that the money he has been using to pay for the carousal comes from his writing rather than from teaching at Deasy's school: "And he showed them glistering coins of the tribute and goldsmith notes the worth of two pounds nineteen shilling that he had, he said, for a song which he writ" (*U* 14.285–87).

Stephen, after performing and drinking for much of the day, has by this point in the narrative given himself over to unabashed self-promotion. Nonetheless, his still fragile ego remains highly vulnerable to the slightest hint of criticism—as readers quickly see when Lynch, his old classmate and putative friend, reminds him of the scantiness of his achievements.

> You have spoken of the past and its phantoms, Stephen said. Why think of them? If I call them into life across the waters of Lethe will not the poor ghosts troop to my call? Who supposes it? I, Bous Stephanoumenos, bullockbefriending bard, am lord and giver of their life. He encircled his gadding hair with a coronal of vineleaves,

> smiling at Vincent. That answer and those leaves, Vincent said to him, will adorn you more fitly when something more, and greatly more, than a capful of light odes can call your genius father. All who wish you well hope this for you. (*U* 14.1112–20)

Though the drunkenness of all of them obscures the fact, Stephen, as the narrative hints with its backward nostalgic glance to the schoolboy nickname that greeted him as he walked past friends swimming in Dublin Bay (*P* 147), is striving for inclusion much as he did fifteen years earlier at Clongowes Wood College. In the process he seems in danger of becoming a man like his father, the one given to overlooking his personal flaws and dwelling on his successes, real or imagined, the man whom Stephen described in the previous novel to his friend Cranly as

> —A medical student, an oarsman, a tenor, an amateur actor, a shouting politician, a small landlord, a small investor, a drinker, a good fellow, a storyteller, somebody's secretary, something in a distillery, a taxgatherer, a bankrupt, and at present a praiser of his own past. (*P* 213)

The danger of succumbing to a younger version of his father adds tension to representations of Stephen for the remainder of the novel. By the time he and Lynch go off to Nighttown, Stephen's dual need for gaining the esteem of fellow Dubliners while maintaining aloofness from the communal engagement that such regard so often requires has come to take precedence over all else, including, most probably, sexual desire. He seeks to capture a complaisant audience for his increasingly disjointed performances by offering to pay for Lynch's visit to the whorehouse. Unfortunately, throughout the chapter, Lynch behaves more like a hostile critic than a supportive interlocutor, an unpleasant fact of which Stephen is all too aware—"You remember fairly accurately all my errors, boasts, mistakes. How long shall I continue to close my eyes to disloyalty? Whetstone!" (*U* 15.2100–101).

The artificial and transient qualities of the experiences in Circe underscore the aching need that propels Stephen through the narrative. Stephen confronts his father in a rancorous exchange with Dedalus/Icarus overtones: "No, I flew. My foes beneath me. And ever shall be. World without end. (*he cries*) *Pater!* Free! . . . Break my spirit, will he? *O merde alors!* (he cries, his vulture talons sharpened) *Hola!* Hillyho!" (*U* 15.3935–41). In a parallel vision of his mother, a much more poignant tone informs the exchange:

> STEPHEN
>
> (*choking with fright, remorse and horror*) They say I killed you, mother. He offended your memory. Cancer did it, not I. Destiny.
>
> THE MOTHER
>
> (*a green rill of bile trickling from a side of her mouth*) You sang that song to me. *Love's bitter mystery.*[8]
>
> STEPHEN
>
> (*eagerly*) Tell me the word, mother, if you know now. The word known to all men. (*U* 15.4185–94)

With terse, abbreviated language the two passages sum up Stephen's complex relations with his parents, made clearer, in my view, when one keeps the attitudes of an exile in mind.

Once Bloom and Stephen leave Nighttown, Stephen's engagement with the narrative discourse decreases dramatically. In Eumaeus his remarks become little more than surly responses that retain his sense of need and defensiveness but give few new insights into his feelings:

> —You suspect, Stephen retorted with a sort of a half laugh, that I may be important because I belong to the *faubourg Saint Patrice* called Ireland for short.
>
> —I would go a step farther, Mr Bloom insinuated.
>
> —But I suspect, Stephen interrupted, that Ireland must be important because it belongs to me.
>
> —We can't change the country. Let us change the subject. (*U* 16.1160–71)

In Ithaca, where all responses are embedded in the question-and answer-format of the chapter, we find only fragmentary moments including him in the discourse. At the same time, Stephen's marginal status remains in the foreground. He cannot and will not go home, and despite Bloom's invitation of a bed, refuses to give up the role of exile.

> Was the proposal of asylum accepted?
>
> Promptly, inexplicably, with amicability, gratefully it was declined. (*U* 17.954–55)

The concluding images remain consistent with what we have seen since Stephen mounted the steps to the roof of the Martello Tower in Telemachus. Over the narrative, he stands as the embodiment of those exilic sensations, presented to us in the opening chapters to establish the emotional orientation. Nonetheless, we will see this same emotional multiplicity evident in other individuals throughout the discourse, from Leopold and Molly Bloom to minor characters like Simon Dedalus and C. P. M'Coy. Idealization counterpoints bitterness, and nostalgia and rancor jockey to replace the sense of certitude that has now been lost like Joyce himself. Joyce, like Kevin Egan, has not forgotten Ireland. Rather, he has articulated a more complex relationship with it.

Consequently, if we see Stephen as existing in the precarious position of trying to sustain his sense of self as an exile even after he is firmly reestablished in Dublin, then Leopold Bloom represents for us the antithetical situation. Bloom, the lifelong Dubliner, continually is searching for integration into the community, yet despite his efforts he finds himself in the position of an internal exile—the Jew among the Catholics, the temperate man among the profligates, the internationalist among the nationalists, and so on. To his chagrin, he can never shed the traits that mark him as an outsider. He finds that among fellow Dubliners he will be tolerated at best or, more often than not, ignored or even shunned.

To underscore the uniqueness of Bloom's position vis a vis his fellow Dubliners, the narrative introduces the motif of the Wandering Jew even before Bloom himself appears, at the end of the Nestor chapter. It begins with Deasy's casual anti-Semitism: "They sinned against the light, Mr Deasy said gravely. And you can see the darkness in their eyes. And that is why they are wanderers on the earth to this day" (*U* 2.361–63). The discourse then goes on with a more complex representation, both rancorously biased and sensitively nostalgic that may come from Stephen's consciousness or that may be the voice of a narrator infected and inflected with conflicting views.

> On the steps of the Paris stock exchange the goldskinned men quoting prices on their gemmed fingers. Gabble of geese. They swarmed loud, uncouth, about the temple, their heads thickplotting under maladroit silk hats. Not theirs: these clothes, this speech, these gestures. Their full slow eyes belied the words, the gestures eager and

> unoffending, but knew the rancours massed about them and knew their zeal was vain. Vain patience to heap and hoard. Time surely would scatter all. A hoard heaped by the roadside: plundered and passing on. Their eyes knew their years of wandering and, patient, knew the dishonours of their flesh. (*U* 2.364–72)

This prologue provides both a typical and a stereotypical approach to Bloom, who appears in a relatively short time and becomes an embodiment and an elaboration of Deasy's allusion. Bloom spends the day meandering, rootless and without promise of subsequent connection, through the city, seemingly in imitation of the epic figure whose Roman rendition of his name gives the novel its title. However, the parallels to Odysseus are at best approximate, and the distinctions between the two figures are as striking as are their similarities.

The variations between the natures and the situations of these characters are important features to emphasize in terms of understanding the degree to which those juxtapositions offer a clearer sense of Bloom's nature. The epic structure of the novel makes it tempting to see Bloom as a highly nuanced version of Odysseus, a modern and modernist rendering of the epic hero, but in fact a more complex situation applies. While Odysseus was a wanderer trying to exercise his legitimate right to return physically home, Bloom more precisely is an exile cut off emotionally from the center of his life.

Calypso, the chapter in which he first appears, lays out a sharp picture of this condition. It begins by showing a physical separation of Bloom and Molly. The floor plan of their typical Dublin row house subtly enforces their condition: Bloom prepares breakfast in the kitchen, on the lowest level of the house, while Molly drowses above him in the bedroom on the top story.[9] The chapter goes on to outline their routines for June 16, elaborating on their separate existences under the same roof: they eat breakfast apart. They plan very different agendas for the day. And they even receive separate correspondence, a letter for Leopold and a postcard for Molly, from their daughter Milly, whom by the way Bloom has exiled to Mullingar. The sense of isolation that accrues early on gives a fuller sense of the complexities and of the mutability of Bloom's memories—both sentimental and slightly rancorous—as he recalls, throughout the chapter, moments with Molly and Milly.

> Milly too. Young kisses: the first. Far away now past. Mrs Marion. Reading, lying back now, counting the strands of her hair, smiling, braiding.
>
> A soft qualm, regret, flowed down his backbone, increasing. Will happen, yes. Prevent. Useless: can't move. Girl's sweet light lips. Will happen too. He felt the flowing qualm spread over him. Useless to move now. Lips kissed, kissing, kissed. Full gluey woman's lips. (*U* 4.444–50)

Nostalgia and rancor alternately punctuate his reminiscences of times spent with Milly and Molly. Feelings blur, but we come to a clearer understanding of Bloom's resignation, with regard both to Molly's impending infidelity and to Milly's burgeoning sexuality, if we see Bloom's comprehension of both conditions refined through the emotional attitudes of an exile. The exilic perspective explains Bloom's detachment, his acceptance of the onset of Milly's sexual assertiveness as she moves from girl to woman and his apathy in the face of the impending pain and humiliation associated with Molly's adultery. His sense of the world comes out of loss, and expecting him to resist it would be to demand that he renounce his exilic state.

Lotus Eaters brings the motif of exile out of the domestic and into the public sphere. In this chapter Bloom moves about Dublin alone in a city filled with exiles, preferring his own company and avoiding any sort of intimate entanglements. He has numerous acquaintances, yet there is no one for whom he has a real attachment. "M'Coy. Get rid of him quickly. Take me out of my way. Hate company when you" (*U* 5.82–83). Even the epistolary relationship that he cultivates with Martha Clifford has a sterile and distant quality to it. "Doing the indignant: a girl of good family like me, respectable character. Could meet one Sunday after the rosary. Thank you: not having any. Usual love scrimmage. Then running round corners" (*U* 5.269–71).

Liminality is the dominant condition among individuals across the city. We see it primarily in Bloom, but it extends by implication to everyone he sees, from the unnamed, solitary boy smoking amid buckets of offal, to the furtive M'Coy seeking to be part of Dignam's funeral without participating, to the ferrety Bantam Lyons hoping to glean an unvoiced tip for the Gold Cup Race. In a scene reminiscent of Bloom in the jakes at the end of Calypso, the chapter concludes with an image of Bloom again alone, this time in the Turkish baths and more significantly imagined by Bloom in an unintentionally ironic self-representation as the progenitor of a race. "He saw his trunk and limbs riprippled over and sustained, buoyed lightly upward, lemonyellow: his navel, bud of flesh: and saw the dark tangled curls of his bush floating, floating hair of the stream around the limp father of thousands, a languid floating flower" (*U* 5.568–72).

The sense of cultivated isolation, a kind of self-imposed solitariness, becomes even clearer in the Hades chapter, and the usefulness of contextualizing it as related to exilic experiences becomes more apparent as readers strive to understand the motivations behind the behavior of all of the men attending Paddy Dignam's funeral. Throughout the chapter Bloom moves among his contemporaries, but time and again the narrative sets him apart from them: He alone does not wish to acknowledge Boylan as the carriage passes him (*U* 6.200–202). He cannot tell the Reuben J. Dodd story properly, so Martin Cunningham intervenes (*U* 6.264–94).

The narrative also introduces the idea that Bloom cultivates a degree of isolation by the standards he sets for himself and by the values he uses to measure others.

> Noisy selfwilled man. Full of his son. He is right. Something to hand on. If little Rudy had lived. See him grow up. Hear his voice in the house. Walking beside Molly in an Eton suit. My son. Me in his eyes. Strange feeling it would be. (*U* 6.74–77)

Even in his charity Bloom stands by himself, the only one whom Martin Cunningham mentions as both making a specific pledge to the Dignam family and actually producing the money (*U* 10.973–76). Cunningham also obliquely singles out Bloom as the only one in the group who has not had to borrow money from Reuben J. Dodd: "Well, nearly all of us" (*U* 6.261). Tom Kernan's effort at forming a group apart from the Catholics is silently rebuffed by the atheist Bloom—"Your heart perhaps but what price the fellow in the six feet by two with his toes to the daisies" (*U* 6.672–73). Nonetheless, he is still vulnerable to John Henry Menton's snub: when Bloom mentions the dinge in Menton's hat, the latter offers nothing more than a cursory thanks, and Bloom thinks, "Thank you. How grand we are this morning" (*U* 6.1033).

Also in the Hades chapter, one sees an expansion of the concept that Dublin is full of individuals cut off from their family life. Bloom remembers hearing gossip that Jack Power keeps a mistress (*U* 6.244–48). He also later recalls snickering stories about Martin Cunningham's wife who periodically destroys their household with her drinking (*U* 6.354). Simon Dedalus bemoans his separation from the wife he drove to her grave, even as he blithely ignores the needs of his children (*U* 6.645–46). It is easy to read all this as simple human misfortune, even individual callousness. However, the concept of exile adds a depth to their acts that might otherwise go unnoticed.

Aeolus reinforces that point of view, and in the process it gives a sense that the treatment of Bloom springs as much or more from the natural reactions of characters steeped in their own isolation as from anti-Semitism. The newspaper office is filled with men cut off from society. From Nannetti, alone in his "reading closet" (*U* 7.75) surrounded by clanging presses, to J. J. O'Molloy, Professor MacHugh, and Myles Crawford each alone in a crowd standing under Nelson's Pillar (*U* 7.1065–75), the readers encounter one individual after another lost within himself while surrounded by others. To underscore the point, the narrative presents instances of Lenehan receiving as much abuse as Bloom, though Lenehan's life as a parasite has conditioned him not to acknowledge, publicly at least, any of the slights he receives. The condition is more general than readers might initially notice, for the men at the *Freeman's Journal* show at best only a minimal regard for one another. In the final analysis, each isolated figure makes his way alone, without the support of anyone else.

The Lestrygonians chapter offers a more elaborate perspective on this same theme of alienation. It shows that Bloom's experience in Lotus Eaters, moving about the city seeking to remain alone and unconnected, was not a unique but a microcosmic view of Dublin life. Bloom never fully engages the people whom he encounters, like Josie Breen or Nosey Flynn. Throughout exchanges in the chapter, we come to see that there is an inherent isolation in them all, and from that isolation come the feelings of rancor and nostalgia that are second nature to the exile.

Of the two, rancor seems to come more easily to one's consciousness. When seeing humanity at a distance, as he does when he stops in the Burton, Bloom can barely restrain his disgust:

> Smells of men. Spaton sawdust, sweetish warmish cigarette smoke, reek of plug, spilt beer, men's beery piss, the stale of ferment.
> His gorge rose.
> Couldn't eat a morsel here. Fellow sharpening knife and fork to eat

> all before him, old chap picking his tootles. Slight spasm, full, chewing the cud. Before and after. Grace after meals. Look on this picture then on that. Scoffing up stewgravy with sopping sippets of bread. Lick it off the plate, man! Get out of this. (*U* 8.670–77)

The disgust he feels here at immersion in human contact stands in paradoxical contrast to the yearning for fellowship he seems to express elsewhere, and underscores his sense of being adrift. The exchange with Josie Breen earlier in the chapter catches Bloom's ambivalence:

> Same blue serge dress she had two years ago, the nap bleaching. Seen its best days. Wispish hair over her ears. And that dowdy toque: three old grapes to take the harm out of it. Shabby genteel. She used to be a tasty dresser. Lines round her mouth. Only a year or so older than Molly.
> See the eye that woman gave her, passing. Cruel. The unfair sex. (*U* 8.265–69)

The only moment of seemingly genuine intimacy comes as he guides the blind piano tuner across the street, and even there he takes the position of scientific detachment. "How on earth did he know that van was there? Must have felt it. See things in their forehead perhaps: kind of sense of volume. Weight or size of it, something blacker than the dark" (*U* 8.1107–9). Throughout Lestrygonians Bloom is, more or less by his own choosing, within and outside the society of Dublin.

As it unfolds, the narrative continues to enforce a dominant view of separation and loss, but it also makes subtle qualifications. Wandering Rocks presents a montage-like tour of the heart of the city, ranging across congested areas to show moments of the satisfaction that comes out of a disposition to remain separate. Father Conmee, lost in thought at the opening of the chapter while on his trip to Artane to see what can be done for one of the Dignam children, and Almidano Artifoni, ignoring the viceregal cavalcade at the end, bracket a host of figures who move about at a remove, content to be only peripherally connected to the world around them.

Even when exchanges take place, as with Dilly Dedalus's conversations first with her father and then with her brother, people speak at cross-purposes, concerned only with stating their own views. As elsewhere, reflections rest on extremes of feelings—from Tom Kernan's self-satisfaction to Lenehan's salacious, and quite probably untrue, account of fondling Molly. Rancor and nostalgia do not dominate the chapter's narrative, but they color the discourse. An awareness of the impact they both exert on individuals in these episodes will inform readers' understanding of characters whose behavior may otherwise seem banal exercises.

Sirens returns attention to Bloom, and it underscores the image of him as the victim. At the same time, as before, keeping the complexity of exile in mind prevents Bloom from slipping into a maudlin stereotype. Early on, the narrative describes Bloom, passing the carriage waiting to take Boylan to his assignation with Molly, with what could be unexpected dignity or heavy-handed irony. "Between the car and window, warily walking, went Bloom, unconquered hero" (*U* 11.341–42). In fact both sentiments aptly describe elements of his nature. He is a conflicted individual who struggles to find the proper way to engage the world that continually holds him at arm's length.

In a literal embodiment of that disposition, Bloom joins those gathering in the Ormond Hotel, but he locates himself in the dining room, away from the central action in the barroom. Though separate from the company in the bar, he keeps a clear sense of what transpires there and, with no hesitation, offers casual judgments of those who are performing in the other room. "Wonder who's playing. Nice touch. Must be Cowley. Musical. Knows whatever note you play. Bad breath he has, poor chap" (*U* 11.560–61). He eats with Richie Goulding but hardly engages in conversation. Instead he recalls Simon Dedalus's dismissive attitude and Richie's no less fawning response. "Brother-in-law: relations. We never speak as we pass by. Rift in the lute I think. Treats him with scorn. See. He admires him all the more. The night Si sang" (*U* 11.789–90).

In moments like this throughout the narrative, we see hints that isolation in Dublin extends well beyond Bloom, and that Bloom, who for the moment at least has grown comfortable in the marginal role of onlooker, occupies a position far more secure than many of the other characters. He observes, critiques, and remains aloof from what transpires. The attitude of exile has become liberating, giving him freedom from the constraints that circumscribe the others even as he retains the ability to move among them.

Cyclops, in contrast, brings to the foreground the vulnerability that also comes as a consequence of Bloom's isolation from the others. A wide-ranging exchange on Irish nationalism turns abruptly and rancorously to several bar patrons questioning Bloom's Irishness.

> —But do you know what a nation means? says John Wyse.
> —Yes, says Bloom.
> —What is it? says John Wyse.
> —A nation? says Bloom. A nation is the same people living in the same place.
> —By God, then, says Ned, laughing, if that's so I'm a nation for I'm living in the same place for the past five years.
> So of course everyone had the laugh at Bloom and says he, trying to muck out of it:
> —Or also living in different places.
> —That covers my case, says Joe.
> —What is your nation if I may ask? says the citizen.
> —Ireland, says Bloom. I was born here. Ireland. (*U* 12.1419–33)

What seems simple fatuous confusion on Bloom's part becomes less ridiculous and more problematic when we see him speaking from the position of an exile. His shifting point of view catches the condition of social ambiguity that has become all too familiar to him, and in all likelihood affects, though unacknowledged, the lives of the others as well.

In an unvoiced reflection of the insecurity that many of the men in the Barney Kiernan's feel regarding identity, hostility builds toward the perceived outsider, and it becomes more overt as individuals underscore Bloom's separateness. First, when Bloom briefly leaves the pub to look for Martin Cunningham, Lenehan falsely asserts that Bloom has gone to collect his winnings from a bet on the Gold Cup Race (*U* 12.1550–51). Then when Bloom returns and does not, as expected of someone who has come into a windfall, buy a round for the house (*U* 12.1759–61), vague resentment builds into a conscious identification of him as other.

At the same time, the narrative neatly plays on iconography to give Bloom's isolation a double-edged significance. When the Citizen's anti-Semitism becomes too much to bear, we see Bloom deftly turning local prejudices back against his tormentor. "And the Saviour was a jew and his father was a jew. Your God" (*U* 12.1805). By invoking Christ, Bloom allies himself with, for Christians, the ultimate exile.

Nausikaa is set on the edge of the water, and as with Stephen in Proteus it puts Bloom in the literal and metaphoric liminal position. As he stands behind the rock, apart from Gerty and the others, his position as exile seems unmistakable. When readers realize he is masturbating in response to Gerty's exhibitionism and hear his callous dismissal of her physical infirmity, he comes closer to invader. Indeed, the coarseness of Bloom's reaction to the lameness of Gerty McDowell would seem quite out of character for the otherwise considerate Bloom had we not the sense of rancor of an exile to explain his harshness. "That's why she's left on the shelf and the others did a sprint. Thought something was wrong by the cut of her jib. Jilted beauty. A defect is ten times worse in a woman. But makes them polite. Glad I didn't know it when she was on show. Hot little devil all the same" (*U* 13.772–76). As in other interpretive instances, invoking the condition of exile does not absolve a character of bad behavior, but it does offer a fuller explanation of motivation.

Just as Lestrygonians reinforces the tone of Lotus Eaters, Oxen of the Sun does the same for our impressions of Hades. In both instances we see Bloom in the company of men, but in Oxen of the Sun as in Hades he still holds himself off from full engagement. "And childe Leopold did up his beaver for to pleasure him and took apertly somewhat in amity for he never drank no manner of mead which he then put by and anon full privily he voided the more part in his neighbor glass and his neighbor nist not of this wile" (*U* 14.161–65). The detachment he shows here calls into question any sense that one may have had from the earlier chapter that it is the hostility of others that has isolated Bloom. As he did in Hades, Bloom holds himself back by choice, and his critical views of others give one the sense that he is not terribly interested in integrating himself into the community. However, as subsequent chapters show, no single impression will give a complete sense of Bloom's consciousness.

The narrative of Circe foregrounds Bloom's sense of exile—dominated by alternating feelings of nostalgia and rancor. In recollections of past, present, and future, of public, private, and domestic life, we see him striving for acclaim while enduring frequent humiliation.

> RUDOLPH
>
> What you making down this pace? Have you no soul? (*with feeble vulture talons he feels the silent face of Bloom*) Are you not my son Leopold, the grandson of Leopold? Are you not my dear son Leo-

pold who left the house of his father and left the god of his fathers Abraham and Jacob? (*U* 15.259–62)

J. J. O'MOLLOY

My client is an infant, a poor foreign immigrant who started scratch as a stowaway and is now trying to turn an honest penny. The trumped up misdemeanour was due to a momentary aberration of heredity, brought on by hallucination, such familiarities as the alleged guilty occurrence being quite permitted in my client's native place, the land of the Pharaoh. (*U* 15.942–47)

BELLO

(*ruthlessly*) No, Leopold Bloom, all is changed by woman's will since you slept horizontal in Sleepy Hollow your night of twenty years. Return and see.

(*Old Sleepy Hollow calls over the wold.*)

SLEEPY HOLLOW

Rip van Wink! Rip van Winkle!

BLOOM

(*in tattered moccasins with a rusty fowlingpiece, tiptoeing, fingertipping, his haggard bony bearded face peering through the diamond panes, cries out*) I see her! It's she! (*U* 15.3153–62)

It is easy to trace a sense of masochism as motivating him throughout these scenes, but that too easily glosses the source with handy psychological labels. More to the point, Bloom finds himself haunted by a desire for place, and his reactions to its absence underscore the centrality of that need in his nature.

The two chapters in which he last appears, Eumaeus and Ithaca, seem to point toward a reestablishment or at least a reoccupation, but does he actually return? Bloom has been perpetuating exile all day in his reluctance to go back to number 7 Eccles Street. He deflects the possibility of a confrontation with Molly with a scheme to bring Stephen back to stay with them.

His physical presence there at the end of the day does not necessarily overturn the exilic feelings that have dominated him. As he goes about the house straightening up Molly's mess, he bumps against a bureau in the rearranged parlor and finds that this little world has changed. Still, as he gets ready for bed, he repeats familiar evening rituals that affirm the normalcy of domestic life even as he feels a sense of displacement, fantasizing about running off to travel the world.[10] While he is slipping into sleep, he gestures toward nostalgia rather than rancor, associating himself with Sinbad the sailor, whose seven voyages propelled by his own restlessness trace cycles of departure and return rather than emphasizing eventual triumph and reintegration—a positive vision concluding a day marked by isolation and failure.

In the final chapter, Penelope, we get extended exposure to Molly—the most poignant and least regarded exile of the group—through reminiscences and speculations on her past, present, and future. Her thoughts, both nostalgic and rancorous, return to Gibraltar and to recollections of her life before marrying Bloom. In the process she underscores the alienated existence that began there and continued throughout her time in Dublin.[11]

Molly both idealizes and romanticizes selected moments from her childhood, focusing on instances of burgeoning sexuality, and punctuates those idyllic recollections with thoughts of the tedium and unpleasantness that she endured in garrison life. Gibraltar, however, stands more as a metaphor for a psychological sense of loss than for anything else. Molly's monologue underscores how isolated she feels and how alienated her existence is.[12] The extravagant sensuality in which she seems to luxuriate while recollecting various sexual exploits comes down to a form of sentimentality, an idealization of a way of life that stands as ephemeral at best. Her outbursts of anger are equally understandable as manifestations of the rancor that has grown up because of the isolation that she feels from any kind of community.

As with Stephen and Bloom, seeing Molly from an exilic perspective enhances rather than reorders the reader's comprehension of her nature. Exile brings a greater poignancy to one's sense of Molly's life. The move from Gibraltar, the death of Rudy, the emotional remoteness of her husband, and the relocation of Milly out of the home are painful experiences in their own right. When one sees each as yet another instance that heightens her isolation, Molly's actions on June 16 take on greater clarity. Adultery with Boylan, despite the graphic sensuality of her monologue—"his wife is fucked yes and damn well fucked too up to my neck nearly" (*U* 18.1510–11)—springs as much or more from deep need for reintegration.[13] The moments of wistfulness that punctuate her monologue, whether in recollections of Hester Stanhope or of longing thoughts of Bloom, Milly, or Rudy, underscore the importance of place as a feature of personal identity, and they remind us of the lack of psychological and emotional connections through the nostalgia and rancor that haunt her consciousness.

Molly has seemed part of the action of the novel for most of the narrative, as salacious, snickering references to her by various men punctuate most chapters in which Bloom appears. Simon Dedalus sums up the views of many in his sneering comment in Sirens, punning on a remark that, at a time when they were financially strapped, Leopold and Molly sold secondhand garments: "Mrs Marion Bloom has left off clothes of all descriptions" (*U* 11.496–97).

At the same time, as Penelope attests through numerous examples, the suggestions of easy availability come to little more than scabrous gossip. Molly has held herself apart from the community, not simply isolated from daily interactions but alienated from the larger society. She sees Dublin and Dubliners from the point of view of an outsider, and takes an unblinking view of the men with whom her husband associates every day:

> theyre a nice lot all of them well theyre not going to get my husband again into their clutches if I can help it making fun of him then behind his back I know well when he goes on with his idiotics because he has sense enough not to squander every penny piece he earns down their gullets and looks after his wife and family goodfornothings. (*U* 18.1275–79)

Nonetheless, in the very harshness of her judgment of those around her, she reflects a sense of loss embodied in the exile's deep and profound longing for genuine integration into community. Recognizing that will give us a more complex understanding of her nature. She is not simply a self-indulgent sensualist. She is troubled by a need for affirmation that can be masked by her frank espousal of animal appetites.

We see this unfolding in Molly's monologue, which presents a varied and complex picture of her nature. It causes readers to revise many of the assumptions that have come from Bloom's uxorious recollections and the poisonous gossip of those men who claim to know her. Molly's very different account of what transpired on the way home from the Glencree Dinner (*U* 18.426–28) unconsciously rebuts Lenehan's salacious suggestions about her (*U* 8.535–73) and suggests that distortion, outright lies, and spite inform a great many of the comments that men have made about

Molly over the course of the narrative. There is no simple pattern for understanding her nature, but by keeping in mind the mutability of an exile's feelings, a reader has a clearer idea of the range of emotions and attitudes that inform her character.

Once one has identified this exilic pattern of sentimentality and rancor in the views of the novel's central characters, it becomes easy to see Dublin as a city full of exiles, isolated characters looking backwards. Simon Dedalus inflates his devotion to the wife he drove to her grave as he excoriates, as unendurable burdens, the children she bore him. Myles Crawford rambles in drunken mania about past glories while expressing little more than bitterness and cynicism for the world that surrounds him. Bob Cowley's periodic benders seem more understandable as the response of a man trapped in grinding routine that can be alleviated only by dissipation. C. P. M'Coy is simply a pale substitute for Bloom, beset with the same sort of alienation yet not given sufficient narrative space to elaborate upon it. Even D. B. Murphy takes on a life as more than a mere late-night blowhard when we see his hyperbolic tales rooted in the pain of the exilic experience.

One sees that by the time he composed *Ulysses*, Joyce had perfected the trope of exile, using his own emotional experiences abroad to capture the isolation of his Dublin in a fashion far more universal than what he conveyed in his short stories. Evidence of it abounds, but the point is not so much to hunt through the narrative to make mechanical associations. The value of orienting one's reading according to issues and experiences related to exile lies in the intensification of our understanding of characters' behavior at various stages of the day. Exilic associations do not reverse our sense of individuals, or even introduce new concepts of their natures, so much as they provide deeper insights into the how and the why of specific thoughts, acts, and deeds.

6

Finnegans Wake and the Exile's Return

by a commodious vicus of recirculation

Ending this study by looking at *Finnegans Wake* has a chronological logic that is obvious at once, but it also aptly sums up the process that I have been advocating throughout the work. My examination of Joyce's canon has sought to trace an oscillation between familiar and unfamiliar. From that, I have endeavored to foster a sense of clear association in the midst of logical disjunction. For me the concept of exile and its consequences, something I have only begun to consider in the past few years, proves an illuminating guide for all these efforts.

Evidence for the efficacy of this approach lies across Joyce's writings and is insistently present in his final work. As the epigraph above suggests, issues of exile and return, themes introduced in the opening paragraphs, run throughout the work. In its capability to engage our deepest attention even as it plunges us into profound confusion, the narrative of *Finnegans Wake* makes a convincing case that the emotional, psychological, spiritual, and physical effects of exile function on Joyce's creative process in a manner that is crucial to grasp if we are to attain a fuller understanding of his final work. In the process it reiterates the need to apprehend that condition across the canon.

While the groundbreaking imaginative features of *Finnegans Wake* command the reader's attention from the first exposure onward, its enforcement of the inherent continuity in all of Joyce's creative acts, unified by the real and human experiences generated by his sense of exile from his native land, exerts equal demands for our attention. Through its thematic and its contextual structures, Joyce's final work provides excellent illustrations of both the specific insights and the general values that one can derive from exploring a very particular kind of isolation. Comprehending that sense of isolation stands as a key feature to understanding Joyce's way of writing.

It is only to reiterate a critical commonplace to note that the form of *Finnegans Wake* is its most overtly arresting feature. The construction of the narrative—as it "moves swiftly sterneward" (*FW* 256.13–14)—challenges the reader's conventional forms of understanding through rhetorical constructions that had not been presented since the eighteenth-century writings of Jonathan Swift and Laurence Sterne. My point, however, is that noting a break from tradition only begins the conversation on interpretive approaches. The genuine challenge comes in answering the question of how to proceed once the difference has been noted.

Starting at the basic level of sentence construction gives one a clear sense of the challenge. Joyce has filled his narrative with neologisms, strained puns, portmanteau words, and sentences and paragraphs that stubbornly resist linear unification. The near familiarity of so much language can prove frustrating, for it teases readers with suggestions of a logical connection while steadfastly avoiding the linguistic closure common to most exchanges.

In this case, however, confusion emerges not from the text but from the expectations that we bring to it. Even the stylistic complexities of *Ulysses* simply overlay the fundamental structure of traditional fictional narration. *Finnegans Wake*, at least on initial reading, does not delineate such familiar interpretive markers. Comprehension comes only after readers have settled on an approach to the work that adopts new perspectives and that relies on different assumptions. My contention is simply that Joyce's previous works have prepared us, just as they prepared him, to undertake the challenge of *Finnegans Wake*, and attention to the context that helped form him as a writer makes the transition in our epistemological approaches far less radical than we might have expected it to be.

Joyce is routinely cited, among other things, as one of the most prominent Irish writers in the canon. Without attempting to diminish his achievements in capturing and conveying the ethos of his native country, I feel that the designation for Joyce becomes much more accurate and much more useful when we see him as an Irish exilic writer. As with my examinations of Joyce's previous works, I find *Finnegans Wake* to be much clearer and more unified when the oscillating perspectives of a writer cut off from his homeland are taken into account.

While the narrative structure of Joyce's writing may seem to lay out patterns of thought and communication completely foreign to common usage, on close inspection one sees that a duality obtains that comes directly out of the liminal, both/and disposition of the exile. The very idiosyncratic condition of the discourse signals its inclination to transmit the deeply personal qualities and experiences of its creator. Thus, in a text that foregrounds phonological variation, it stands as reasonable to see its discourse emerging from the impulse to outline the linguistic experiences of almost anyone forced to struggle with a new language in an unfamiliar setting. With this in mind, one can see its polyglot semantic construction evoking the disoriented and disconcerted sensations of the transplanted individual struggling to master the mutable speech patterns of the country in which he or she resides.

The more one recognizes instances of the application of this perspective, the more one sees its useful interpretive connections. An all too common experience of the displaced is a sense of only tentative comprehension of the world now inhabited. Exiles, already traumatized by displacement, also face the culture shock of finding they have at best a tenuous grip on the process of communicating with the natives who surround them.

This is true for all foreign speakers, however fluent, for the cultural complexity reflected in the argot of every society embeds challenges in the most straightforward of exchanges. Idiomatic customs make logical structures for expression increasingly difficult for the foreigner to discern, and this condition takes on a pan-national flavor in *Finnegans Wake*. Words, phrases, sentences, and paragraphs from dozens of different languages puncture, mangle, and ultimately transform the putative English narrative that propels the discourse forward. They evoke for native speakers that sense of instant disorientation that can overtake even the most accomplished polyglots living in countries not their own. A witticm widely attributed to another Irish writer, George Bernard Shaw—"England and America are two countries divided by a common language"—offers an apt summation.

I frankly never grasped the full significance of the linguistic choreography of *Finnegans Wake* until my wife and I moved to Miami from Milwaukee in 2009. In a city where English is only one of many languages one regularly hears on the street and where the cultural context can shift from North American to European to Caribbean to South American in a matter of a few city blocks, we quickly became aware that we were surrounded by transplanted individuals from around the world who came to maturity speaking a host of very different languages from English, yet who have labored quite successfully to master this non-native tongue. Nonetheless, and this was a realization slow in coming, despite all their efforts a fundamental difference obtains. Spanish, Portuguese, French, Creole, Russian, Turkish, and many more languages remain integral parts of the consciousness of many who have been in America for decades.

Recognizing the multiplicity—both/and, insider/outsider, native/foreign—in this diversity, however, is neither the endpoint of grasping the Miami experience nor particularly accurate when seen as a stark division. Like the language of *Finnegans Wake*, the experiences of belonging and not belonging do not form sharply separate entities in the individual consciousness. They bleed into one another so that, in the process of becoming conscious of uniqueness, one is continually reminded of a sense of amalgamation.

As I have found in numerous instances, a foreign-born individual who has lived in America for decades and has spoken English for all or most of that time remains unsure of many aspects of the language, and time and again will hesitantly ask questions about proper verb construction, preferred idiomatic usage, or a simple choice of preposition. The striking feature of the situation is that those asking questions invariably speak English with a precision and sophistication surpassing many of those who have been immersed in the language from birth. It is always a powerful revelation to see that the self-consciousness and uncertainty of speaking a foreign language never completely disappears, and it can impose itself on even the most self-assured of speakers.

Though there is no biographical proof, I think it reasonable to wonder if, despite his fluency in several languages, Joyce, like every other non-native speaker I have encountered, experienced that uneasiness. (Truth be told, I have experienced very much the same insecurity and hesitation, with far less competence to sustain me, throughout my own fumbling attempts to learn Spanish, and this has unfolded in the face of a populace that has been unfailingly generous with my faltering efforts to communicate.) Admittedly, it is an opinion for which I have not solid proof, but for my argument the point itself is moot.

Whether Joyce did or not have the personal experience of linguistic uncertainty as he conversed in Italian, French, or German, as a language teacher and as a student of languages he would have seen the condition assert itself in others time and again in Trieste, Rome, Zurich, Paris, and elsewhere. More to the point, he would have understood that every foreign phrase that an exile uses with hesitancy would remind that individual of the ongoing state of separation not only from the native country but also from the society of the current country. That insistent insecurity that can punctuate the speech patterns of any and every foreign speaker conveys very powerfully the mutability of language upon which the discourse of *Finnegans Wake* is founded.

The word itself forms a leitmotif in *Finnegans Wake*, appearing most often in its variant form "hesitency." Most commonly, it has been explained as a reference to the misspelling of the word by Richard Piggott in a document that he forged to implicate falsely Charles Stewart Parnell in the Phoenix Park murders.[1] While that explanation gives a useful local gloss of the word's application, it takes a broader meaning from the sense of its evoking the confusion found in anyone's struggle to articulate ideas in an unfamiliar idiom.[2]

Reading *Finnegans Wake* from the perspective of an exile goes beyond simply illuminating the linguistic form of the narrative. The work's thematic development, at once both maddeningly familiar and undeniably distant, presents the same challenge to see aspects of foreignness and of familiarity in a hypostatic union. References accumulate from the most basic level upward. Portmanteau words signal multiple allusions elaborated in the exposition of sentences, paragraphs, and passages. Readers will struggle to find a single point of understanding, while knowing instinctively that others elude them.[3]

Like the literal exile, the reader is in a liminal state, existing on the periphery, never achieving integration and never experiencing expulsion. The consequence is an estrangement from the text without a complete separation. The both/and condition of the narrative of *Finnegans Wake* has long been a critical commonplace. However, seeing it as a consequence of an exilic status brings to the foreground imaginative connections that heretofore have gone unremarked.

Setting out to interpret Joyce's idiosyncratic presentation of form and context is an experience not unlike that of the exile trying to achieve integration and continually finding the results are approximate at best. The reader of *Finnegans Wake*, pursuing a general sense of the meaning of the text, in fact constructs a highly subjective impression of it that only approaches to greater and lesser degrees the personal impressions of all of the other readers who have come to Joyce's final work. While that may seem to mimic any reading experience, it remains a unique impression because of the referentiality we employ. A work becomes part of our experience often to the extent that we can identify it with other works. Acknowledging the association by no means marks the end of one's interpretive experience, but it does provide important analytical orientation at the outset. Joyce's narrative strategy has for decades strained the comprehensive capabilities of individuals long accustomed to the familiar process of invoking experiences with previous fictional works to regularize all of our reading experience. *Finnegans Wake* does not make that approach impossible to apply, but, by underscoring the uniqueness of our encounters with Joyce's text, it impels us toward new reference points for determining structural patterns to guide our readings.[4]

Seeing this disjunction between traditional interpretive associations and the new models that *Finnegans Wake* pushes us to discern clarifies for me the source of the anger and disgust that close friends and ardent supporters, like Ezra Pound and Stanislaus Joyce, quickly expressed after seeing early fragments of *Finnegans Wake*. Their disapproval goes to the heart of their own backgrounds. They were themselves exiles, or nearly so, familiar with the physical displacement and linguistic and cultural disorientation, and of course in the past they had generally been strong advocates of Joyce's previous experimentation.[5] Nonetheless, they balked at the construction of *Finnegans Wake* and seemed to crave in their reading of it some opportunity to apply traditional associations to other familiar works of fiction.[6] Like expatriates who never really accept their new environment—whether as denizens of Harry's New York Bar at 5, rue Daunou, between the avenue de l'Opéra and the rue de la Paix in Paris, or as residents of colonial enclaves across the British empire—a number of Joyce's former supporters could not or would not give themselves over to the exile experience.

One finds this same impulse to regularize the work into familiar interpretive patterns in the critical responses to *Finnegans Wake* that have appeared over the last ninety or so years. Those reactions, particularly given the fragmentary way in which the text was introduced to readers over the decade and a half preceding its full publication, are completely understandable. Nonetheless, the insights of numerous early scholars working without benefit of the full text markedly increased our understanding of Joyce's last work.[7] At the same time, without dismissing the insightful work compiled by critics over the decades, I would like to conclude my study by showing how reading *Finnegans Wake* and its existing criticism from the exilic point of view greatly enhances our ability to comprehend the complexities of the work.

Its piecemeal dissemination made it inevitable that understanding of Joyce's last work would likewise evolve in a piecemeal fashion. Beginning in 1924, fifteen years before it appeared as a completed work, Joyce fell into the practice of steadily publishing segments of *Finnegans Wake* in a range of little magazines. Critics responded just as exiles respond to their episodic exposure to the new environment in which they find themselves—through analogies and comparisons to the world they have left behind. Readers began to form strong opinions on the meaning of *Finnegans Wake* based on the diverse segments that appeared. Like the exile trying to discern a full understanding of a foreign environment by extrapolating from discrete, random, and often unconnected moments, critics felt compelled to project a sense of the finished text of Joyce's work well before seeing it as a unified whole.

One of the most pervasive, and ultimately misleading, views, derived from a passage in a November 1926 letter from Joyce to Harriet Shaw Weaver, is that the narrative text approximates a dream. The specific passage giving rise to that assumption provokes exactly the proleptic move that I have described above. Without using the term "sleep" or "dream," Joyce observes to Weaver: "One great part of every human experience is passed in a state which cannot be rendered sensible by the use of wideawake language, cut and dry grammar and goahead plot" (*Letters* III.146). To the casual observer, eschewing "wideawake language" might logically point to a dream vocabulary, but to the reader oriented to the possibility that Joyce was drawing upon his often fragmented engagement with the world, this sounds very much like a generalization of human perceptions based on the way an exile struggles to grasp a new environment.

However, having already seen how persons like Ezra Pound and Stanislaus Joyce—themselves displaced from their native countries—could be oblivious to evocations of exilic impressions, one cannot be surprised at the tendency of other readers, without such shared experiences, to discern a more commonplace narrative structure. Shortly after *Finnegans Wake* was published in May 1939, Edmund Wilson took up the dream idea in an influential essay that attempted an overview of Joyce's book.[8] Once proffered, the idea quickly caught on. Five years after Wilson's essay appeared, Joseph Campbell and Henry Morton Robinson endorsed that approach in a book that became extremely popular.[9]

From that time onward, a great many critics have simply proceeded according to the assumption that the dream and the dreamer's perspective dominated the narrative structure. However, sophisticated readers increasingly have felt the need to qualify that position. Clive Hart serves as a very good example of the process, refining our sense of the term "dream" to produce a broader interpretive flexibility that, through an analogy with conventional narratives, ends up effacing the significance of seeing the narrative as a dream state:

> Like the anonymous narrator of more conventional "third-person" novels, the Dreamer is omniscient; we are involved in his dream as we are involved in any narrative; in each case the narrator's identity is almost entirely irrelevant. Like Stephen's Artist-God, Joyce's Dreamer has been "refined out of existence."[10]

John Bishop offers a slightly less specific qualification, though one equally uncomfortable with a rigorous application of dream imagery: "People have customarily treated the book, at Joyce's invitation, as the 'representation of a dream' though not about a dream in any pedestrian sense of that word."[11] Bernard Benstock and Patrick Parrinder, among others, have more frankly and directly questioned the usefulness of this approach to the narrative.[12] Derek Attridge has endeavored to occupy a middle ground, saying that the paradigm of the dream and dreamer may be "one among a number of such [interpretive] contexts which, though incompatible with one another, all have some potential value."[13] At the same time, a number of highly regarded studies continue to pursue the idea of a dream as the framework of the narrative.[14] Nonetheless, while the intensity of the opinion still varies, a growing number of critics have come to see that viewing *Finnegans Wake* as a dream narrative has had a dead-end effect, an interpretive strategy that explains without illuminating any of the complexities in the narrative discourse.[15]

The more one probes the paradigmatic applicability of dreams and dreaming to the narrative structure of *Finnegans Wake*, the more shortcomings emerge. The initial appeal of the analogy comes from a sense that the chaos of a dream is unified by a self-contained rationality that justifies all that occurs, no matter how bizarre. However, this process of rationalization functions as a self-generating and unsupported system of cognition that cannot be reproduced, even in other dreams by the same dreamer. In contrast, the chaos that characterizes the exilic experience follows a universal pattern replicated, at least in a general way, from exile to exile. Seeing *Finnegans Wake* from the template of the exilic experience provides a discernable unity applicable from reader to reader.

The previous chapters have already demonstrated the efficacy of a point of view attuned to the author's displacement in interpretation of Joyce's other writings. Tracing the exilic impulse in *Finnegans Wake*, by contrast, offers a larger and more coherent interpretive approach to Joyce's last work. As is the case in readings of *Dubliners*, *A Portrait of the Artist as a Young Man*, *Exiles*, and *Ulysses* that follow the same approach, identification of exilic issues in the thematic threads and character developments of *Finnegans Wake* will enhance the reader's ability to understand specific issues in the text in greater detail, and they will allow one to relate various parts of the work to a larger motivation that unifies it.

This becomes the final piece in a unified approach to Joyce's canon, and it captures the imaginative perspective that the author brought to bear on his process of composition. The exilic point of view engages Joyce's works through an awareness of important assumptions and attitudes that shaped his writings. Just as our understanding of his books increases as we develop a greater knowledge of the cultural context—history, religion, customs, and beliefs—from which his writing emerged, so also are we enhanced by a clearer understanding of the attitudes and issues that engaged his consciousness during the process of creation.

Ideas of exile illuminate interpretations because they help readers address key issues of identity, grounded in the family, that run through Joyce's narrative. Authorial self-perception clearly affects the imaginative process, and impressions tied to the context of separation and loss have a unique impact upon the structure of the narrative and by extension upon a reader's comprehension of it. The importance of community and its relation to the individual, in a gamut of feelings from positive to negative in almost every context imaginable, take on permanent forms fixed at a particular moment from the point of view of exilic experiences. Awareness of the impact of exile—physically, emotionally, culturally, and spiritually—grounds the reader's sensibilities in a clearly discernible point of view that offers clarity and at the same time suggests a variety of responses. As with earlier works, the exilic perspective oscillates between imaginative possibilities without prescribing a single interpretation.

Examples presented throughout this study have shown that nostalgia and rancor dominate the exile's view of the homeland. Retrospection stands as the animating force behind these feelings, and that feature emerges time and again, in every aspect of the form and content of Joyce's final work. As the title to this chapter suggests, in *Finnegans Wake* Joyce both summarizes and reconsiders the concepts of exile and return that run throughout the narratives of Joyce's canon. He announces his commitment in the fractured lines that open his work:

> riverrun, past Eve and Adam's, from swerve of shore to bend of bay, brings us by a commodious vicus of recirculation back to Howth Castle and Environs. (*FW* 1.1–3)

As many previous commentators have noted, this initial passage underscores the circularity that calls into question habits of linear reading and challenges the very concept of a narrative opening. It will encapsulate the circular, cyclical structure of *Finnegans Wake* as it completes the sentence that begins on the final page of the novel:

> A way a lone a last a loved a long the (*FW* 628.15–16)

Taken together, these fragments offer a complex description of individual isolation juxtaposed with the inclusionary movement of the River Liffey carried by tide and current through the city center, past the Hill of Howth, and out into Dublin Bay, tracing the oscillating, mutable cadences of the narrative on top of the formal shape of its discourse. The rhythmic movement of the water running into and out of the River Liffey represents more than tidal oscillations. It evokes the constancy and continuity of regular fluctuation while in fact tracing the path of erosion and evolution. The simultaneity of fluid stasis and activity within the banks of the Liffey catches the turbulent view of the exile superimposing impressions of the past upon the contemporary world from which he or she remains barred.[16]

One has ample indication of the interpretive potential of exile as it calls forth the condition of contradiction that runs throughout Joyce's writing. Both in selections focusing on the diverse characterizations and in the microcosmic and macrocosmic treatments of diverse topics, a sense of exile effectively enriches any reading one might wish to pursue. Let me focus briefly on several of the central characters to illustrate how my approach can enhance our grasp of their complex natures.

Humphrey Chimpden Earwicker stands out as a paramount example of the shifting roles of an exile. His nickname, Here Comes Everybody, underscores the mutability and transitory features of the character. At different times the narrative puts him in the role of an innkeeper, a Norwegian captain, and a Russian general and links him archetypally to King Roderick O'Connor, Tim Finnegan, Napoleon, and numerous other historical and fictional figures.[17] However, while HCE perhaps most readily evokes associations with the wanderings of an exile, it seems to me equally important to examine the detail in which exilic attitudes are woven into the features of other central characters.

After Earwicker, the figure most overtly associated with the concept of exile is Shem the Penman, with the text's blunt though deft summation of him as "self exiled in upon his ego" (*FW* 184.6–7) catching both the physical isolation and the solipsistic alienation dominating the consciousness of the displaced, self-absorbed artist. The link can hardly be surprising with the tantalizing, near-autobiographical evocation of Joyce's own nature that comes out of the first detailed presentation of the character in the novel's seventh chapter. The discourse unfolds from "a poor trait of the artless" (*FW* 114.32) into a detailed look at the character:

> Shem is as short for Shemus as Jem is joky for Jacob. A few toughnecks are still getatable who pretend that aboriginally he was of respectable stemming (he was an outlex between the lines of Ragonar Blaubarb and Horrild Hairwire and an inlaw to Capt. the Hon. and Rev. Mr. Bbyrdwood de Trop Blogg was among his most distant connections) but every honest to goodness man in the land of the space of today knows that his back life will not stand being written about in black and white. Putting truth and untruth together a shot may be made at what this hybrid actually was like to look at. (*FW* 169.1–10)

In the process, the representation of Shem offers the most useful suggestions regarding how the concepts of exile and the experiences of the exile inform the creative process. Most particularly, the conflicting images of marginalization ("an outlex between the lines") and connection ("and an inlaw") catch the duality of identity with which many exiles struggle. Seeing Shem, and by extension Joyce, from this perspective greatly enhances our understanding so that "a shot may be made at what this hybrid actually was like to look at."

This theme continues and is expanded throughout chapter 7. It provides a consistent view of Shem as a marginalized figure who retains links to central societal elements. It also shows in detail how much more useful than the idea of a dreamlike state the exilic concept can be to explain the aura of disassociation that runs across the discourse.

In chapter 7's lengthy description of Shem the Penman, the narrative explicitly alludes at several points to the exilic impulse, showing it as a force that takes over the artist will he/nil he: "He even ran away with hunself and became a farsoonerite, saying he would far sooner muddle through the hash of lentils in Europe than meddle with Irrland's split little pea" (*FW* 171.4–6). Furthermore, the narrative explores features of the condition that obtain as much internally as externally. Here a recognition of the self-contained features of the exile experience—like Milton's Satan carrying hell with him wherever he goes—gives poignancy and complexity to the nature of Shem and the other central figures who might otherwise simply seem baffling, inconsistent representations of the subconscious. Thus, in a Satanic evocation, when living in

> The house O'Shea or O'Shame, *Quivapieno,* known as the Haunted Inkbottle, no number Brimstone Walk, Asia in Ireland, as it was infested with the raps, with his penname SHUT sepia-scraped on the doorplate and a blind of black sailcloth over its wan phwinshogue, in which the soulcontracted son of the secret cell groped through life at the expense of the taxpayers. (*FW* 182.30–35)

Shem finds himself "self exiled in upon his ego" (*FW* 184.6–7). The artist, like Lucifer, is a paradigmatic exile, voluntarily cut off from the forces with which he most closely continues to identify. Exile gives pathos to what might otherwise seem the often buffoonish features and behavior of the isolated central characters of *Finnegans Wake.*[18]

Elsewhere in *Finnegans Wake,* Joyce brings archetypal connections into play as he conflates and contrasts the wanderings of St. Laurence O'Toole with the meanderings of Shem. The narrative recollects a St. Laurence free from the sentimental attachment to home felt by many exiles: "Libera, nostalgia! Beate Laurentie O'Tuli, Euro pra nobis!" (*FW* 228.25–26). Glugg, Shem in the role of the Devil in the riddling game, the "Mime of Mick, Nick and the Maggies" (*FW* 219.1–259.10), takes the alternative point of view toward his origins, with a good measure of rancor and a bitter sense of the exile's fate:

> He would si through severalls of sanctuaries maywhatmay mightwhomight so as to meet somewhere, if produced on a demi panssion for his whole lofetime, payment in goo to slee music and poisonal comfany, following which, like Ipsey Secumbe, when he fingon to foil the fluter, she could have all the g.s. M. she moohooed after fore and rickwards to herslF, including science of sonorous silence, while he, being brung up on soul butter, have recourse of course to poetry. With tears for his coronaichon, such as engines weep. Was liffe worth leaving? Nej! (*FW* 230.17–25)

Shem as exile is not a new concept, and others have already called attention to exilic allusions in the narrative. Wim Van Mierlo and Ingeborg Landuyt have shown particular astuteness in examining Joyce's efforts at the blending of Catholic tradition and Irish history. Their clever tracing of a range of references to exilic Irish saints—specifically St. Laurence O'Toole, St. Brendan the Navigator, St. Columbanus, St. Columkille, and St. Patrick—illustrates how one finds displacement from community serving as a common denominator of Irish national identity.[19]

Those insights suggest to me a larger sustained pattern within the discourse. The intertwining of figures whose lives left archetypal impressions upon Irish culture with stories that highlight their exilic status makes a grand statement about identity in Joyce's narrative. It joins themes of nationalism and exile in a fashion that invites readers to see the Irish character as represented not only in *Finnegans Wake* but in all his fiction in terms of the longing and grief produced by traumatic separation from one's homeland. Exile does not sum up Irish identity, but it stands as an important contributing feature.

Joyce underscores this proposition by extending the impact of exile across the narrative experiences of his characters. Throughout book III of *Finnegans Wake* (403.1–590.30)—given the title "Shaun the Post" by the author—exile is personified as a condition haunting the individual. It opens with the speaker "dropping asleep somepart in nonland" (*FW* 403.18). For me what is important is not the act of sleeping but the soporific condition associated with a location that negates associations of place with one's homeland, and even though Joyce has set Shaun in Ireland in the first chapter of book III, by the second he seems to be going to America as an economic emigrant (like the tenor John McCormack, whom Joyce had known in Dublin). Nonetheless, the aura of the separation he feels from his home and the isolation he experiences from family is demonstrated across the narrative with an insistent determination, even if most of the alienation in fact stands as a self-generated condition.[20] As Joyce says in a 24 May 1924 letter to Harriet Shaw Weaver, in this section Shaun takes the role of "a postman traveling backwards in the night through events already narrated. It is written in the form of a *via crucis* of 14 stations but in reality it is only a barrel rolling down the river Liffey" (*Letters* I.214). Though Joyce suggests parodic implications, the Way of the Cross, tracing Christ's passion and death on Good Friday, evokes yet another archetypal exile and the sufferings he endures in consequence of His separation from the Father.

In the next chapter Shaun has become Jaun, now wandering around aimlessly in "his bruised brogues" (*FW* 429.4–5). The narrative continues the paschal imagery to which Joyce alluded in his letter to Weaver. Jaun gives an ineffectual Lenten lecture to Issy and the girls of St. Bride's school and then, after an unsuccessful attempt to ascend into heaven, lingers briefly as "rural Haun" (*FW* 471.35).[21]

Finally in III.3 Shaun becomes Yawn. There he is cross-examined by the four old men inquiring about, among other things, his place of origin, his language, and his family. The narrative presents us with a series of bitter accounts of restless and unsatisfying travel. Like any exile forced from his country, Shaun responds with coarse rancor, at one point saying, "Fik yew! I'm through. Won. Toe. Adry. You watch my smoke" (*FW* 469.27–28).

The most complex and engaging rendering of the exilic impulses of rancor and nostalgia appears near the end of *Finnegans Wake* with Anna Livia Plurabelle's extended recollections of her past, both before and after her marriage to Humphrey Chimpden Earwicker, and her grim sense of the present and of the future that she now faces. Like Molly's soliloquy in the Penelope chapter of *Ulysses*, ALP's disquisition summarizes, extends, and corrects images, ideas, and themes that have run throughout the narrative. It is particularly useful in summarizing references to the exilic experience and its impact upon our understanding of the discourse.

Although Anna Livia's role as an exilic figure has developed over the course of the narrative, it comes into high relief in the final few pages. There attention centers on ALP's decision to go into exile. Though it is never fully explained, the choice is seemingly forced upon her by HCE's decision to depose her as matriarch, installing a younger woman in her position. A loss of identity translates into a loss of place:

> But you're changing, acoolsha, you're changing from me, I can feel. Or is it me is? I'm getting mixed. Brightening up and tightening down. Yes, you're changing, sonhusband, and you're turning, I can feel you, for a daughterwife from the hills again. Imlamaya. And she is coming. Swimming in my hindmoist. Diveltaking on me tail. Just a whisk brisk sly spry spink spank sprint of a thing theresomere, saultering. Saltarella come to her own. (*FW* 626.35–627.6)

To understand fully ALP's unconcealed bitterness, the reader needs to see that it goes beyond simple wounded pride. The desolation that she expresses reflects exactly the kind of rancor one feels over any abrupt displacement that cuts one off from the life one has previously known. The emphasis on the process of evolution within the account of what is unfolding, the old giving way to the new, only serves to heighten our sense of the speaker's anger at the circumstances that are disrupting her life and her contempt for those who are forcing this change upon her.

There is also a strong intimation that the condition of displacement is in fact being reversed. From what she says, it becomes clear that ALP has been an exile for as long as she has known HCE, and her origins and the sense of loss that she now feels come out gradually in nostalgic recollections of bits of her life as a young girl in a different place. That is, she traces a recurring pattern of suffering, first in confronting what she is losing at the moment and then in recounting what she previously lost when she became a wife. The tender beginning shows the idealization of her past, but the harsh denunciations that follow underscore the fragility of sentimental recollections in the face of displacement:

> For she'll be sweet for you as I was sweet when I came down out of me mother. My great blue bedroom, the air so quiet, scarce a cloud. In peace and silence. I could have stayed up there for always only. It's something fails us. First we feel. Then we fall. (*FW* 627.7–11)

As with so many of Joyce's characters and, of course, the author himself, her exile is self-imposed, and in this case it again takes us back to Miltonic images. In her litany of regrets, Anna Livia explains her condition by a vague general reference to some personal flaw, evoking though not mimicking the expulsion of Lucifer from heaven. "I could have stayed up there for always only. It's something fails us. First we feel. Then we fall." It is the self-exile's anthem, and words close to what Joyce might have used to sum up his departure from Ireland.

As I have said throughout this study, the clinical accuracy of those sentiments matters far less than the emotional disposition of the individual who uttered them. Seeing Joyce seeing himself as an exile gives us insight into his process of composition. By extension that gives us a way of reading.

The amalgamated tone of the exile's response is clear in the resignation that comes out of what ALP is saying—"Anyway let her rain for my time is come. I done me best when I was let. Thinking always if I go all goes" (*FW* 627.12–14). That does not mean that resignation alone sets the context of our reading. For no sooner are those sentiments uttered than Anna Livia slips into a bitter condemnation of the family, and more particularly the husband, she is about to leave:

> A hundred cares, a tithe of troubles and is there one who understands me? One in a thousand of years of the nights? All me life I have been lived among them but now they are becoming lothed to me. And I am lothing their little warm tricks. And lothing their mean cosy turns. And all the greedy gushes out through their small souls. And all the lazy leaks down over their brash bodies. How small it's all! And me letting on to meself always. And lilting on all the time. I thought you were all glittering with the noblest of carriage. You're only a bumpkin. I thought you the great in all things, in guilt and in glory. You're but a puny. (*FW* 627.14–24)

While the disquisition seems straightforward, the exilic perspective allows us to discern a complexity not immediately evident. This is not simply the raging of a spurned wife. These are the sentiments of the outsider, one who has never felt a part of the world in which she found herself. Here and over the course of the narrative, that duality of being in but not of the community runs through the perceptions of nearly all of the major characters.

ALP's feelings, her mixture of rancor and nostalgia for both her past and her present conditions, become strikingly clear as she reminisces about the world she left behind:

> Home! My people were not their sort out beyond there so far as I can. For all the bold and bad and bleary they are blamed, the seahags. No! Nor for all our wild dances in all their wild din. I can seen meself among them, allaniuvia pulchrabelled. How she was handsome, the wild Amazia, when she would seize to my other breast! And what is she weird, haughty Niluna, that she will snatch from my ownest hair! For 'tis they are the stormies. (*FW* 627.24–31)

The pun on Amazia as both revelation and Amazon makes a strong feminist statement and plays nicely against Niluna, glossed by Adaline Glasheen as Cleopatra, so that force and beauty are united as defining female attributes.[22] At the same time, as with any of Joyce's allusions, the prudent reader will always remain attentive to multiplicity. In fact, one can easily argue that the feelings expressed by ALP have a broader applicability when seen from the exilic perspective. She aches specifically and sentimentally for the world shaped by strong women, but she also reflects the deeper sense of longing, shared by many, for a world now lost and idealized in recollections.

However, given the trauma of the moment, rancor is never far from ALP's sentiments, and the narrative challenges us to discern the full complexity of the experience:

> But I'm loothing them that's here and all I lothe. Loonely in me loneness. For all their faults. I am passing out. O bitter ending! I'll slip away before they're up. They'll never see. Nor know. Nor miss me. (*FW* 627.33–36)

The passage clearly catches up feelings of anger and anguish as more than the expression of unreflective emotion. The feelings articulated go well beyond the simple pain of isolation. They explore the stages of emotion when anger leads to anguish over the sense that everything ALP has done will come to nothing once she has ceased to be a figure in their lives.

Emblematic of exilic sensations, no single feeling predominates or even holds ALP's attention for long. Anger gives way to desire as she thinks of return, reconciliation, and reintegration:

> And it's old and old it's sad and old it's sad and weary I go back to you, my cold father, my cold mad father, my cold mad feary father, till the near sight of the mere size of him, the moyles and moyles of

> it, moananoaning, makes me seasilt saltsick and I rush, my only, into your arms. . . . Yes. Carry me along, taddy, like you done through the toy fair! If I seen him bearing down on me now under whitespread wings like he'd come from Arkangels, I sink I'd die down over his feet, humbly dumbly, only to washup. (*FW* 627.36–628.11)

What might seem like simple yearning for the past turns into something more complex from the exilic point of view. The world she evokes in her soliloquy, like those of many exiles, may or may not exist. Its material location is far less important, for understanding ALP and analogous characters throughout the narrative, than is our sense of it a as construction of emotional refuge, a place for the exile to turn that remains inviolate no matter what the conditions surrounding her.

As the narrative seemingly comes to an end the exilic journey is revived with both the promise of comprehension and the impulsion toward completion:

> A gull. Gulls. Far calls. Coming, far! End here. Us then. Finn, again! Take. Bussoftlhee, mememormee! Till thousendsthee. Lps. The keys to. Given! A way a lone a last a loved a long the (*FW* 628.13–16)

The discourse only seems to break off. In fact, it turns us back to the opening lines of *Finnegans Wake* to begin again the process of exploration, comprehension, and unification, without ever the sense that the task will be completed.

In just this fashion, *Finnegans Wake* sums up the aesthetic experience conferred by all of Joyce's writings. The exilic point of view is not meant as a neat summary or a template-like device for generating meaning. Rather, in all of his works exile maintains the intermediary position between apprehension and comprehension. It is not a specific orientation toward reading but the observation of emphatic issues that inform Joyce's process of creation without predicting the final results.

So, too, this study does not aspire to draw all meaning from his writings. In fact, it does not propose any meaning. Rather, it points readers to a crucial element for orienting their own interpretation. Some may not agree that "The keys to. Given!" but I do hope that my study leads them "A way a lone a last a loved a long the"

Notes

The Context of Exile: A Critical Introduction

1. For a range of examinations of ideas that call into question the integrity of concepts like Nation, State, Community, Ethnicity, and Nationalism, see Triandis, *Analysis of Subjective Culture*; Said, *Orientalism*; Anderson, *Imagined Communities;* Smith, *Ethnic Origins of Nations*; Gellner, *Nations and Nationalism*; Bhabha, *Nation and Narration*; Billig, *Banal Nationalism*.

2. Beckett, *Waiting for Godot*, 3.

3. Admittedly, Stephen seems to have less confidence in the process than does Joyce—"See now. There all the time without you: and ever shall be, world without end" (*U* 3.27–28)—but that too is as it should be. The dynamic interaction of Joyce and his readers, not simply their static absorption of Stephen's thoughts, brings meaning to the narrative.

4. Said, "The Mind of Winter," 54.

5. Said, "Reflections on Exile," 137.

6. Ibid.

7. Colley, *Nostalgia and Recollection*, 57.

8. This continues well into the present with established poets like Eamonn Wall coming to America from County Wexford, Ireland, because there is no system in place for them to work as artists in their native country. See his *From the Sin-é Café to the Black Hills*.

9. For examples of assessments of Wilde's Irishness by noted Irish authors and critics, see McCormack, *Wilde the Irishman*.

10. Edward Said gives a useful survey of this process, and an early indication of the direction his own criticism would take, in *Joseph Conrad and the Fiction of Autobiography*.

11. Kurzke, *Thomas Mann*.

12. The feelings of both authors come across quite clearly in two essays, both reprinted in Robinson, *Altogether Elsewhere*: Joseph Conrad's "Poland Revisited" (331–52), originally written in 1915, and Thomas Mann's "The Exiled Writer's Relationship to His Homeland" (100–105), originally delivered as a talk at a writers' congress in California in 1943.

13. See in particular Boym's introductory remarks in her book *The Future of Nostalgia*.

14. Starobinski, "The Idea of Nostalgia." See also Casey, "The World of Nostalgia."

15. For an example of how another critic has applied nostalgia to literary works, see Rubenstein, *Home Matters*.

16. For a detailed examination of this condition, see my essay "The Myth of Hidden Ireland."

17. O'Donoghue, "The Mule Duignan," in *Outliving*, 56.

18. An equally eloquent and starkly painful representation of the rancorous world of Irish exiles appears in the 2007 film *Kings*, directed by Tom Collins. It depicts the lives of five Irish laborers twenty years after leaving County Galway to work construction in London. It alternates between recollections of their youth in Ireland and a day spent at the funeral of one of the group, whose suicide sums up the despair evident to greater or lesser degrees in all their lives.

19. See "St. Columba," *Catholic Encyclopedia* online, newadvent.org/cathen/04136a.htm.

20. See Kiernan, *Irish Exiles in Australia*, and Miller, *Emigrants and Exiles*.

21. Donnelly, *The Great Irish Potato Famine*.

22. Arensberg and Kimball explore this phenomenon and other aspects of Ireland's agrarian economy in detail in their definitive work on the topic, *Family and Community in Ireland*. For a useful survey of reactions to the Great Famine by contemporaneous poets (1845–50), see Morash, *The Hungry Voice*.

23. Miller's study of the Irish emigrant experience, *Emigrants and Exiles*, includes reference to the sense of nostalgia mentioned above.

24. In an essay specifically assessing Joyce's attitudes toward exile, Van Mierlo notes Joyce's references to "American Wake" in the early notes for *Finnegans Wake*. See his "Greater Ireland beyond the Sea," 190–91.

25. One finds a good overview of prose works of the period in J. F. Foster's *Fictions of the Irish Literary Revival*. For a broader view of the movement and period, see McMahon's *Grand Opportunity*.

26. The Dun Emer Press was established by Yeats's sister Elizabeth in 1902. For a gloss of the references in this passage, see Gifford, *"Ulysses" Annotated*, 20.

27. John Millington Synge, Joyce's contemporary, had similar experiences. He spent little of his short adult life in Ireland, and his work garnered little praise outside the Irish National Theatre crowd.

Chapter 1. Joyce's Exilic Self-Conception

1. For more detailed evidence of Joyce's sentiments and self-perceptions, see Ellmann, *James Joyce*, 283–318, 333–49, 535, 655–58.

2. See *Letters of James Joyce*. He certainly retained ambivalent feelings for Ireland for much of his life, and he expressed a wide range of feelings throughout his years of correspondence. For example, a 9 December 1912 letter of condolence to his aunt Josephine on the death of her husband, his uncle William Murray, shows a tender recollection of Joyce's family ties (I.72). Another letter to Josephine on 14 October 1921 makes inquiries about various Dublin neighbors—the Powells, the Dillons, Mrs. Gallaher, Mrs. Clinch, and Mrs. Russell—and his father (I.174). In contrast, a letter to his brother Stannie and another to Nora in August 1909 when Joyce was in Dublin struggling to get his short

stories published are full of acrimony (II.238–40). One can continue through all three volumes and find multiple examples of Joyce's alternating feelings.

3. See for example Joyce, *Selected Letters*, 37, 68, 76, 102, 111, 127, 139, 178.

4. Accounts of Joyce's life vary in emphasis, and reflect the particular circumstances from which the particular biography emerged. Nonetheless, they all underscore Joyce's fundamental sense of the need to escape the social, cultural, and familial institutions governing Irish life. Among the earliest studies, Herbert Gorman's *James Joyce: His First Forty Years* and *James Joyce: A Definitive Biography* were shaped by Joyce's direct influence. The two most extensive examinations of Joyce's motives for leaving Ireland remain the Ellmann biography *James Joyce* and Hélène Cixous's *The Exile of James Joyce*. They have been supplemented over the years by a number of important works. See, for example, Bradley, *James Joyce's Schooldays*; Costello, *James Joyce: The Years of Growth*; McCourt, *The Years of Bloom*; and Bowker, *James Joyce: A New Biography*. A selection of shorter studies includes Daiches, "James Joyce: The Artist as Exile"; Engel, "Contrived Lives"; Martin, "Joyce, Wagner, and the Wandering Jew"; Ardizzone, "Self-Imposed Exile in Joyce and Beckett"; Cawelti, "Eliot, Joyce, and Exile"; Guo, "Exile Writer, Intellectualized Aesthetics and Obscure Art"; and Tseng, "Exile, Cunning, Silence." All of these works recognize the momentous impact exerted by exile on Joyce's life and writing, though there is a broad disparity among their views on the specific effects of that experience.

5. See R. F. Foster, *W. B. Yeats: A Life*, vol. 1; Hill, *Lady Gregory*; Rose, *Katharine Tynan*; Eglinton, *A Memoir of AE*.

6. Indeed, the cultural claustrophobia of Dublin impressed upon Joyce the disadvantages of remaining in Ireland well before he left in 1904. Three years previously he had already articulated this view in his article "The Day of the Rabblement." Joyce wrote it to protest the parochialism of the Irish Literary Theatre, and when it was rejected by *St. Stephen's*, a journal published by University College Dublin, he brought it out as a broadside. At one point he observed, admittedly with a tone of melodrama, "A nation which never advanced so far as a miracle-play affords no literary model to the artist, and he must look abroad" (*Critical Writings*, 70). The bitterness he felt over Irish provincialism and the claustrophobic creative atmosphere that the mandarins of Irish intellectual life were enforcing was certainly foremost in Joyce's mind when he composed his satirical poem "The Holy Office" around August 1904 (ibid., 149–52). His sense of the course of action that would be forced upon any individual with independent views by the parochial atmosphere of his native country was still evident in a talk he gave in Trieste on 27 April 1907 titled "Ireland, Island of Saints and Sages" when he noted, "No one who has any self-respect stays in Ireland, but flees afar as though from a country that has undergone the visitation of an angered Jove" (ibid., 171).

7. S. Joyce, *My Brother's Keeper*. See also his *Complete Dublin Diary*.

8. In "James Clarence Mangan" (*Critical Writings*, 175–86), the companion Trieste lecture to the one quoted in note 6, Joyce expands an essay written as a college undergraduate in an examination of the life of the nineteenth-century Irish poet to illustrate the challenges imposed by a circumscribed environment that any Irish artist faced, though the tone is markedly less harsh and pointedly aware of the difficulties that

a colonial environment imposed upon a writer's search for identity. He continues this theme, acknowledging flaws in the Irish character while excoriating the British for their heavy-handed rule, in a series of articles for the Trieste newspaper *Il Piccolo della Sera*—"Fenianism," "Home Rule Comes of Age," "Ireland at the Bar," and "The Shade of Parnell" (ibid., 187–201, 209–13, 223–28).

9. See, for example, two pieces on life in the West of Ireland, "The City of the Tribes" and "The Mirage of the Fisherman of Aran," that appeared in *Il Piccolo della Sera* in 1912 (ibid., 229–37).

10. S. Joyce, *My Brother's Keeper*, 46, 42.

11. See for example his 3 April 1923 letter to his aunt Josephine Murray in *Letters* III.75–76.

12. Quoted in Ardizzone, "Self-Imposed Exile in Joyce and Beckett," 43.

13. For instances of this, see *Letters* I.198, II.153, 157, 472–73, III.75–76.

14. See for example Hélène Cixous's *Exile of James Joyce*. See also Schechner, *Joyce in Nighttown*; Brivic, *Joyce between Freud and Jung*; Benstock, *James Joyce: The Undiscover'd Country*; Kelly, *Our Joyce*; Johnson-Roullier, *Reading on the Edge*.

15. For example, Pinguentini, *James Joyce in Italia*; Staley and Lewis, *Reflections on James Joyce*; McCourt, *The Years of Bloom*.

16. Fairhall, *James Joyce and the Question of History*; Spoo, *James Joyce and the Language of History*.

17. Lloyd, *Anomalous States*; Duffy, *The Subaltern "Ulysses"*; Nolan, *James Joyce and Nationalism*; Cheng, *Joyce, Race, and Empire*; Orr, *Joyce, Imperialism, and Postcolonialism*.

18. In addition to works cited earlier in this study, the references include these memoirs and biographies: Gogarty, *As I Was Going Down Sackville Street*; Byrne, *Silent Years*; Colum and Colum, *Our Friend James Joyce*; Power, *Conversations with James Joyce*; Curran, *James Joyce Remembered*; Budgen, *Myselves When Young*; Beja, *James Joyce: A Literary Life*; Maddox, *Nora*; Jackson and Costello, *John Stanislaus Joyce*; Shloss, *Lucia Joyce*.

19. Power, *From the Old Waterford House*, 63–64.

20. Cheng explores this attitude, albeit from a postcolonial perspective, in the *Dubliners* chapter of *Joyce, Race, and Empire*, 128–47.

21. A study similar to my concerns from the opposite perspective, that of the emergence of "Englishness" in the colonial context, is Baucom's *Out of Place*.

22. See, for example, Levin and Shattuck, "First Flight to Ithaca"; Torchiana, "Joyce's 'Eveline' and the Blessed Margaret Mary Alacoque"; Gabler, "The Seven Lost Years of *A Portrait of the Artist as a Young Man*"; Melchiori, *Joyce in Rome*; Seidel, *Epic Geography*.

23. For further information, see McCourt, *Years of Bloom*, 198–201.

Chapter 2. *Dubliners*: The First Glimpse of Ireland from Abroad

1. See also *Letters* II.48–50, 53–54, and Ellmann, *James Joyce*, 181–85.

2. I began exploring these ideas in 1989 in my *Reading the Book of Himself*. The current study takes those assumptions and focuses them on the exilic experience.

3. I first came across what J. P. Riquelme has felicitously labeled Joyce's oscillating perspectives when I was reading his *Teller and Tale in Joyce's Fiction*. I have used Riquelme's term throughout this study, though I do not claim to apply it in quite the same way

he does. Nonetheless, for me it is a marvelous encapsulation of the rhythm of Joyce's narratives.

4. Ellmann, *James Joyce*, 254.

5. Walzl, "Gabriel and Michael."

6. For a breakdown of this process, see appendix B, "A Chronology of the Initial Composition and Revisions of the Stories of *Dubliners*," in Gillespie, *Reading the Book of Himself*, 216–17.

7. Although he does not emphasize the contrast of rancor and sympathy as I do, Kershner employs a similar dialectic form in his Bakhtinian study of the cultural context from which *Dubliners* emerged in his *Joyce, Bakhtin, and Popular Literature*.

8. Nicholas Fargnoli offers a detailed and erudite explanation of the possible meanings of *epicleti* in Fargnoli and Gillespie's *Critical Companion*, 273. Steppe takes the argument further, asserting that the term derives from a misreading of Joyce's handwriting; see his "Merry Greeks." See also Schork, *Latin and Roman Culture in Joyce*, 6, and Lernout, *Help My Unbelief*, 20.

9. Existing manuscript material for all of the renderings of "The Sisters" prior to its 1914 publication in *Dubliners* has been collected in *Dubliners: A Facsimile of Drafts and Manuscripts*, vol. 4 in the *James Joyce Archive*. As with any interpretation, different readers will find different levels of nostalgia and rancor. What will be evident to anyone surveying these drafts, however, is a marked shift in the temperament of the discourse.

10. Walzl, "Joyce's 'The Sisters.'"

11. Margot Norris offers an excellent survey of the most common responses to "The Sisters" in her *Suspicious Readings*, 16–18. While other critics have offered additional commentary on the story since Walzl's essay appeared, Norris's overview shows that the fundamental interpretive assumption—that the stories represent a harsh critique of the city and its citizens—remains the same.

12. See Morrissey's "Joyce's Revision of 'The Sisters.'"

13. Joyce, "The Sisters," 676.

14. Ibid.

15. That is not to say that the sisters are docile servants. Garry Leonard makes an interesting point, that in Eliza's slips of the tongue—"Freeman's General" for "Freeman's Journal" and "rheumatic wheels" for "pneumatic wheels"—she is offering her own form of resistance to her brother and his punctilious insistence on linguistic accuracy. See *Reading "Dubliners" Again*, 44.

16. Walzl, "Joyce's 'The Sisters,'" 381.

17. Not everyone shares Walzl's certainty about the application of the title. Norris notes other critics, such as Peter Spielberg and Fritz Senn, who remain perplexed by the title; see her *Suspicious Readings*, 23.

18. In *The Years of Bloom* John McCourt argues convincingly that Joyce's living in Trieste produced a transition away from dismissive, even hostile, attitudes toward women. Nicholas Fargnoli, in private correspondence, echoes this view and cites the letter of 6 September 1906 as evidence that the change coincided with Joyce's stay in Rome from 31 July 1906 to 7 March 1907.

19. For the time line of composition and revision, see Gillespie, *Reading the Book of Himself*, 216.

20. For a discussion of the story's anomalous qualities, see Gillespie and Weir, "'After the Race' and the Problem of Belonging."

21. Igoe tells the story in *James Joyce's Dublin Houses*, 3–5. For an account of Joyce's disputes with British consul A. Percy Bennett in World War I Zurich, see Ellmann, 423–40.

22. Some critics have gone so far as to suggest that in "Ivy Day" Joyce was recycling the poem he wrote at age nine. See, for example, Chapman, "Joyce and Yeats."

23. Richard Ellmann's biography as well as passages in the author's letters have led some critics to assume misogyny or, at the very least, a poor understanding of women as an animating feature of both Joyce's life and his works. A number of critics have defended Joyce's attitudes toward women. See, for example, Adams, *James Joyce: Common Sense and Beyond*; O'Brien, "Some Determinants of Molly Bloom"; Heilbrun, afterword to *Women in Joyce*; Keane, *Terrible Beauty*. A number of other critical studies have sought to refute these views. See Henke and Unkeless, *Women in Joyce*; Brown, *James Joyce and Sexuality*; Restuccia, *Joyce and the Law of the Father*; Henke, *James Joyce and the Politics of Desire*. Perhaps the most balanced view of both sides comes from Norris, *Joyce's Web*.

24. Shortly after the Watergate scandal, the columnist Jimmy Breslin spoke of the innate differences between the disgraced president, Richard Nixon, and the Democratic Speaker of the House of Representatives, Tip O'Neill. Breslin made no distinction between the morality of the political actions of the two men, but he noted that the Quaker faith in which Nixon was raised had no mechanism for forgiveness, while O'Neill's Catholicism had the sacrament of Confession. For Nixon this meant that any fall was permanent and irreversible, while for O'Neill anything could be forgiven and a fresh start enjoyed.

Chapter 3. Stephen Dedalus's Lifelong Exile

1. Along these lines, Gregory Castle offers an extended look at the formation of Stephen's point of view from a more individualized perspective than that followed in my analytical approach. Castle, in a traditional and meticulously argued assessment, traces the bildungsroman impulse as it reacts to modernist issues. See his "Coming of Age in the Age of Empire," also incorporated into his longer work *Reading the Modernist Bildungsroman*.

2. As noted throughout this chapter, Stephen's nature has been examined from a range of perspectives, and the exilic point of view is only the latest. Perhaps the most insightful extended assessment of Stephen is Edmund L. Epstein's *Ordeal of Stephen Dedalus*.

3. Gorman reiterated this theme in his expanded biography, *James Joyce*, published seventeen years later.

4. See, for example, Bettelheim, *The Uses of Enchantment*, and Zipes, *Breaking the Magic Spell* and *Happily Ever After*.

5. That position is implicit in most of Hugh Kenner's writing on Joyce, and it serves as the anchoring thesis of his book-length study of Joyce's second novel, *Ulysses*.

6. The words baby tuckoo sings are a variation of the chorus of "Lilly Dale," a popular

song by the nineteenth-century American songwriter H. S. Thompson about a dying girl, often performed in blackface minstrel shows. It is every bit as grim as "The Lass of Aughrim" referenced in "The Dead," but here it undergoes an interesting modification. The transcription has changed the line "o'er her little green grave" in the original to the more nostalgic "On the little green place."

7. Gillespie, *Reading the Book of Himself*, 67–84.

8. One finds a very detailed schematic breakdown of *Portrait* in John Paul Riquelme's *Teller and Tale in Joyce's Fiction*, 232–34. Although I do not take quite the same approach to the structure of the narrative, Riquelme's term "oscillating perspectives" evokes the image of the discursive rhythms of Joyce's novel.

9. For a thumbnail sketch of the concepts of nonlinearity, see the appendix, "The Rise of Nonlinear Science," in Gillespie, *The Aesthetics of Chaos*, 113–17.

10. Sheldon Brivic has also examined Stephen's perception of the world, though he takes a very different point of view. See his "Stephen Dedalus's Fantasies of Reality."

11. The uniqueness of the nostalgia and rancor that grow out of the exilic condition as opposed simply to feelings of homesickness is the distinction already emphasized in this study's introduction in reference to the work of Svetlana Boym.

12. One finds one of the most careful overviews of this crucial passage in an essay by Hans Walter Gabler, "The Christmas Dinner Scene." Gabler's assessment lays out the key features of the passage and allows subsequent readings, like this one, to build on his delineation of the fundamental structure.

13. The classic essay on Joyce's use, and modification, of the standard Catholic retreat is Thrane's "Joyce's Sermon on Hell."

14. Kenner, *Dublin's Joyce*, 127.

15. For an alternative view on the concept of forging and on Stephen's perceptions from a Dickensian point of view, see Osteen, "The Great Expectations of Stephen Dedalus."

Chapter 4. Re-Viewing Richard: Nostalgia and Rancor in *Exiles*

1. James W. Douglass's relatively early response to the play catches the discomfort felt by many critics in reconciling it with Joyce's other works. See "James Joyce's *Exiles*." Fifteen years later, in *Joyce's Voices*, Hugh Kenner saw it as farce slipping into a "strenuous drama of ideals" (25).

2. MacNicholas, "The Stage History of *Exiles*," 9.

3. Ibid., 23. MacNicholas has made other important contributions to understanding the play. See in particular his "Joyce's *Exiles*," "James Joyce's *Exiles* and the Incorporated Stage Society," and *James Joyce's "Exiles": A Textual Companion*.

4. Shepherd-Barr, "Reconsidering Joyce's *Exiles* in Its Theatrical Context."

5. Hickman, "'Not . . . love verses at all, I perceive': Joyce's Minor Works," 87–88.

6. Barthes, "Death of the Author," 146–47.

7. For example, Rabaté, "The Modernity of *Exiles*"; Ragland-Sullivan, "Psychosis Adumbrated"; Sanner, "Exchanging Letters and Silence."

8. Mahaffey, "Love, Race, and *Exiles*."

9. De Marco, *Early Joyce and the Writing of "Exiles,"* 13–14.

10. One finds examples of this approach in Bowen, "*Exiles*: The Confessional Mode"; S. Pearce, "'Like a Stone'"; and Kershner, "Playing for Keeps."

11. Emphasis on the exilic condition gives further significance to Richard's surname. By having Richard deny any relation to the Irish patriot Archibald Hamilton Rowan (*E* 45), Joyce calls the exile experience into the audience's mind. Hamilton Rowan is mentioned in *Portrait* as having stayed at Clongowes Woods Castle while fleeing English authorities on his way to France (*P* 8). His peripatetic life was marked by enforced absences from Ireland and frequent public and private expressions of a deep love for his country. The name Joyce chose for his exile, while it certainly leaves open the possibility of an ironic reading, raises again the concept of nostalgia having an equal pull with rancor. Along these lines, Joyce uses Buck Mulligan skillfully to call attention to the irony of Stephen's surname: "The mockery of it. . . . Your absurd name! An ancient Greek" (*U* I.33).

12. See Ellmann, *James Joyce*, 70.

13. Ellmann claims that Joyce drew this account from the death of his grandfather (*James Joyce*, 14).

14. One finds a good account of Joyce's father in Jackson and Costello's biography *John Stanislaus Joyce*.

15. It is tempting to ask: What was the need for the inversion of parental roles? Why not simply present fictionalized versions of the sympathetic Mary Joyce and the intolerant John Joyce like the ones found in *Portrait*? The most satisfying explanation comes from the title of the play. Joyce's love for Dante Alighieri gave him a keen sense of the tradition of exile and of its consequences. The sympathy of Mary Joyce and the antagonism of his father were predictable reactions that one might expect in any family. By inverting them, the exilic experience is made more unique and more privileged.

16. Burgin, "Paranoiac Space," 29.

17. Although I do not examine her role in detail here, Bertha plays an important part in the dramatic development of the play. For a more focused discussion of her, and one with a markedly different emphasis, see Brivic's "Structure and Meaning in Joyce's *Exiles*." See also Loughman's "Bertha, Victress, in Joyce's *Exiles*."

18. Of course, the possible irony of the phrase comparing Richard Rowan to Jonathan Swift remains, but a sense of Richard's ambivalent feelings expands possibilities for interpretation. While Swift certainly had a harsh view of Irish excesses, immortalized in his representations of the Yahoos, his courageous defense of the Irish economy in "The Drapier's Letters" and his attack on imperialist exploitation in "A Modest Proposal" showed a profound attachment to that country.

Chapter 5. *Ulysses*: Exiles on Main Street

1. I use the slash here not out of coyness but rather from the conviction that *Ulysses* proves equally amenable to modernist or postmodernist interpretive perspectives. One might make the same argument for *A Portrait of the Artist as a Young Man*.

2. For an extremely detailed and lucid overview of the process, see Bradbury and McFarlane, *Modernism*.

3. Beebe provides a very useful delineation of the traditional view of the relation of *Ulysses* to modernism in his "*Ulysses* and the Age of Modernism." Even after four decades, it remains a good starting point for anyone attempting to get a sense of the context from which Joyce's novel emerged.

4. See Huesel, "Parallax as a Metaphor for the Structure of *Ulysses*."

5. For an alternative perspective on how social, cultural, and political context shapes both the composition and the comprehension of *Ulysses*, see Enda Duffy's *The Subaltern "Ulysses."*

6. I use the term *sous rature* in the sense made popular by Jacques Derrida, borrowing from Martin Heidegger, in *Of Grammatology*.

7. I discuss this idea in greater detail in *Reading the Book of Himself*, 173–99.

8. May Dedalus is quoting a line from Yeats's "Who Goes with Fergus?" Bloom will hear Stephen reciting verses from that poem at the end of the Circe chapter, though he will misidentify them as a reference to a "Miss Ferguson."

9. A floor plan of the house, giving a clear sense of its physical disposition, appears in Gunn and Hart's *James Joyce's Dublin*.

10. See also Gibson, "'An aberration of the light of reason.'"

11. See Herring, "The Bedsteadfastness of Molly Bloom" and "Toward an Historical Molly Bloom." Herring attempts to give a greater context to Molly and her background by taking an expanded look at Molly's life in Gibraltar.

12. For a good summary of the range of perspectives that readers have taken with Molly, see R. Pearce, *Molly Blooms*.

13. A number of critics have examined the complexities of Molly's attitude toward Boylan and toward her infidelity. Heather Cook Callow offers a summary of views from Richard Ellmann, Stanley Sultan, Robert Adams, David Hayman, and others in her "'Marion of the Bountiful Bosoms.'" See also Kenner's idiosyncratic but engaging argument in "Molly's Masterstroke," which, together with the numerous responses to Kenner, itself produced a subcategory of Joyce criticism.

Chapter 6. *Finnegans Wake* and the Exile's Return

1. See McCarthy, Beja, and Seesholtz, "Joyce and the Phoenix Park Murders," 81.

2. For a detailed study of its development in Joyce's composition process, see Van Hulle's "Hesitancy in Joyce's and Beckett's Manuscripts."

3. One finds excellent examples of efforts to grasp the text's referentiality in works like Adaline Glasheen's *Third Census of "Finnegans Wake"* and Roland McHugh's *Annotations to "Finnegans Wake."* These critics and authors of similar works themselves acknowledge that they offer only one level of understanding, and even that remains speculative.

4. Associative habits of comprehension stand as such integral features of the interpretive process that we give them little conscious thought. Nonetheless, we engage in countless forms of categorization—genres of writing, types of fictional styles, works appealing to particular groups, and many more types of associations—all in efforts to facilitate understanding. We read by comparison.

5. Ezra Pound, the poster boy for avant-garde writing that thrived upon the impulse to shock the petit bourgeois, and a strong and loyal supporter of Joyce's work, nevertheless found the close of the Calypso passage in *Ulysses* particularly disturbing:

> [Bloom] kicked open the crazy door of the jakes. Better be careful not to get these trousers dirty for the funeral. He went in, bowing his head under the low lintel. Leaving the door ajar, amid the stench of mouldy limewash and stale cobwebs he undid his braces.
>
> Asquat on the cuckstool he folded out his paper, turning its pages over on his bared knees. Something new and easy. No great hurry. Keep it a bit.
>
> Quietly he read, restraining himself, the first column and, yielding but resisting, began the second. Midway, his last resistance yielding, he allowed his bowels to ease themselves quietly as he read, reading still patiently that slight constipation of yesterday quite gone. Hope it's not too big bring on piles again. No, just right. So. Ah!
>
> He tore away half the prize story sharply and wiped himself with it. Then he girded up his trousers, braced and buttoned himself. He pulled back the jerky shaky door of the jakes and came forth from the gloom into the air. (*U* 4.494–541)

After reading an early version of that chapter, the usually flamboyant Pound warned Joyce in a 7 June 1918 letter (*Pound/Joyce*, 131) that such an explicit description had gone too far:

> Section 4 [the Calypso episode] has excellent things in it; but you overdo the matter. Leave the stool to Geo. Robey [a popular English music hall comedian]. He has been doing "down where the asparagus grows" for some time.
>
> I think certain things simply bad writing, in this section. Bad because you waste the violence. You use a stronger word than you need, and this is bad art, just as any needless superlative is bad art.

6. See, for example, a 22 October 1925 letter from Joyce to Harriet Shaw Weaver describing various reactions of friends and family (*Letters* I.235) and a 15 November 1926 letter to Joyce from Ezra Pound (*Letters* III.145–46) suggesting that both the writing and the reading of the work were a waste of time.

7. Joyce may have been responding to this criticism when he has Shaun claim that Shem planned to "wipe alley english spooker, multaphoniaksically spuking, off the face of the erse" (*FW* 178.6–7).

8. Wilson, "The Dream of H. C. Earwicker."

9. Campbell and Robinson, *A Skeleton Key to "Finnegans Wake."*

10. Hart, *Structure and Motif in "Finnegans Wake,"* 82–83.

11. Bishop, *Joyce's Book of the Dark*, 6.

12. Benstock, *James Joyce*; Parrinder, *James Joyce*.

13. Attridge, "*Finnegans Wake*: The Dream of Interpretation."

14. See, for example, Bishop, *Joyce's Book of the Dark*; Gordon, "*Finnegans Wake*": *A Plot Summary*; Begnal, *Dreamscheme*.

15. For an overview of this debate, see Fargnoli and Gillespie, *Critical Companion*, 91.

16. The applicability of turbulence, particularly in nonlinear terms, stands as an important issue in its own right, and several Joyce critics have turned to physics for metaphors for interpretation. For a more detailed examination of its applicability to Joyce, see Rice's *Joyce, Chaos, and Complexity* and Mackey's *Chaos Theory and James Joyce's Everyman*.

17. For an overview of some of the allusions incorporated in HCE's monogram, see Benstock's "Here Comes Everybody—Including Lyonel the Second."

18. For a detailed examination of the entire chapter, albeit from a very different and much more linear perspective, see my "An Inquisition of Chapter Seven of *Finnegans Wake*."

19. Van Mierlo and Landuyt, "Catholicism, Nationalism, and Exile."

20. This is only one of many references to aspects of sleep—falling asleep, being asleep, or waking from sleep. While it is not impossible to dream of sleeping, its unlikeliness further undermines, for me, the dream as a structuring device for *Finnegans Wake*.

21. Joyce discussed this chapter with Harriet Shaw Weaver in June 1924 and August 1928. See *Letters* I.216, 263–64.

22. Glasheen, *Third Census of "Finnegans Wake,"* 206.

Bibliography

Adams, Robert M. *James Joyce: Common Sense and Beyond.* New York: Random House, 1966.

Anderson, Benedict. *Imagined Communities: Reflections on the Origin and Spread of Nationalism.* Rev. ed. London: Verso, 1991.

Ardizzone, Patrizia. "Self-Imposed Exile in Joyce and Beckett." *Textus* 10 (1997): 41–58.

Arensberg, Conrad M., and Solon T. Kimball. *Family and Community in Ireland.* 2nd ed. Cambridge, Mass.: Harvard University Press, 1968.

Attridge, Derek. "*Finnegans Wake*: The Dream of Interpretation." *James Joyce Quarterly* 27 (1989): 11–29.

Barthes, Roland. "The Death of the Author." In *Image-Music-Text*, 142–48. Translated by Stephen Heath. New York: Hill and Wang, 1977.

Baucom, Ian. *Out of Place: Englishness, Empire, and the Locations of Identity.* Princeton, N.J.: Princeton University Press, 1999.

Beckett, Samuel. *Waiting for Godot.* New York: Grove, 1954.

Beebe, Maurice. "*Ulysses* and the Age of Modernism." *James Joyce Quarterly* 10 (Fall 1972): 172–88.

Begnal, Michael H. *Dreamscheme: Narrative and Voice in "Finnegans Wake."* Syracuse, N.Y.: Syracuse University Press, 1988.

Beja, Morris. *James Joyce: A Literary Life.* Columbus: Ohio State University Press, 1992.

Benstock, Bernard. "Here Comes Everybody—Including Lyonel the Second." *James Joyce Quarterly* 21 (Summer 1984): 370–71.

———. *James Joyce.* New York: Frederick Ungar, 1985.

———. *James Joyce: The Undiscover'd Country.* New York: Barnes and Noble, 1977.

Bettelheim, Bruno. *The Uses of Enchantment: The Meaning and Importance of Fairy Tales.* New York: Knopf, 1976.

Bhabha, Homi K., ed. *Nation and Narration.* New York: Routledge and Kegan Paul, 1990.

Billig, Michael. *Banal Nationalism.* London: Sage, 1995.

Bishop, John. *Joyce's Book of the Dark: "Finnegans Wake."* Madison: University of Wisconsin Press, 1986.

Bowen, Zack. "*Exiles*: The Confessional Mode." *James Joyce Quarterly* 29 (Spring 1992): 581–86.

Bowker, Gordon. *James Joyce: A New Biography.* New York: Farrar, Straus and Giroux, 2012.

Boyle, Robert. *James Joyce's Pauline Vision: A Catholic Exposition.* Carbondale: Southern Illinois University Press, 1978.

Boym, Svetlana. *The Future of Nostalgia.* New York: Basic Books, 2001.

Bradbury, Malcolm, and James McFarlane, eds. *Modernism: A Guide to European Literature, 1890–1930.* London: Penguin, 1978.

Bradley, Bruce. *James Joyce's Schooldays.* New York: St. Martin's, 1982.

Brivic, Sheldon. *Joyce between Freud and Jung.* Port Washington, N.Y.: Kennikat Press, 1980.

———. "Stephen Dedalus's Fantasies of Reality: A Žižekian View." *James Joyce Quarterly* 41 (Fall 2003/Winter 2004): 69–78.

———. "Structure and Meaning in Joyce's *Exiles*." *James Joyce Quarterly* 6 (Fall 1968): 29–52.

Brown, Richard. *James Joyce and Sexuality.* Cambridge: Cambridge University Press, 1985.

Budgen, Frank. *Myselves When Young.* Oxford: Oxford University Press, 1970.

Burgin, Victor. "Paranoiac Space." *Visual Anthropology Review* 7 (1991): 22–30.

Byrne, J. F. *Silent Years: An Autobiography with Memoirs of James Joyce and Our Ireland.* New York: Farrar, Straus and Young, 1953.

Callow, Heather Cook. "'Marion of the Bountiful Bosoms': Molly Bloom and the Nightmare of History." *Twentieth Century Literature* 36 (Winter 1990): 464–76.

Campbell, Joseph, and Henry Morton Robinson. *A Skeleton Key to "Finnegans Wake."* New York: Harcourt, Brace, 1944.

Casey, Edward S. "The World of Nostalgia." *Man and World* 20 (1987): 361–84.

Castle, Gregory. "Coming of Age in the Age of Empire: Joyce's Modernist *Bildungsroman*." *James Joyce Quarterly* 40 (Summer 2003): 665–94.

———. *Reading the Modernist Bildungsroman.* Gainesville: University Press of Florida, 2006.

Cawelti, John G. "Eliot, Joyce, and Exile." *ANQ* 14 (2001): 38–45.

Chapman, Wayne K. "Joyce and Yeats: Easter 1916 and the Great War." *New Hibernia Review* 10 (Winter 2006): 137–51.

Cheng, Vincent J. *Joyce, Race, and Empire.* Cambridge: Cambridge University Press, 1995.

Cixous, Hélène. *The Exile of James Joyce.* Translated by Sally A. J. Purcell. New York: David Lewis, 1972.

Colley, Ann C. *Nostalgia and Recollection in Victorian Culture.* New York: St. Martin's, 1998.

Colum, Mary, and Padraic Colum. *Our Friend James Joyce.* Garden City, N.Y.: Doubleday, 1958.

Costello, Peter. *James Joyce: The Years of Growth, 1882–1915.* New York: Pantheon, 1992.

Curran, C. P. *James Joyce Remembered.* Oxford: Oxford University Press, 1968.

Daiches, David. "James Joyce: The Artist as Exile." *College English* 2 (December 1940): 197–206.

De Marco, Nicola. *The Early Joyce and the Writing of "Exiles."* Rome: Aracne, 2008.

Derrida, Jacques. *Of Grammatology.* Translated by Gayatri Chakravorty Spivak. Baltimore: Johns Hopkins University Press, 1976.

Donnelly, James S., Jr. *The Great Irish Potato Famine*. Charleston, S.C.: History Press, 2008.

Douglass, James W. "James Joyce's *Exiles*: A Portrait of the Artist." *Renascence* 15 (1963): 82–87.

Duffy, Enda. *The Subaltern "Ulysses."* Minneapolis: University of Minnesota Press, 1994.

Eglinton, John [William Kirkpatrick Magee]. *A Memoir of AE (George William Russell)*. London: Macmillan, 1937.

Ellmann, Richard. *James Joyce*. Rev. ed. New York: Oxford University Press, 1982.

Engel, Monroe. "Contrived Lives: Joyce and Lawrence." In Kiely and Hildebidle, *Modernism Reconsidered*, 65–80.

Epstein, Edmund L. *The Ordeal of Stephen Dedalus: The Conflict of Generations in James Joyce's "A Portrait of the Artist as a Young Man."* Carbondale: Southern Illinois University Press, 1971.

Fairhall, James. *James Joyce and the Question of History*. Cambridge: Cambridge University Press, 1993.

Fargnoli, A. Nicholas, and Michael Patrick Gillespie. *Critical Companion to James Joyce*. New York: Checkmark, 2006.

Foster, John Wilson. *Fictions of the Irish Literary Revival*. Syracuse, N.Y.: Syracuse University Press, 1987.

Foster, R. F. *W. B. Yeats: A Life*. Vol. 1, *The Apprentice Mage*. New York: Oxford University Press, 1997.

Gabler, Hans Walter. "The Christmas Dinner Scene, Parnell's Death, and the Genesis of *A Portrait of the Artist as a Young Man*." *James Joyce Quarterly* 13 (Fall 1975): 27–38.

———. "The Seven Lost Years of *A Portrait of the Artist as a Young Man*." In *Approaches to Joyce's "Portrait": Ten Essays*, edited by Thomas F. Staley and Bernard Benstock, 25–60. Pittsburgh, Pa.: University of Pittsburgh Press, 1976.

Gellner, Ernest. *Nations and Nationalism*. Oxford: Blackwell, 1983.

Gibson, Andrew. "'An aberration of the light of reason': Science and Cultural Politics in 'Ithaca.'" *European Joyce Studies* 6 (1996): 133–74.

Gifford, Don. *"Ulysses" Annotated: Notes for James Joyce's "Ulysses."* With Robert J. Seidman. 2nd ed. Berkeley: University of California Press, 1988.

Gillespie, Michael Patrick. *The Aesthetics of Chaos: Nonlinear Thinking and Contemporary Literary Criticism*. Gainesville: University Press of Florida, 2003.

———. "An Inquisition of Chapter Seven of *Finnegans Wake*." *Renascence* 35 (Winter 1983): 138–51.

———. "The Myth of Hidden Ireland: The Corrosive Effect of Place in *The Quiet Man*." *New Hibernia Review* 6 (Summer 2002): 18–32.

———. *Reading the Book of Himself: Narrative Strategies in the Works of James Joyce*. Columbus: Ohio State University Press, 1989.

Gillespie, Michael Patrick, and David Weir. "'After the Race' and the Problem of Belonging." In *Collaborative "Dubliners": Joyce in Dialogue*, edited by Vicki Mahaffey, 108–24. Syracuse, N.Y.: Syracuse University Press, 2012.

Glasheen, Adaline. *Third Census of "Finnegans Wake": An Index of the Characters and Their Roles*. Berkeley: University of California Press, 1977.

Gogarty, Oliver St. John. *As I Was Going Down Sackville Street*. London: Rich and Cowan, 1937.

Gordon, John. *Finnegans Wake: A Plot Summary*. Syracuse, N.Y.: Syracuse University Press, 1986.

Gorman, Herbert S. *James Joyce: A Definitive Biography*. London: John Lane, 1941.

———. *James Joyce: His First Forty Years*. New York: B. W. Huebsch, 1924.

Gunn, Ian, and Clive Hart. *James Joyce's Dublin: A Topographical Guide to the Dublin of "Ulysses."* London: Thames and Hudson, 2004.

Guo, Jun. "Exile Writer, Intellectualized Aesthetics and Obscure Art: Interpreting James Joyce and His Artistic Aspiration." *James Joyce Journal* 14 (Winter 2008): 117–32.

Hart, Clive. *Structure and Motif in "Finnegans Wake."* London: Faber and Faber, 1962.

Heilbrun, Carolyn G. Afterword to Henke and Unkeless, *Women in Joyce*, 215–16.

Henke, Suzette A. *James Joyce and the Politics of Desire*. New York: Routledge, 1990.

Henke, Suzette, and Elaine Unkeless, eds. *Women in Joyce*. Urbana: University of Illinois Press, 1982.

Herring, Phillip F. "The Bedsteadfastness of Molly Bloom." *Modern Fiction Studies* 15 (1969): 49–61.

———. "Toward an Historical Molly Bloom." *English Literary History* 45 (1978): 501–21.

Hickman, Miranda. "'Not . . . love verses at all, I perceive': Joyce's Minor Works." In *James Joyce*, edited by Sean Latham, 83–104. Dublin: Irish Academic Press, 2009.

Hill, Judith. *Lady Gregory: An Irish Life*. Wilton, Cork: Collins, 2011.

Huesel, Barbara Stevens. "Parallax as a Metaphor for the Structure of *Ulysses*." *Studies in the Novel* 15 (Summer 1983): 135–46.

Igoe, Vivian. *James Joyce's Dublin Houses and Nora Barnacle's Galway*. London: Mandarin, 1990.

Jackson, John Wyse, and Peter Costello. *John Stanislaus Joyce*. New York: St. Martin's, 1997.

Johnson-Roullier, Cyraina E. *Reading on the Edge: Exiles, Modernities, and Cultural Transformation in Proust, Joyce, and Baldwin*. Albany: State University of New York Press, 2000.

Joyce, James. *The Critical Writings of James Joyce*. Edited by Ellsworth Mason and Richard Ellmann. New York: Viking, 1959.

———. *Dubliners*. Edited by Margot Norris. New York: W. W. Norton, 2006.

———. *Exiles*. New York: Penguin, 1973.

———. *Finnegans Wake*. New York: Viking, 1939.

———. *Giacomo Joyce*. Edited by Richard Ellmann. New York: Viking, 1968.

———. *The James Joyce Archive*. 63 vols. General editor, Michael Groden. New York: Garland, 1978.

———. *Letters of James Joyce*. Vol. I, edited by Stuart Gilbert; vols. II and III, edited by Richard Ellmann. New York: Viking, 1957–66.

———. *A Portrait of the Artist as a Young Man*. Edited by John Paul Riquelme. New York: W. W. Norton, 2007.

———. *Selected Letters of James Joyce*. Edited by Richard Ellmann. New York: Viking, 1975.

———. "The Sisters." *Irish Homestead*, 13 August 1904, 676–77.

———. *Stephen Hero*. Edited by Theodore Spencer, with additional pages edited by John J. Slocum and Herbert Cahoon. New York: New Directions, 1963.

———. *Ulysses*. Edited by Hans Walter Gabler. New York: Random House, 1986.

Joyce, Stanislaus. *The Complete Dublin Diary of Stanislaus Joyce*. Ithaca, N.Y.: Cornell University Press, 1971.

———. *My Brother's Keeper: James Joyce's Early Years*. Edited by Richard Ellmann. New York: Viking, 1958.

Kain, Richard M. *Fabulous Voyager: A Study of James Joyce's "Ulysses."* New York: Viking, 1947.

Keane, Patrick J. *Terrible Beauty: Yeats, Joyce, Ireland, and the Myth of the Devouring Female*. Columbia: University of Missouri Press, 1988.

Kelly, Joseph. *Our Joyce: From Outcast to Icon*. Austin: University of Texas Press, 1998.

Kenner, Hugh. *Dublin's Joyce*. Bloomington: Indiana University Press, 1956.

———. *Joyce's Voices*. Berkeley: University of California Press, 1978.

———. "Molly's Masterstroke." *James Joyce Quarterly* 10 (Fall 1972): 19–28.

———. *Ulysses*. Rev. ed. Baltimore: Johns Hopkins University Press, 1987.

Kershner, R. B. *Joyce, Bakhtin, and Popular Literature*. Chapel Hill: University of North Carolina Press, 1989.

———. "Playing for Keeps: *Exiles* and University College Dublin." *European Joyce Studies* 15 (2003): 137–49.

Kiely, Robert, and John Hildebidle, eds. *Modernism Reconsidered*. Cambridge, Mass.: Harvard University Press, 1983.

Kiernan, T. J. *The Irish Exiles in Australia*. Melbourne: Burns and Oates, 1954.

Kurzke, Hermann. *Thomas Mann: Life as a Work of Art*. Translated by Leslie Wilson. Princeton, N.J.: Princeton University Press, 2002.

Leonard, Garry M. *Reading "Dubliners" Again: A Lacanian Perspective*. Syracuse, N.Y.: Syracuse University Press, 1993.

Lernout, Geert. *Help My Unbelief: James Joyce and Religion*. London: Continuum, 2010.

Levin, Richard, and Charles Shattuck. "First Flight to Ithaca: A New Reading of Joyce's *Dubliners*." *Accent* 4 (Winter 1944): 75–99.

Lloyd, David. *Anomalous States: Irish Writing and the Post-Colonial Moment*. Dublin: Lilliput, 1993.

Loughman, Celeste. "Bertha, Victress, in Joyce's *Exiles*." *James Joyce Quarterly* 19 (Fall 1981): 69–72.

Mackey, Peter Francis. *Chaos Theory and James Joyce's Everyman*. Gainesville: University Press of Florida, 1999.

MacNicholas, John. "James Joyce's *Exiles* and the Incorporated Stage Society." *ICarbS* 4 (1978): 11–16.

———. *James Joyce's "Exiles": A Textual Companion*. New York: Garland, 1979.

———. "Joyce's *Exiles*: The Argument for Doubt." *James Joyce Quarterly* 11 (Fall 1973): 33–40.

———. "The Stage History of *Exiles*." *James Joyce Quarterly* 19 (Fall 1981): 9–26.

Maddox, Brenda. *Nora: A Biography of Nora Joyce*. New York: Ballantine, 1989.

Mahaffey, Vicki. "Love, Race, and *Exiles*: The Bleak Side of *Ulysses*." *Joyce Studies Annual* (2007): 92–108.

Martin, Timothy P. "Joyce, Wagner, and the Wandering Jew." *Comparative Literature* 42 (Winter 1990): 49–72.

McCarthy, Patrick A., Morris Beja, and Mel Seesholtz. "Joyce and the Phoenix Park Murders: A Forum." *Irish Renaissance Annual* 4 (1983): 76–84.

McCormack, Jerusha, ed. *Wilde the Irishman*. New Haven, Conn.: Yale University Press, 1998.

McCourt, John. *The Years of Bloom: James Joyce in Trieste, 1904–1920*. Madison: University of Wisconsin Press, 2000.

McHugh, Roland. *Annotations to "Finnegans Wake."* 3rd ed. Baltimore: Johns Hopkins University Press, 2006.

McMahon, Timothy G. *Grand Opportunity: The Gaelic Revival and Irish Society: 1893–1920*. Syracuse, N.Y.: Syracuse University Press, 2008.

Melchiori, Giorgio, ed. *Joyce in Rome: The Genesis of "Ulysses."* Rome: Bulzoni, 1984.

Milbauer, Asher Z. *Transcending Exile: Conrad, Nabokov, I. B. Singer*. Miami: Florida International University Press, 1985.

Miller, Kerby A. *Emigrants and Exiles: Ireland and the Irish Exodus to North America*. New York: Oxford University Press, 1985.

Morash, Christopher, ed. *The Hungry Voice: The Poetry of the Irish Famine*. 2nd ed. Dublin: Irish Academic Press, 2009.

Morrissey, L. J. "Joyce's Revision of 'The Sisters': From Epicleti to Modern Fiction." *James Joyce Quarterly* 24 (Fall 1986): 33–54.

Nolan, Emer. *James Joyce and Nationalism*. London: Routledge, 1994.

Norris, Margot. *Joyce's Web: The Social Unraveling of Modernism*. Austin: University of Texas Press, 1992.

———. *Suspicious Readings of Joyce's "Dubliners."* Philadelphia: University of Pennsylvania Press, 2003

O'Brien, Darcy. "Some Determinants of Molly Bloom." In *Approaches to "Ulysses": Ten Essays*, edited by Thomas F. Staley and Bernard Benstock, 137–55. Pittsburgh, Pa.: University of Pittsburgh Press, 1970.

O'Donoghue, Bernard. *Outliving*. London: Chatto and Windus, 2003.

Orr, Leonard, ed. *Joyce, Imperialism, and Postcolonialism*. Syracuse, N.Y.: Syracuse University Press, 2008.

Osteen, Mark. "The Great Expectations of Stephen Dedalus." *James Joyce Quarterly* 41 (Fall 2003/Winter 2004): 169–84.

Parrinder, Patrick. *James Joyce*. Cambridge: Cambridge University Press, 1984.

Pearce, Richard, ed. *Molly Blooms: A Polylogue on "Penelope" and Cultural Studies*. Madison: University of Wisconsin Press, 1994.

Pearce, Sandra Manoogian. "'Like a Stone': Joyce's Eucharistic Imagery in *Exiles*." *James Joyce Quarterly* 29 (Spring 1992): 587–91.

Pinguentini, Gianni. *James Joyce in Italia*. Verona: Ghidini e Fiorini, 1966.

Pound, Ezra. *Pound/Joyce: The Letters of Ezra Pound to James Joyce, with Pound's Essays on Joyce*. Edited by Forrest Read. New York: New Directions, 1967.

Power, Arthur. *Conversations with James Joyce*. Edited by Clive Hart. New York: Barnes and Noble, 1974.

———. *From the Old Waterford House: Recollections of a Soldier and Artist*. 1944. Waterford: Ballylough, 2003.

Rabaté, Jean-Michel. "The Modernity of *Exiles*." *European Joyce Studies* 1 (1989): 22–39.

Ragland-Sullivan, Ellie. "Psychosis Adumbrated: Lacan and Sublimation of the Sexual Divide in Joyce's *Exiles*." *James Joyce Quarterly* 29 (Fall 1991): 47–62.

Restuccia, Frances L. *Joyce and the Law of the Father*. New Haven, Conn.: Yale University Press, 1989.

Rice, Thomas Jackson. *Joyce, Chaos, and Complexity*. Urbana: University of Illinois Press, 1997.

Riquelme, John Paul. *Teller and Tale in Joyce's Fiction: Oscillating Perspectives*. Baltimore: Johns Hopkins University Press, 1983.

Robinson, Marc, ed. *Altogether Elsewhere: Writers on Exile*. London: Faber and Faber, 1994.

Rose, Marilyn Gaddis. *Katharine Tynan*. Cranbury, N.J.: Associated University Presses, 1974.

Rubenstein, Roberta. *Home Matters: Longing and Belonging, Nostalgia and Mourning in Women's Fiction*. New York: Palgrave, 2001.

Said, Edward W. *Joseph Conrad and the Fiction of Autobiography*. Cambridge, Mass.: Harvard University Press, 1966.

———. "The Mind of Winter: Reflections on Life in Exile." *Harper's*, September 1984, 49–55.

———. *Orientalism*. New York: Pantheon, 1978.

———. "Reflections on Exile." In Robinson, *Altogether Elsewhere*, 137–49.

Sanner, Kristin N. "Exchanging Letters and Silence: Moments of Empowerment in *Exiles*." *James Joyce Quarterly* 39 (Winter 2002): 275–88.

Schechner, Mark. *Joyce in Nighttown: A Psychoanalytic Inquiry into "Ulysses."* Berkeley: University of California Press, 1974.

Schork, R. J. *Latin and Roman Culture in Joyce*. Gainesville: University Press of Florida, 1997.

Seidel, Michael. *Epic Geography: James Joyce's "Ulysses."* Princeton, N.J.: Princeton University Press, 1976.

Shepherd-Barr, Kirsten. "Reconsidering Joyce's *Exiles* in Its Theatrical Context." *Theatre Research International* 28 (2003): 169–80.

Shloss, Carol Loeb. *Lucia Joyce: To Dance in the Wake*. New York: Farrar, Straus and Giroux, 2003.

Smith, Anthony D. *The Ethnic Origins of Nations*. Oxford: Basil Blackwell, 1986.

Spoo, Robert. *James Joyce and the Language of History: Dedalus's Nightmare*. Oxford: Oxford University Press, 1994.

Staley, Thomas F., and Randolph Lewis, eds. *Reflections on James Joyce: Stuart Gilbert's Paris Journal*. Austin: University of Texas Press, 1993.

Starobinski, Jean. "The Idea of Nostalgia." Translated by William S. Kemp. *Diogenes* 54 (1966): 81–103.

Steppe, Wolfhard. "The Merry Greeks (With a Farewell to *epicleti*)." *James Joyce Quarterly* 32 (Spring/Summer 1995): 597–617.

Thrane, James R. "Joyce's Sermon on Hell: Its Source and Its Backgrounds." *Modern Philology* 57 (February 1960): 172–98.

Torchiana, Donald T. "Joyce's 'Eveline' and the Blessed Margaret Mary Alacoque." *James Joyce Quarterly* 6 (Fall 1968): 22–28.

Triandis, Harry C. *The Analysis of Subjective Culture*. New York: Wiley, 1972.

Tseng, Li-Ling. "Exile, Cunning, Silence: Trajectory of Art of Exile from Joyce's *Ulysses* to Beckett's *Trilogy*." *Concentric* 35 (March 2009): 205–28.

Van Hulle, Dirk. "Hesitancy in Joyce's and Beckett's Manuscripts." *Texas Studies in Language and Literature* 51 (Spring 2009): 17–27.

Van Mierlo, Wim. "The Greater Ireland beyond the Sea: James Joyce, Exile, and Irish Emigration." In *Joyce, Ireland, Britain*, edited by Andrew Gibson and Len Platt, 178–97. Gainesville: University Press of Florida, 2006.

Van Mierlo, Wim, and Ingeborg Landuyt. "Catholicism, Nationalism, and Exile: Sheed and Ward's *Irish Way* in VI.B.34." *Genetic Joyce Studies* 2 (Spring 2002). www.geneticjoycestudies.org/GJS2WimInge.htm.

Wall, Eamonn. *From the Sin-é Café to the Black Hills: Notes on the New Irish*. Madison: University of Wisconsin Press, 2000.

Walzl, Florence L. "Gabriel and Michael: The Conclusion of 'The Dead.'" *James Joyce Quarterly* 4 (Fall 1966): 17–31.

———. "Joyce's 'The Sisters': A Development." *James Joyce Quarterly* 10 (Summer 1973): 375–421.

Wilson, Edmund. "The Dream of H. C. Earwicker." *New Republic* 91 (July 12, 1939): 270–74.

Zipes, Jack. *Breaking the Magic Spell: Radical Theories of Folk and Fairy Tales*. Austin: University of Texas Press, 1979.

———. *Happily Ever After: Fairy Tales, Children, and the Culture Industry*. New York: Routledge, 1997.

Index

MICHAEL PATRICK GILLESPIE, after receiving his Ph.D. from the University of Wisconsin in 1980, taught for twenty-nine years at Marquette University, ultimately as the inaugural Louise Edna Goeden Professor of English. He has written a dozen books (on the works of James Joyce, Oscar Wilde, William Kennedy, chaos theory, and Irish film) and two monographs, has edited seven other works including two volumes in the Norton Critical Edition of authors, and has written more than eighty articles and book chapters relating to English and Irish studies, in addition to serving on the advisory boards of a half dozen scholarly journals and as a reader for thirteen university presses. He has received fellowships or grants from the National Endowment for the Humanities, the American Philosophical Society, the Humanities Research Center, the William Andrews Clark Library, the American Council of Learned Societies, the Wisconsin Humanities Council, and Marquette University. A featured speaker in the Joseph Schick Lecture Series and the Lawrence McBride Memorial Lectures, and the only American recipient of the Charles Fanning Medal for Distinguished Work in Irish Studies, he has been named a Distinguished Scholar by Florida International University. Gillespie has been on the Board of Trustees of the International James Joyce Foundation and on the Board of Consultants for the Zurich James Joyce Foundation and has been secretary, vice president, and president of the American Conference for Irish Studies.

Since 2009 he has been at Florida International University, where he serves as professor of English and director of the Center for the Humanities in an Urban Environment. He is at present working on a critical edition of James Joyce's *Exiles*. Putting backspin on a golf ball lofted onto a green is a skill that still eludes him.

THE FLORIDA JAMES JOYCE SERIES
Edited by Sebastian D. G. Knowles

The Autobiographical Novel of Co-Consciousness: Goncharov, Woolf, and Joyce, by Galya Diment (1994)
Bloom's Old Sweet Song: Essays on Joyce and Music, by Zack Bowen (1995)
Joyce's Iritis and the Irritated Text: The Dis-lexic Ulysses, by Roy Gottfried (1995)
Joyce, Milton, and the Theory of Influence, by Patrick Colm Hogan (1995)
Reauthorizing Joyce, by Vicki Mahaffey (paperback edition, 1995)
Shaw and Joyce: "The Last Word in Stolentelling," by Martha Fodaski Black (1995)
Bely, Joyce, and Döblin: Peripatetics in the City Novel, by Peter I. Barta (1996)
Jocoserious Joyce: The Fate of Folly in Ulysses, by Robert H. Bell (paperback edition, 1996)
Joyce and Popular Culture, edited by R. B. Kershner (1996)
Joyce and the Jews: Culture and Texts, by Ira B. Nadel (paperback edition, 1996)
Narrative Design in Finnegans Wake: *The Wake Lock Picked*, by Harry Burrell (1996)
Gender in Joyce, edited by Jolanta W. Wawrzycka and Marlena G. Corcoran (1997)
Latin and Roman Culture in Joyce, by R. J. Schork (1997)
Reading Joyce Politically, by Trevor L. Williams (1997)
Advertising and Commodity Culture in Joyce, by Garry Leonard (1998)
Greek and Hellenic Culture in Joyce, by R. J. Schork (1998)
Joyce, Joyceans, and the Rhetoric of Citation, by Eloise Knowlton (1998)
Joyce's Music and Noise: Theme and Variation in His Writings, by Jack W. Weaver (1998)
Reading Derrida Reading Joyce, by Alan Roughley (1999)
Joyce through the Ages: A Nonlinear View, edited by Michael Patrick Gillespie (1999)
Chaos Theory and James Joyce's Everyman, by Peter Francis Mackey (1999)
Joyce's Comic Portrait, by Roy Gottfried (2000)
Joyce and Hagiography: Saints Above!, by R. J. Schork (2000)
Voices and Values in Joyce's Ulysses, by Weldon Thornton (2000)
The Dublin Helix: The Life of Language in Joyce's Ulysses, by Sebastian D. G. Knowles (2001)
Joyce Beyond Marx: History and Desire in Ulysses *and* Finnegans Wake, by Patrick McGee (2001)
Joyce's Metamorphosis, by Stanley Sultan (2001)
Joycean Temporalities: Debts, Promises, and Countersignatures, by Tony Thwaites (2001)
Joyce and the Victorians, by Tracey Teets Schwarze (2002)
Joyce's Ulysses *as National Epic: Epic Mimesis and the Political History of the Nation State*, by Andras Ungar (2002)
James Joyce's "Fraudstuff," by Kimberly J. Devlin (2002)
Rite of Passage in the Narratives of Dante and Joyce, by Jennifer Margaret Fraser (2002)
Joyce and the Scene of Modernity, by David Spurr (2002)
Joyce and the Early Freudians: A Synchronic Dialogue of Texts, by Jean Kimball (2003)
Twenty-first Joyce, edited by Ellen Carol Jones and Morris Beja (2004)
Joyce on the Threshold, edited by Anne Fogarty and Timothy Martin (2005)

Wake Rites: The Ancient Irish Rituals of Finnegans Wake, by George Cinclair Gibson (2005)
Ulysses *in Critical Perspective*, edited by Michael Patrick Gillespie and A. Nicholas Fargnoli (2006)
Joyce and the Narrative Structure of Incest, by Jen Shelton (2006)
Joyce, Ireland, Britain, edited by Andrew Gibson and Len Platt (2006)
Joyce in Trieste: An Album of Risky Readings, edited by Sebastian D. G. Knowles, Geert Lernout, and John McCourt (2007)
Joyce's Rare View: The Nature of Things in Finnegans Wake, by Richard Beckman (2007)
Joyce's Misbelief, by Roy Gottfried (2007)
James Joyce's Painful Case, by Cóilín Owens (2008)
Cannibal Joyce, by Thomas Jackson Rice (2008)
Manuscript Genetics, Joyce's Know-How, Beckett's Nohow, by Dirk Van Hulle (2008)
Catholic Nostalgia in Joyce and Company, by Mary Lowe-Evans (2008)
A Guide through Finnegans Wake, by Edmund Lloyd Epstein (2009)
Bloomsday 100: Essays on Ulysses, edited by Morris Beja and Anne Fogarty (2009)
Joyce, Medicine, and Modernity, by Vike Martina Plock (2010; first paperback edition, 2012)
Who's Afraid of James Joyce?, by Karen R. Lawrence (2010; first paperback edition, 2012)
Ulysses *in Focus: Genetic, Textual, and Personal Views*, by Michael Groden (2010; first paperback edition, 2012)
Foundational Essays in James Joyce Studies, edited by Michael Patrick Gillespie (2011)
Empire and Pilgrimage in Conrad and Joyce, by Agata Szczeszak-Brewer (2011)
The Poetry of James Joyce Reconsidered, edited by Marc C. Conner (2012; first paperback edition, 2015)
The German Joyce, by Robert K. Weninger (2012)
Joyce and Militarism, by Greg Winston (2012)
Renascent Joyce, edited by Daniel Ferrer, Sam Slote, and André Topia (2013; first paperback edition, 2014)
Before Daybreak: "After the Race" and the Origins of Joyce's Art, by Cóilín Owens (2013; first paperback edition, 2014)
Modernists at Odds: Reconsidering Joyce and Lawrence, edited by Matthew J. Kochis and Heather L. Lusty (2015)
The Ecology of Finnegans Wake, by Alison Lacivita (2015)
James Joyce and the Exilic Imagination, by Michael Patrick Gillespie (2015)

www.ingramcontent.com/pod-product-compliance
Lightning Source LLC
Chambersburg PA
CBHW060803310726
48980CB00002B/212
* 9 7 8 0 8 1 3 0 6 0 6 5 1 *